THE COMPLETE GUIDE TO TRANSGENDER IN THE WORKPLACE

THE COMPLETE GUIDE TO TRANSGENDER IN THE WORKPLACE

Vanessa Sheridan

Foreword by John L. Sullivan

PRAEGER

An Imprint of ABC-CLIO, LLC

A B C 🦋 C L I O

Santa Barbara, California • Denver, Colorado • Oxford, England

Library of Congress Cataloging-in-Publication Data

Sheridan, Vanessa, 1949–
   The complete guide to transgender in the workplace / Vanessa Sheridan ;
   foreword by John L. Sullivan.
     p. cm.
   Includes bibliographical references and index.
   ISBN 978–0–313–36584–3 (hbk. : alk. paper) — ISBN 978–0–313–36585–0
   (ebook : alk. paper)
   1. Transgender people—Employment. 2. Diversity in the workplace. 1. Title.
HF5549.5.S47S54 2009
658.30086'6—dc22   2009010074

13 12 11 10 9   1 2 3 4 5

This book is also available on the World Wide Web as an eBook.
Visit www.abc-clio.com for details.

ABC-CLIO, LLC
130 Cremona Drive, P.O. Box 1911
Santa Barbara, California 93116-1911

This book is printed on acid-free paper ∞

Manufactured in the United States of America

It is not our purpose to become each other; it is to recognize each other, to learn to see the other and honor him for what he is.
—Hermann Hesse

Contents

Appendices

Foreword

We have made significant progress in the past 15 years in our efforts to create fully inclusive workplaces for lesbian, gay, bisexual, and transgender (LGBT) Americans. We still have a great deal of work to do, especially with and for our transgender colleagues, but we now have a much better idea of what we need to do to get us where we need to be.

It would be nice if we could simply state that inclusion is the "right thing to do" and let that be our guiding principle. Unfortunately, that is frequently not a sufficient basis for companies, and individuals, to make the correct decision. So, we need to look at the broader benefits, especially to a company's success, which will motivate and drive these actions.

We have made progress because companies recognize the financial benefits of having a fully engaged workforce. Hiring and retaining the "best and the brightest" is the mantra of every successful company. Creating exceptions based on criteria other than work performance, such as race, age, national origin, sexual orientation, gender identity, or gender expression, should not be acceptable because they are not relevant to a company's success.

Many steps have been taken to create inclusive work environments, especially for the gay and lesbian communities. Companies have adopted nondiscrimination policies and have implemented domestic partner benefit programs. Companies have recognized the imperative of creating an environment where employees feel safe and valued in the workplace. That ability for gay and lesbian employees to bring their whole selves to work enables greater productivity as employees. Instead of asking these employees to "check a portion of themselves at the door," inclusive companies require that employees bring 100 percent of themselves to the job. In this environment, they dedicate their time on the job to contributing to the corporate success; no time or energy is wasted in attempting to hide who they truly are.

But, full inclusion in the workplace is significant beyond what it means for the corporate bottom line. There are additional benefits to the community beyond increased productivity in the workplace. By creating a safe environment for all employees, companies create a place where gay and lesbian employees can share the stories of their lives along with their colleagues. These conversations about the daily ups and downs of their lives, and how much they are the same ups and downs that everyone faces, break down the barriers of "difference" and allow a greater understanding of how much we all have in common. Conversations about life partners and daily routines remove the mystery, destroy the myths, and confirm that everyone is so much the same in so many ways.

However, the progress made with the gay and lesbian community in the workplace has not fully extended to our transgender colleagues and friends. The mystery and myths remain. The fear of the unknown is still extremely high. Companies must take what they have learned from our early successes in diversity and apply those lessons to the transgender community as well. Those lessons learned include creating an environment of inclusion for all; encouraging open and honest dialogue in an effort at continuous learning; promoting understanding; and ultimately embracing inclusion of all in the workplace.

The statistics support the premise that today's most successful companies are creating fully inclusive environments through policy changes and diversity programs (see the rapid progression of transgender-inclusive polices scored by the HRC Corporate Equality Index). This book provides the guidance and insight necessary for companies to extend their policies and practices of inclusion to the transgender community, so that ALL employees can truly feel safe and valued in the workplace.

John L. Sullivan
Senior Vice President, General Counsel and Corporate Secretary
Imation Corp.
Oakdale, Minnesota

Introduction

In the year 2000, only three *Fortune* 500 companies included gender identity in their employee nondiscrimination policies. Since then, nearly a third of the *Fortune* 500—over 175—companies have made the strategic business decision to be transgender-inclusive. That is a significant shift in business thinking within a relatively short time span, and it carries powerful implications for the future of transgender inclusion within organizations.

These are no ordinary times, and this is not business as usual. The transgender phenomenon has become an observable, legitimately identifiable area of business interest, and there is a need for resources to assist companies in dealing with this new workplace issue. In response to that need, this book will provide

- Useful tools for organizational change;
- Practical guidelines for those who seek to deal effectively with this new business subject;
- Insightful tips, suggestions, ideas, and models for organizations and individuals;
- A starting point for meaningful workplace conversations.

Welcome, gentle reader, to a world that is adapting to gender-based realities in new and unprecedented ways.

A WORD ABOUT THE AUTHOR

My name is Vanessa Sheridan. At a very early age, I intuitively understood that I was "different." That difference is manifested in my life as a transgender identity. The discovery and personal acceptance of this identity set me on a journey of exploration that has taken me in some unexpected but interesting directions.

Being transgender means that one is not always readily understood or accepted by everyone in society. There are plenty of myths and misconceptions about what it means to be transgender, and those inaccurate perceptions can impact the business world in many ways. Misconceptions about transgender persons may cloud the judgment of people and organizations, causing them to make unfortunate decisions about hiring and/or working with transgender individuals. This book was born of a desire to address those issues in a pragmatic way, offering factual information and reasonable alternatives that will benefit the business community.

Some consider me to be an expert on the leading-edge business topic of transgender in the workplace. Since 1991 I have been speaking, writing, and consulting with organizations of all sizes to help raise awareness of the transgender phenomenon. I am the author of two previous books on transgender spirituality. Both of those books were finalists for Lambda Literary Awards. Over the years I have worked extensively with businesses, including *Fortune* 500 companies, helping them improve their organizational cultures by providing practical advice, resources, training, speaking/presenting services, strategies, and guidelines relative to transgender as an increasingly significant workplace inclusion issue.

I am both pleased and humbled to say that you are holding a groundbreaking book. It is the first book on the topic of transgender in the workplace ever to be released by a mainstream publishing house. My belief is that it will not be the last: others are certain to follow as the transgender phenomenon becomes increasingly relevant throughout the business community. My hope is that you will find the book useful and informative, and that it will provide information to help improve your organization.

TAKING THIS SERIOUSLY

The fact that transgender inclusion issues are beginning to be taken seriously within corporate America is cause for both wonder and hope. It is also a good reason to ask some important questions. For example, just how seriously are transgender-related issues being taken in today's workplaces? How seriously *should* they be taken? What are the business implications of taking these issues seriously? How will organizational leaders deal with issues such as ethics, social responsibility, accountability, and training relative to transgender inclusion concerns in the workplace? You are invited to read on and determine those answers for yourself.

Gender variance "has accompanied human existence since antiquity,"[1] and "transitioning from one sex to the other, either permanently or temporarily, has occurred in most human societies throughout recorded history."[2] However, transgender in the workplace is only now becoming a timely, leading-edge, and legitimate area of business interest. The issue represents a value proposition for organizations. It deserves air and light so it can become part of the larger discussion about organizational pluralistic concerns.

Every successful business wants to save time and costs while improving their productivity, revenue, and profitability. Organizations strive to generate innovative solutions to problems, provide those solutions to their employees and customers, and improve the products and services that their end users ultimately purchase and receive. Growing numbers of companies will attest that learning about the increasingly relevant topic of transgender in the workplace—and then putting that knowledge into practice in the work environment —is a practical, effective way to move ahead in productively meeting organizational business goals.

Throughout society, the private sector remains ahead of the political discussions that surround the transgender phenomenon. While politicians engage in endless debate about the implications of equal protections and civil rights, the business community is moving steadily to encourage fairness and equality for its employees. Increasingly, corporate America is embracing the many benefits of a pluralistic workforce. There is a reason for that: different worldviews, backgrounds, and experiences in corporate work teams typically result in improvements for all concerned, including the team, the service or product that is being offered, the organization, and the people that the organization serves.

These are groundbreaking trends in today's global business community. For increasing numbers of organizations, transgender in the workplace—particularly within the context of strategic efforts to strengthen business practices through an intentional pursuit of workforce pluralism—is proving to be a useful, practical tool for both cultural improvement and enhancing the bottom line.

SUCCESS, SURVIVAL, AND SOLUTIONS

Microsoft CEO Steve Ballmer believes that success and long-term survival for his organization depend on three distinct elements: innovation, big, bold goals, and an ability to do things that are compelling.[3] Many of us would probably agree with Ballmer that those elements are essential for success and long-term survival in our own organizations as well. Business growth and continued success usually accrue to the smartest, most creative, and most strategic. Today, responsible strategies for organizational progress increasingly include the development and implementation of appropriate employee policies, guidelines, procedures, and awareness training in the new business area of transgender.

Providing "smart" solutions to internal organizational concerns can result in a competitive business edge that is often manifested in improved work styles and productivity, positively enhanced organizational cultures, streamlined organizational processes, and quick, useful, easy access to a remarkable depth of information. This book will provide some practical business resources by focusing on the timely and socially relevant issue of transgender. Keeping ahead of the curve on this leading-edge business topic will provide organizations with a definite marketplace advantage over their competitors. This, in turn, can help generate significant returns on their investment in human capital.

Today's successful business organizations strive to get the most out of every asset, including parts, systems, technologies, facilities, and employees. As new information and technological advances are introduced to the workplace, new applications—along with major implications for business in the global economy—will continue to arise. Change is fuel, and many forward-thinking organizations are achieving greater effectiveness by recognizing that transgender-inclusive initiatives can help drive the business changes that are necessary to ensure growth.

United States' workplaces tend to mirror the composition of the nation itself. In the workplace, people from all areas of life—different races, ages, income levels, religious and spiritual beliefs, sexual orientations, and gender identities—are brought together and are expected to somehow make it work. As the business world becomes more diverse every day, awareness of and sensitivity to various diversity issues become employability hot buttons.

Transgender in the workplace is a complex and often misunderstood subject for many in our society. Consequently, it is essential for organizations to present a valid business case for transgender diversity while providing accurate information, appropriate training, and access to relevant resources about this newly emerging business issue. Hopefully, reading this book will be a valuable step in that direction, providing an impetus as well as specific tools to help your organization create positive, lasting change.

Please keep in mind, however, that the book cannot do the work for you. Take the ideas, suggestions, information, and other tools contained in these pages, combine them with your own and/or existing resources, and determine how best to apply them thoughtfully and effectively within the larger context of your organization's business situation. That is how this book can be most helpful in bringing about the diversity-related changes that will create a unique business advantage for your company.

FROM FEAR AND IGNORANCE TO KNOWLEDGE AND GROWTH

An irrational fear of benign human difference can create potential difficulties and/or problematic situations in a workplace. After all, most of us are products of our culture: we have been conditioned by the sharply polarized paradigms and ideals of gender that have been prevalent in society for a long, long time. It is always easier—and usually more convenient—to judge others than to understand them. Unfortunately, people often fear what they do not understand. Fluid, flexible, "different," and/or adaptable concepts of gender—especially those based on widely varying human qualities rather than on immutable physical characteristics such as chromosomes, genitalia, or other body parts—may create tremendous anxiety in some people. This anxiety can, in turn, generate an almost palpable fear of the unknown, or the "other," that transgender represents to such persons. Unfortunately, those who remain uninformed—and thus irrationally fearful—about a human issue such as transgender often pay a price for clinging to their unfounded fears: they miss out on an opportunity to become more knowledgeable about the scope of the human condition. Our fears hold us back and limit our lives. In the workplace, they often restrict us from doing our best work and becoming our best selves. Such fear-laden mind-sets are one-way tickets to a mediocre, pedestrian, unproductive, uninspiring, and ultimately unhappy existence during our hours on the job.

Recognition of the inherent dangers represented by that restrictive, life-shrinking fear of human difference combined with a desire to promote the concept of pluralism as a vital business principle are the primary reasons for this book's existence. Hopefully, the information contained in these pages will help readers to

- Address their fears of the unknown by placing an emphasis on the often misunderstood transgender phenomenon as it intersects with the workplace;
- Drag those fears kicking and screaming into the light of day;
- Examine fears about the transgender "other" carefully and unflinchingly;
- Render those fears powerless through the tools of knowledge and enlightenment.

Once the grip of fear and ignorance is loosened through the acquisition of knowledge, we can begin to learn and grow and more fully become the extraordinary people we are all capable of being, and our organizations can become better, more just, fair, and humane places to work. Greater knowledge and awareness will be present in the hearts and minds and attitudes and actions of the human beings who come to work every day to create common cause through their efforts.

HELP FOR BUSINESS PROFESSIONALS

This book is designed to provide a basic understanding and overview of the transgender phenomenon from a business-oriented perspective. However, it will not be enough for today's business organizations to possess only a limited awareness of a human issue that is so complex and significant in its implications for society. If we seek to be more successful in our fields of endeavor, we must also be equipped with a basic understanding of transgender as it exists in the real world. That is why many pragmatic suggestions, examples, and potential guidelines for organizations and their leaders are included in these pages.

Throughout the book you will discover a variety of facts, ideas, and opinions about transgender. You will be introduced to definitions of important transgender-related terms. (As we will soon learn, using the proper terminology when talking to or about transgender persons is important.) You will also find some real-life accounts of transgender individuals, along with workplace models to help your organization develop and implement specific nondiscriminatory employee policies.

The *Oxford English Dictionary* defines *transgender* as an "identity that does not conform unambiguously to conventional notions of male or female gender, but combines or moves between these." Obviously, this is not an issue with which most people are overly acquainted. Often, what we know—or think we know—about transgender can be inaccurate or misinformed. Despite widespread cultural unfamiliarity with the phenomenon, transgender is a basic human rights concern that deserves attention.

In developing a greater understanding of transgender workers, this book will focus primarily on the positive qualities that are associated with human difference, not on pathology. (There is already an abundance of material that uniformly and unfairly portrays all transgender individuals as mentally disturbed. This book will not accommodate or perpetuate that outmoded myth.) Transpersons are not sick, perverted, or mentally unbalanced simply because they are transgender. It is important for society to become increasingly aware of how "biological, psychological, and social forces shape us into unique human beings with a wide variety of sex and gender expression."[4] Transgender is but one of those distinctive manifestations that is present and ubiquitous within the human condition.

The book's final section of appendices offers a variety of helpful resources and additional information about the transgender phenomenon, including some recommended readings and suggested Web sites. The International Gender Bill of Rights, an important human rights document, can be found here, along with Alcatel-Lucent Technologies' and IBM Corporation's Equal Opportunity Policy Statements. These documents may potentially serve as prototypes, models, and/or inspirations for organizations interested in crafting their own transgender-inclusive Equal Employment Opportunity statements. In addition, the Equality Principles—a document providing helpful strategies for organizations that seek to promote fairness and respect for everyone at work—are included in this section.

This book's goals are to

1. Provide useful, practical information and a variety of resources to help organizations deal successfully with the transgender phenomenon as a legitimate area of business interest;

2. Help organizations move beyond ignorance and discrimination in order to develop respect for the remarkable human diversity and remarkable possibilities that transgender workers represent.

Having access to information about transgender is one thing, but acting appropriately and effectively on that information is quite another. The poet Virgil wrote, "Fortune favors the bold," which is often true in business—but boldness needs to be combined with strategic thought and effective planning to achieve success. By becoming better informed and then taking appropriate action, business organizations can create more dynamic, innovative, and productive workplaces where every person, regardless of gender, can be free to be himself or herself and perform his or her best work in a culturally healthy environment that is conducive to success.

YOU HAVE TO DO THE WORK!

This book is rooted in one simple premise: People in the workplace deserve to be evaluated not on whether they fit into a specific gender role or meet arbitrary social standards of gender identity, characteristics, and expression but on whether they can do the job.

Most transgender employees are *not* looking for special treatment or special rights. They only want to be respected for who they are as workers and as people. But to be respected as workers, they first need to be hired to work. Obtaining meaningful employment is a critical issue for many gender-variant individuals. Unemployment and underemployment are rampant within the transgender community, which ultimately leads to poverty and all the problems associated with that unfortunate state.

According to the National Center for Transgender Equality (NCTE),

Transgender people have the right to work, in fair conditions and for equal pay. The opportunity to work is a fundamental aspect of human rights. By working, people sustain themselves and their loved ones. We can gain dignity and self-worth through our employment, and our work can even contribute to the wellbeing of the larger world ... Transgender people continue to face extensive discrimination in employment, often being unable to find work in our fields of expertise or losing jobs due to prejudice. Unemployment and underemployment are among the greatest challenges facing us.[5]

The information in these pages will provide a helpful resource for transgender workers, their employers and coworkers, and those who care about the status of transgender persons in the workplace. In addition, the book offers ideas and encouragement for transgender individuals who may be struggling with coming out[6] issues on the job. The book also presents suggestions for organizations that seek to treat their gender-variant employees and transgender customers fairly. (As we will discover, transgender customers are a demographic group that is becoming increasingly viable, visible, and targeted in terms of corporate marketing strategies. Many business organizations will want to expand their efforts to include this potential—and, at least to this point, mostly overlooked—group as part of their comprehensive marketing strategies.)

An organization may potentially be viewed as a giant crayon box. Businesses that make the choice to be transgender-inclusive in their policies and practices will be able to add one more color to their box, and that means the possibilities for success will be increased proportionately. Hopefully, your organization will choose to add this new transgender-inclusive color as well, thereby increasing its options and possibilities—and thus its opportunities—to be successful in today's competitive marketplace.

CHAPTER 1

What Is Transgender?

The term *transgender* has been used in so many different contexts and has acquired so many nuanced implications that it is sometimes difficult to define the word in a way that will be meaningful for everyone. Transpeople tend to come in all sorts of unique packages, which can add to the layers of mystery that surround the phenomenon. Some gender-variant persons hate being identified by a label at all, which only brings more complexity to the terminology issue.

The word *transgender* is an umbrella term that covers a wide variety of ideas and manifestations, all relating to gender and its remarkable potential for unique personal expression. Its scope may include (but is certainly not limited to) primary and secondary transsexuals, pre- and postoperative transsexuals, cross-dressers, intersex persons, drag queens and kings, androgynous individuals, Two-Spirit persons (who are usually Native American and/or indigenous people), bi-gendered persons, multi-gendered individuals, and a host of other types of gender variance that exist within the human condition. Transgender is a very big tent that covers a lot of territory, with much of it difficult to categorize. Expressions of gender fluidity can sometimes be hard to name or describe, much less classify. In *Song of Myself*, Whitman wrote, "I am large, I contain multitudes"—and so it is with transgender persons. (Please be aware: Transgender is not synonymous with schizophrenia. We are not talking about multiple personality disorder here, and gender variance is not mental illness.)

A useful understanding of the term is this: *transgender* includes everything not covered by our culture's narrow terms for "man" and "woman." Writer Emi Koyama says, "Some use [the word *transgender*] to refer to people whose behavior or expression do not match with their gender. Some use it to describe a gender outside of the man/woman binary. Some use it to describe the condition of having no gender or multiple genders. Other possibilities include people who perform genders or deliberately play with/on gender as well as being gender-deviant in other ways."[1]

In essence, *transgender* encompasses almost all manifestations of blurring or crossing gender barriers.[2] Those gender barriers are maintained by society in an ongoing though subjective attempt to categorize and label people. The arbitrary rules of gender are firmly enforced through a variety of explicit and covert methods that permeate the entire culture. British transgender activist Christine Burns tells us, "Being a trans person isn't about having sex in some way that sounds inherently deviant. It's about struggling for identity as a result of the sex you were labeled at birth, and doing no more than to address that in ways you want people to see and understand."[3]

UNDERSTANDING THE DIFFERENCES BETWEEN SEX AND GENDER

While *sex* is primarily a biological term that applies to almost all human and animal species, the concept of *gender* is a social construct that is "affected by social and cultural influences and may not be biologically determined."[4] Since gender is not biological in its manifestations, it is found only in human cultures. Helen Boyd tells us that confusion and consternation are "what happens when two really important words—gender and sex—get used interchangeably. Because gender is about identity—whether a person is masculine or feminine, no matter if they're male or female, and sex is about biology, chromosomes, and genitalia."[5]

Gender is not sex, and sex is not gender. Despite those vitally important distinctions, many people still tend to confuse and/or conflate the two, sometimes with disadvantageous results. Male-to-female transsexual author Donna Rose says, "Sex is a 'body' thing. It is the mere presence or absence of a Y chromosome, causing a body to develop the physical attributes that define a human body male, or female."[6] Sex is a naturally occurring physical element of our existence—but in our seemingly inescapable desire for assigning people and things to categories, we human beings simply made gender up.

Despite its cultural origins, gender is an extremely powerful force that inexorably shapes and molds society in innumerable ways.

In this culture, we have come to think of and accept gender categorization as a completely natural occurrence, much like a person's physical sex, when in actuality it is nothing of the sort. Just because we are accustomed to thinking about a thing or situation in a certain way does not necessarily mean it is inherently natural to human beings: it only means it has become widely accepted and is perceived as socially or statistically normative. Anthropologists are well aware that cultural norms—including those involving gender—can and do vary significantly from society to society.

Helen Boyd has written, "Gender is mostly described by the words 'feminine' and 'masculine,' and although many rue the day that gender was built upon the sexual binary, and some rue the day that the sexual binary ever came to be accepted as fact, those two words tidily summarize what we mean by gender, most of the time."[7] Some have inferred, perhaps crudely but accurately, that sex is about what is between the legs, while gender is about what is between the ears. In other words, sex is rooted in biology, while gender is culturally created and therefore subjectively conceived and manifested. We will examine these significant human distinctions and understandings about sex and gender as our exploration continues.

CROSSING THE BORDERS OF GENDER

Transgender persons are explorers and pioneers. They do not necessarily desire to be gender transgressors, but by default they are anyway. The need for personalized gender-variant expression drives transpeople to cross and/or transcend society's gender boundaries, or at least to blur the arbitrary, culturally designated lines of gender categorization.

David Steinberg writes that transgender persons represent

a willingness to step outside the inflexible gender binary that would divide human beings strictly into the categories of male and female, and that would assign this gender designation solely on the basis of the genitals a person finds themselves with at birth. As archaeologists and anthropologists are rapidly learning, gender transgression is an issue that has existed throughout history and across all cultures. Yet the idea that one's gender does not always conform to one's birth genitals, and that it is possible to actively reject the gender assumptions and expectations of parents, friends, and family in favor of the gender identification a person feels from within, is only now emerging in Western culture from shadow worlds of social dismissal and ridicule into the light of public discussion and increasing societal acceptance.[8]

Accordingly, increasing numbers of transgender individuals are moving from the darkness of ignorance, obscurity, and oppression into greater public awareness and are, at least in some cases, obtaining the respect and acceptance they deserve.

CONFRONTING NEGATIVITY

Despite the fact that most transpersons personally identify as heterosexual, the gay, lesbian, bisexual, and transgender communities share two fundamental issues that make these groups natural allies. First, individuals in each of these communities desire the freedom to openly be themselves without undue persecution or retribution from society. Second, neither group's members consciously or willfully "chose" their internal orientation or identity. Consider the issue pragmatically: Who would intentionally choose a gender identity or sexual orientation that places them at odds with the rest of society, making them vulnerable to cultural scorn, ridicule, retribution, and/or even potential violence for their perceived "difference"? Reasoning through this question only adds credibility to the premise that a transgender identity and/or a same-sex orientation are innate characteristics, not chosen ones.

Writing about discrimination against transpersons, transman Matt Kailey says, "Gay men, lesbians, bisexual people, transfolk—we all have something in common. The core of our commonality is gender—we are labeled and discriminated against based on our gender. The second layer is the form that discrimination takes—murders, assaults, destruction of property, failure to get jobs or housing, inadequate health care, the inability to marry, the denial of partner benefits and society's narrow definition of 'family' that does not include us."[9]As this book continues, we will learn more about the social discrimination that is frequently visited upon transpeople.

There are some who insist that the existence of a transgender identity or of transgender behavior is actually a type of moral failing, signifying a descent into degradation and abject hedonism. They claim that the transgender phenomenon is not a natural occurrence at all but is instead the inevitable result of a series of "bad" decisions that produce small moral compromises. These compromises relentlessly weaken the will, erode the conscience, and engender unnatural feelings and desires. Like falling dominoes, this process precipitates a more pronounced downward spiral of immorality that leads to "destructive transgender behavior," the impulsive adoption of a "false transgender identity," and the degradation and decadence of a sad, self-indulgent "transgender lifestyle" (whatever *that* is). This theory of willfully chosen transgender immorality appears to tie up all the loose ends, creating an explanatory package that allows detractors to pigeonhole and easily categorize transpersons as moral degenerates.

There is only one small problem with the "moral failing" explanation for transgender: It is not true.

The vast majority of transpersons do not engage in corrupt or destructive personal behaviors that are detrimental to themselves or society. Moreover, transpeople do not capriciously create or "adopt" an artificial transgender identity. Instead, they discover and painstakingly learn to recognize, eventually accept, and adapt their lives to accommodate the reality of their existing internal transgender identity. Then, quite logically, these gender-variant individuals desire to dress, name themselves, and behave in ways that align more congruently with an individually experienced transgender reality. Most transgender individuals do not weakly succumb to the "moral degradation" of a "transgender lifestyle"; instead, they recognize their personal truth, they learn to deal constructively with it, and they live in ways that may perhaps be unique or somewhat different but that are nevertheless rooted in a positive, ethical approach to life. (Just so we are clear on this point, there is no such thing as a "transgender lifestyle." There are only transgender human beings who are living their lives.) There is nothing inherently "artificial" or degrading about recognizing, affirming, and taking action to fully express who and what one truly is in a benign manner. Surely such courageous journeys of self-discovery and acts of personal integrity pose no legitimate threat to society.

While all of us are aware of certain individuals whose lives appear to be the depressing products of terrible decisions, poor choices, or harmful moral compromises, the existence of a gender-variant identity and subsequent transgender behaviors cannot be legitimately linked to a lack of personal ethics or morals. One certainly does not have to be transgender to make faulty ethical decisions or exhibit immorality, as some of our politicians, business leaders, television/media personalities, religious authority figures, and other powerful individuals in society prove regularly. Generally speaking, transgender and immorality are mutually exclusive concepts.

The issue of transgender is not about moral choices or ethical dilemmas because gender variance is, in and of itself, neither immoral nor unethical. Transgender is simply a naturally occurring part of the human condition, at least for those whose lives are touched and influenced by its existence. It is not a whimsical or immoral "choice" that is made arbitrarily. Once again, no one chooses to be transgender: transgender chooses the individual. Transgender simply *is*, and therefore, moral/ethical judgments with regard to its existence are irrelevant.

One reason to be aware of the connotations associated with the word "lifestyle" is the implication that all transgender persons think and/or behave in the same way. In reality, nothing could be further from the truth. Just as there is no "straight lifestyle," neither is there a "transgender lifestyle." There are only transgender people trying to make a living and exercise their inalienable right as citizens to pursue happiness. (The Constitution of the United States does not automatically convey the right to happiness, only the right to pursue it. As many can attest, finding and holding onto happiness is something else altogether.)

People who use the term "lifestyle" to disparage the existence, appearance, or behaviors of gender-variant individuals are probably not overly interested in a careful or respectful assessment of the complex facts surrounding the transgender phenomenon. Instead, these detractors often seem to be more concerned with reinforcing their own biases toward transfolk and communicating those biases to others. If someone uses the term "lifestyle" when referring to a transperson, they are most likely not speaking about the transgender individual from a position of approval or acceptance—and their own prejudicial slip may well be showing.

Being transgender usually involves a journey toward a personal recognition and acceptance. It is about living life as the gender-variant person you understand yourself to be. Millions of transpeople around the world have made this pivotal, life-changing discovery about themselves. That insight has changed their lives forever, often for the better. Anyone who insists that a legitimate transgender identity is a willful choice or a capricious, arbitrary, self-serving "preference" is operating from a place of ignorance, self-delusion, faulty logic, deliberate deception, and/or premeditated obfuscation.

Healthy choices for a transperson include purposely addressing, accepting, and dealing with their internal transgender reality, not in denying or continuing to repress that personal truth. An individual cannot suppress something so central to their very essence forever; eventually the need for transgender expression surfaces in one way or another. A human being cannot deny an intrinsic identity without eventually suffering some negative consequences. What is the transperson supposed to do: ignore their transgender nature and/or pretend it does not exist, which is not a viable or effective long-term option? The need for personal acceptance always comes back and bubbles up in some form anyway. Should the transgender individual try to repress or hide her or his transgender identity, which usually leads to socially and/or self-imposed guilt, shame, and any number of other mental/physical/emotional/spiritual health problems? Or should the transperson make the decision to recognize, accept, and affirm the fact that, for whatever reason, they are indeed gender-variant? And if being transgender is their personal reality, should they not also intentionally seek out ways to help them embrace that unique gender status through appropriate methods of expression, thereby seizing the opportunity to learn and grow as unique people who are on a remarkable gender journey?

Transgender people who come to fully accept their distinctive gender identity usually have few regrets, for their unique gift of gender allows them to experience life from a distinct perspective as whole, healthy transgender human beings. Dallas Denny, editor of *Transgender Tapestry* (arguably the transgender community's most esteemed and widely read quarterly journal), has written, "Being true to oneself is an internal process; it may or may not lead to external changes ... it's about accepting who you are."[10] Real, lasting change and personal growth are human experiences that always begin from the inside.

Imagine for a moment that you are heterosexual but are not permitted to do anything at work that openly expresses or identifies your sexual orientation. For instance, you cannot wear a wedding ring. You cannot talk about who you are dating or who your relationship partner might be. You cannot openly discuss your engagement or your wedding anniversary. You cannot display pictures of your spouse or children on your desk or on your wall. How would you feel in such a situation? Oppressed, perhaps? Limited? Angry? Resentful? Frustrated because of having to deny a significant part of who you are as a human being? Fearful of recrimination or of losing your position if someone should find out that you are straight? Do you think you would be able to do your best and most productive work if you were forced into such a repressive situation on the job? Now imagine how gender-variant employees feel when they must keep their gender identity a secret in the workplace. Thankfully, increasing numbers of organizations are developing and implementing nondiscrimination policies, procedures, and guidelines to help remedy that unjust situation for their transgender workers.

According to Miqqui Alicia Gilbert, cross-dresser and college professor, the presence of gender-based oppression is why "we of the transgender world often watch with envy [while] the gay and lesbian universe becomes safer, more secure, and more normalized. We fight for inclusion in human rights legislation, for reasonable portrayal in the media, for acceptance, and for the acknowledgment that we exist."[11] While we applaud the hard-earned progress that lesbians and gays have made throughout society, transfolk still have a long way to go in terms of achieving full equality and widespread social acceptance. Selisse Berry, executive director of Out & Equal Workplace Advocates, makes this clear when she says, "People are finally much more comfortable with the words gay and lesbian. They're not familiar with what the word transgender even means, and sometimes people's only connection is either drag queens, prostitution or some movie."[12]

THE INCREDIBLE VARIETY OF TRANSGENDER PERSONS

To further nuance our knowledge of the transgender phenomenon, let us consider some of the kinds of people who populate the remarkably diverse transgender community. In *The Praeger Handbook of Transsexuality: Changing Gender to Match Mindset*, Rachel Ann Heath writes, "The 'trans' idea disrupts the binary gender divide and leads to a gender continuum from male to female, just like the colors of a rainbow." (Some prefer to think of transgender as a spectrum, which implies a continuous sequence or range. This is as opposed to a continuum, which is finite and dependent upon two distinct polarities for its beginning and end.)

The sheer variety of gender variance may come as a surprise to you, especially if you are one of those who labor under the misconception that all transgender persons are transsexual. (They are not. In fact, most gender-variant people are not transsexual at all—only a relatively small percentage of all transgender individuals fully identify as transsexual.)

Transgender persons may include but, as any knowledgeable gender specialist can tell you, are certainly not limited to the following:

- *Primary and secondary transsexuals*—Primary transsexualism is often identified by its early arrival, with many primary transsexuals reporting engaging in experiences and activities usually identified with the opposite sex, including cross-dressing experiences, and often at very young ages. Secondary transsexualism tends to manifest itself somewhat later in life, sometimes after a period of possible fetishistic cross-dressing, when the gender-variant individual begins to pursue a more permanent self-identity with the opposite sex. The development of a secondary transsexual identity often occurs around the time of puberty.

- *Preoperative and postoperative transsexuals*, who can be either male-to-female or female-to-male.[13] These are individuals who possess an innate desire to physically change the sex that was assigned to them at birth in order to achieve greater congruency between their personal internal awareness, their gender identity, and their physical body/outward appearance. While growing up, many adult transsexual persons intuitively sensed that they were really a girl or a boy on the inside despite their external appearance and no matter what the rest of the world may have told them. That internal awareness became increasingly insistent in spite of the masculine or feminine socialization process they may have experienced. They somehow spontaneously knew about this incongruency all throughout childhood, during adolescence, and into adulthood. It was not a passing phase, and they did not grow out of it. There was always a nagging feeling of incompleteness, a sense that something was not right and ought to be corrected. The core identity of the transsexual is already male or female, at least on an internal basis, and manifests itself emotionally and psychologically regardless of the person's external appearance, body type, or genitalia. Therefore, most primary transsexuals are interested in pursuing transition in order to make their body and external appearance physically align with the gender that is already present within the mind and heart.[14] It is not a question of wanting to change one's sex just because it seems like a fun thing to do. Transsexuals literally know and understand themselves to have been born into the wrong body. Many of them are determined to rectify that untenable circumstance so they may lessen their personal anxiety and live happy, harmonious, and fulfilled lives. A complete change of physical sex is a significant, life-altering initiative that is usually pursued through a combination of medical assessment and diagnosis, long-term psychological counseling, hormonal therapy, the one-to-two-year real life test, sexual reassignment surgery,[15] and other supervised medical procedures. However, due to the extensive medical expenses and other costs associated with such a complex undertaking (often $100,000 or more), and because most medical insurance companies refuse to cover these costs, the majority of transsexuals never undergo sexual reassignment surgery.

- *Transgenderists*, who are persons that live full- or part-time in a gender other than their birth sex, with no apparent desire to pursue sexual reassignment surgery. These individuals usually do not identify as or consider themselves to be transsexual, at least in terms of wishing to physically change their sex or alter their genitalia. An example of a transgenderist might be a person with a penis who is happily living her life completely as a woman, or a person with a vagina who lives his life full-time as a man. (The sheer numbers of people who are doing so at this very moment might surprise you.)

- *Cross-dressers*, who are persons whose form of external gender expression may differ from the usual social expectations for their birth sex. This is often manifested through wearing the clothing and/or adopting the appearance and behavior of the opposite gender. Contrary to the fallacious but widespread notion that all people who dress as the opposite sex are homosexual, most reliable research indicates that the majority of cross-dressers are actually heterosexual in their orientation. Many are married and have children. Also, most cross-dressers are not transsexual and have no desire to physically change their sex. For the cross-dresser, it is usually about gender expression, not a gay sexual orientation or sex-change operations.

- *Transvestite, transvestism, and transvestitism*, which are clinical terms that carry potentially negative connotations and/or implications of mental illness. These terms are often perceived as pejorative and pathologizing by those who wear the clothing of the opposite sex. *Cross-dresser*, a word that more accurately describes the behavior and avoids the attendant pathological or clinical implications, is the preferred term.

- *"Mannish" or "passing" females*—These are persons whose form of gender expression is usually masculine and who are often assumed to be lesbians, though in actuality their sexual orientation may have little or nothing to do with their form of gender expression. One can certainly be heterosexual and still be a mannish female (or a feminine male, for that matter). As we have learned, sexual orientation and gender identity/expression are not necessarily synonymous.

- *"Feminine" males* are persons whose appearance and/or behaviors are culturally perceived as feminine in their outward manifestations. These individuals are often assumed to be homosexual. Nevertheless, as we have previously noted, assumptions about someone's sexual orientation—particularly assumptions based on gender expression—can be problematic and/or incorrect. It is usually better not to assume in such instances, though many people do it anyway as a matter, of course. Gender is one of the very first things we notice about another person, and our social conditioning prompts us to immediately begin making generalizations and assumptions about how we will treat or react to that person. However, intentionally refusing to assume you know someone else's gender allows you to get to know the person as a human being first. That way you can more easily avoid jumping to inaccurate conclusions.

- *Intersex* persons, or persons with ambiguous genitalia—"Intersex" is a term preferred by persons who were previously dubbed "sexually ambiguous" or "hermaphrodites" by the medical community and others. Intersex persons are found within the natural arc of the gender spectrum, somewhere between the dichotomous polarities of male and female. These individuals are not completely male, nor are they completely female: they are in between those two extremes of gender. They are, therefore, intersex. Intersex involves "visually obvious departures from the normal sex organs in boys and girls as well as developmental effects caused by abnormal chromosomal configurations and abnormal physiological responses to sex hormones."[16] People identified as intersex are individuals whose sex was assigned immediately at birth but who may manifest certain physical characteristics, expressions, or identities that vary or differ in some way from the birth sex that was assigned without their consent. It is also possible that a person may become intersex as the result of an accident or due to some medical action, such as a gender transition surgery. "The Intersex Society of North America presents on its website [www.isna.org] the statistic that one in every one hundred people, at birth, has a body that differs from the standard male or female body in some way."[17] What we are discussing here is a variation from the statistical norm in terms of genitalia and/or other sexual/physical characteristics. It is important to be aware that intersex is not a disease: it is only a difference.

Transgender often manifests itself differently in various cultures around the world, but the phenomenon has always been a part of human society and has historically been expressed in many unique ways. Labeling transgender people can be risky, particularly when the categories begin to overlap and/or when people exhibit certain gender characteristics that are difficult to pigeonhole. Just as Mother Nature herself can defy categorization, often laughing in the face of our feeble human attempts to subject the nonquantifiable mysteries of life to arbitrary classification, classifying people as transgender can be a complicated and perplexing business.

WHY DOES TRANSGENDER EXIST?

As of this writing, no one really knows why transgender exists—and do not believe anyone who tries to tell you otherwise. Scientists, theologians, anthropologists, physicians, psychotherapists, and sociologists have studied the transgender phenomenon at length, but no one can explain with full certainty why some people are gender-variant and others are not.

One of the motivations for transgender feelings and behaviors in some persons, especially transsexual individuals, involves the presence of a medically diagnosed condition that psychology has labeled *gender dysphoria*. This term is often used to describe ongoing or recurrent intense feelings of gender-based discomfort, anxiety, pain, and anguish. These feelings exist because of a perceived incongruency between one's internal sense of self and the sex that was assigned to them at birth.

Gender dysphoria is a diagnostic term that some transgender persons have come to strongly resent. A psychological diagnosis of "gender dysphoria" can connote or imply a clinical stigma, suggesting that someone who is transgender and in psychological or emotional distress is automatically mentally ill and therefore somehow deficient or less than competent. As the transgender community becomes increasingly active on its own behalf, transgender-related diagnoses by the medical/psychological community are receiving increased scrutiny, opposition, and sometimes outright rejection. The impetus behind these negative responses to a diagnosis of gender dysphoria is rooted in the concept of self-determination. Many transgender people believe that no person or institution has the authoritarian right to decide an individual's gender status or to determine how they ought to respond to a gender-related situation. Instead, they are convinced that such decisions ought to be a private and personal matter, not medically determined.

Try placing yourself in the shoes of the transgender individual: how would you like to be diagnosed and classified as mentally ill, not because you are somehow flawed, sick, or perverted but simply because of an arbitrary classification to which a psychiatrist or some other socially powerful gatekeeper has decided to assign you? Especially when you know it is not really you that is sick, but society and its unbending, unfair gender-based expectations? Wouldn't it make you angry? Wouldn't you resent being treated like that? Wouldn't you, as an autonomous human being, want to reserve the right to determine your own gender status, particularly if you knew that society's initial assignment of your gender—based solely upon the appearance of your genitals at birth—was inaccurate?

An individual's designated anatomical sex is an arbitrary medical assignment, based almost exclusively upon the appearance of a person's genitalia and/or body type at the moment of birth. Usually, the doctor looks at the baby's body, checks the genitals, and says, "It's a boy," or "It's a girl," and that is the end of it. Case closed, at least for most people. The majority of infants are able to grow up secure in the knowledge that their sex and accompanying gender roles/expectations are fixed and appropriate for them. That is the way it has always been, and for most folks that is how it will continue to be for the foreseeable future.

For a certain percentage of people, however, the gender journey is just beginning. We are learning that the center of gender awareness is not the genitals, as was previously believed, but that it is actually located in the brain. All transgender individuals intuitively wrestle on some level with cognitive dissonance relative to their natal gender assignment, but the struggle for gender congruency can be particularly acute for transsexual and intersex persons. The arbitrary gender/sex assignment by medical professionals at a person's birth may potentially be damaging for those who, for whatever reason, do not fully align with the established cultural paradigm that informs and accompanies such determinations.

A transgender identity is an internal phenomenon that often manifests itself early in life. Some transgender children recognize their unique gender situation almost immediately and know it instinctively from a very early age. The lucky ones are able to identify, accept, and act upon their inner transgender identity without punishment or condemnation during childhood. They have supportive, loving families and friends who allow and even encourage the transchild to simply be who they are. How fortunate (and rare) these children are! More commonly, gender-variant children come to an awareness of gender difference during their maturation/socialization process, often around the time of puberty's onset. Most struggle to remain in the gender of their assigned sex due to family and/or cultural expectations, even though they may experience intense emotional suffering and much internal distress as a result. They want to fit in and try to do so, but it is extremely difficult and sometimes impossible for the transperson to maintain a façade of social "normality" when they know at their core that something important is askew.

The difficulties of juggling puberty, burgeoning sexuality, and the adolescent desire for family/social acceptance are often more pronounced for the transgender child than for the average young person. Sometimes the difficulties and accompanying feelings of alienation and despair can become overwhelming, which accounts in large measure for the abnormally high percentage of suicide attempts among transgender young persons. Rejection by family members and/or society at large may become so painful that suicide seems the only option. (Some reports indicate that the rate of suicide attempts for transgender youth runs as high as 50 percent.)

Some transpeople make the decision to correct their recognized gender anomaly and go through a shift that holds major implications for every aspect of their existence. At a certain point, often in the middle of their lives, some transsexuals and transgenderists have had enough: they cannot (or refuse to) meet society's inflexible gender-based expectations any longer. They initiate a gender transition in order to ameliorate the intense emotional conflict of their gender situation. They begin living and working in a manner that is more harmonious with their internal gender identity, manifesting a personal awareness that may run counter to the arbitrary gender expectations that were assigned to them at birth.

The ramifications of transitioning can be significant because these transgender persons must then "out" themselves to their families, friends, employers, coworkers, and everyone else in their lives. This necessary "outing" is why our organizations and workplaces have a specific responsibility to respect the dignity and integrity of employees who come out as transgender and/or transition to a new social gender while remaining on the job. These transpersons are doing their best to live openly and be truthful about who and what they are. Imagine the bravery and commitment it takes to begin a life-altering transition like that, especially in public for all to see! Such courageous, honest decisions deserve to be affirmed and supported in our workplaces, not ridiculed or rejected.

It seems logical that business organizations would desire to employ people who are willing to be truthful and courageous. Coming out publicly as gender-variant is an act of bravery and integrity. However, coming out also makes the transperson vulnerable in ways that most people will never experience. For this reason, coming out—especially in one's place of employment—can be one of the most difficult and potentially heroic things imaginable.

THEORIES OF TRANSGENDER CAUSATION

As we have discovered, no single theory explains all of transgender. A theory is, at best, a way to highlight a singular idea—and transgender has so far proven to be too broad, rich, and varied a concept to be limited to a single causal theory. In fact, "No one knows whether [transgender] is a biological result or a mix of the biological, the psychological, and the cultural."[18]

Nevertheless, mounting evidence indicates the existence of a legitimate connection between transgender and biology. A document from the International Conference on Transgender Law and Employment Policy states, "there is a broad consensus among medical researchers that transgenderism is rooted in complex biological factors that are fixed at birth. This research confirms what transgendered [*sic*] people know and experience on a much more personal basis: being transgendered is not a choice nor a 'lifestyle,' but a difficult, uninvited challenge."[19] There are several theories about the actual cause(s) of transgender, and we will briefly examine a few of them in this chapter.

Etiology is the study of causation, and the etiological origins of the transgender phenomenon continue to be hotly disputed. Most researchers have tended to align themselves in the familiar nature versus nurture formation, where prenatal theories of hormonal imbalances and chromosomal irregularities contend with postnatal notions of opposite-sex psychological imprinting and family-system concepts of dominant and/or absent parents.

Increasingly, however, research seems to indicate that there may be a strong correlation between elements such as prenatal hormonal factors and fetal development that ultimately lead to the existence of an internal transgender identity. In fact, medical researchers indicate they have already discovered a link between testosterone levels during pregnancy and the ensuing gender-role behavior of preschool girls. "The study found that the more testosterone a girl was exposed to in the womb, the more likely she was at a young age to engage in tomboy-like behavior, such as playing with toys that boys typically prefer ... Researchers say previous studies in animals have found a similar relationship between maternal testosterone levels and behavior."[20]

If this link between testosterone levels and tomboyish behavior in girls proves over time to be significantly influential, it may at least partially explain why some females seem to naturally gravitate toward more traditionally "masculine" behaviors and appearances. The impact of hormonal levels during pregnancy is a major factor in the development of fetal brains. Following this same line of reasoning, we might extrapolate that exposure to increased levels of estrogen (or perhaps to a diminished level of testosterone) in the womb could potentially lead to typically "feminine" brain development that might induce more feminine thought patterns and associated feminine behaviors in males.

If this hormonal link and its accompanying influence are ultimately proven to be primary causes of either masculine or feminine brain development and/or associated transgender-related actions, surely it would be appropriate to avoid discriminating against people for exhibiting benign gender-based behaviors that were biologically imprinted *en utero*. Why should an individual be held in social contempt or suffer cultural sanctions due to the existence of a nonthreatening and biologically innate situation to which they were organically predisposed during the gestation period? How can anyone continue to insist that benign transgender thoughts and feelings are arbitrarily and willfully chosen (and therefore potentially sinful or immoral) if transpersons are hormonally induced toward those thoughts, feelings, and accompanying behaviors during pregnancy? If certain people are shaped and molded in this way by hormonal or other biological influences, then surely it is unreasonable to insist that behaviors in response to those influences are indicative of a willful decision or an arbitrarily chosen "lifestyle" for transpeople.

To be sure, there are other types of internal and/or developmentally related predispositions that are dangerous and/or destructive to society—for example, an inclination toward pedophilia or pyromania or other psychosexual aberrations and abnormalities that bring harm to people or property. Transgender, however, is *not* a dangerous or destructive internal predisposition. In and of itself, a transgender identity or gender-variant mode of expression harms no one.

Gilbert observes that an exclusivist, judgmental attitude about gender often "pushes young people, especially young boys, into the arms of homophobia as they fear being labeled fags or fairies. At the grade school age there is great confusion between gender role variation and sexual orientation. If a young boy does something 'girly' or feminine, it is his sexual orientation that is attacked because the assumption ... dictates that any feminine male must be attracted to males."[21] Such assumptions about sexuality can be inaccurate, not to mention patently unjust and blatantly bigoted. Transgender appearances and/or behaviors are not automatically equivalent to a homosexual orientation.

It is not being "different" that makes growing up a challenge for transgender young people. The real challenge lies in navigating safely through a society that does not understand or accept them. The primary obstacles to health and happiness for many young transpersons usually come in the forms of lack of support, acceptance, and affirmation from an uninformed, prejudiced public that insists on equating gender with sexuality.

Here is what surgeon Don Laub, a doctor who has performed hundreds of successful male-to-female surgeries on transsexual patients, has to say about biological determinism and behaviors:

There have been a number of experiments, corroborated over and over, at Wisconsin, at Oregon, at Stanford. They injected lab animals—cats, rats, dogs, and monkeys—with opposite-sex hormones shortly before birth. And that was it. No matter what kind of conditioning you used on those mammals, they behaved consistently like the opposite sex, like the gender of the hormone with which they were injected. And I think that's what we'll find, eventually: a biological answer.[22]

Hormonal and/or other biological factors certainly appear to be significant elements that may precipitate gender-based behaviors and identities. However, and in fairness, we must also consider the vital roles that environment, family, school, religion, and other social influences can play in human development. Unless we grow up alone on a desert island or live as a hermit in a cave, society and its institutions powerfully influence us in many ways. We do not live our lives in a social vacuum, and we are all impacted by the presence of cultural factors. But surely environmental, relational, circumstantial, and/or other such influences are not the only reasons for the existence of a transgender identity and/or accompanying transgender behaviors—for if they are, how then can we explain the presence of a transgender identity and/or behaviors in some children who grow up in the very same environment and social milieu as other children, often in the same family, who exhibit no inclination whatsoever toward transgender? What additional elements might possibly account for such a fundamental divergence in terms of gender identity and expression among siblings raised in the same home?

Some have cited Carl Jung's theory of *anima* and *animus* as a possible rationale for the existence of a transgender identity. This psychological premise implies that transgender behavior is an outer expression of the deeper, more subconscious aspects of one's personality. A Jungian hypothesis of transgender would presumably encompass internalized personal qualities (such as a gender-variant identity) that are demonstrated through an external manifestation of some kind such as masculine or feminine dress, appearance, behaviors, speech, movements, and gestures.

Referring to an innate desire for transgender expression, Dr. William Stayton, Head of the University of Pennsylvania's Department of Human Sexuality, says, "Truth is, you can't change it."[23] Most knowledgeable helping professionals now try to counsel the transgender individual to deal honestly and forthrightly with their gender situation rather than attempt to eradicate it, because denial and/or efforts at repression of a legitimately innate gender identity simply do not work over extended periods of time.[24] People can always make decisions about specific behaviors in which they will engage, but they cannot change their inborn, immutable gender identity any more than they can change their fingerprints.

A BRIEF DISCUSSION OF SOME TRANSGENDER SUBGROUPS

Perhaps the largest subgroup of transgender persons are *cross-dressers* who are heterosexual males, although there are also plenty of females who cross-dress. Accurate numbers for the male-to-female cross-dressing population are difficult to obtain because of the social stigma that is subjectively attached to the behavior and appearance of men who innately desire feminine expression and who dress/act accordingly. (Due to the more relaxed standards of dress that society generally permits for females, it may potentially be somewhat easier for them to cross-dress in public without fear of reprisal.)

Most male-to-female cross-dressers remain closeted due to a fear of retaliation for transgressing socially sanctioned and culturally enforced gender norms. Homophobia and gay bashing are still rampant in our society. The terror of being labeled a sissy or of being attacked for being perceived as gay is one of the primary reasons why many straight cross-dressers keep themselves hidden from public view.

Most cross-dressers tend to lead lives that are quite ordinary and "normal" in almost all other respects. Many cross-dressers are heterosexually married, and many have children. Unlike transsexuals, who deal with a very different though equally legitimate set of transgender circumstances and internal desires, cross-dressers have no desire to change their physical sex. They only seek to dress and behave in a transgender manner as a means of individual gender expression and personal fulfillment. Unless it is manifested as a "fetishistic paraphelia" (i.e., a psychosexual disorder) as defined by the DSM-IV-TR,[25] the act of cross-dressing is not considered to be indicative of a mental illness. Also, until or unless there is an impairment in some vital area of human functioning or someone is harmed by the activity, cross-dressing is viewed as being within the parameters for normal variations of human behavior.

On the other hand, *transgenderists* (i.e., transpersons who are not interested in sexual reassignment surgery but still live part- or full-time in the opposite gender role) and *transsexuals* tend to differ significantly from cross-dressers in their internal understanding of who they are. Unlike their cross-dressing siblings, transgenderists and transsexuals are people who come to feel and believe that they can no longer continue to live or function within the framework of gender expectations associated with the physical sex assigned to them at birth.

Intersex persons are slowly emerging from the shadows to become a more visible element of society. We respectfully note that some intersex individuals do not identify with or consider themselves to be transgender, and feel they have differing experiences, histories, and needs than transgender persons. They believe that the transgender community does not necessarily reflect, include, or represent their unique intersex perspectives and experiences. This viewpoint on the part of some intersex persons deserves to be acknowledged. However, for this book's purposes, we will, with the most honorable and well meaning of intentions, include intersexuals as part of the very large and diverse transgender family and/or community.

According to sociology professor and intersex expert Dr. Sharon E. Preves, babies born with ambiguous genitalia (i.e., genitals that are difficult to classify as either male or female) number about 1 in 2,000, which is approximately the same frequency as babies born with Down's syndrome or cystic fibrosis. This type of birth is not statistically unusual.[26]

The birth of an intersex infant may occur frequently, but the medical community and society as a whole still seem to have trouble coping with the issue. In an article about Preves's book, *Intersex and Identity: The Contested Self,* John Townsend writes about "the callously systematized way that medicine and general society suffocate intersex people."[27] Townsend also says that "Society's urge to fit everybody into two discrete sexes has become so all-encompassing that the common medical practice has been to perform a surgical correction of ambiguous genitalia soon after birth, most often to female."[28]

That almost certainly happens because it is easier for surgeons to construct realistic female genitalia than operative male sexual organs. Helen Boyd writes, "Sometimes a girl is born with a sealed labia and a large clitoris and is declared a boy in the delivery room. Sometimes boys are born with what are referred to as 'micropenises' (and yes, doctors have a special ruler for measuring), who, if they are otherwise of indeterminate sex, are 'turned into' girls. (One surgeon actually crassly stated, 'It's easier to dig a hole than build a pole.' Charming.)"[29] As a result of these arbitrary actions on the part of physicians, "many intersexed individuals have found themselves unable to adjust to their involuntary gender assignment and deeply resent [such uninvited surgical procedures]."[30]

According to the Gay & Lesbian Alliance Against Defamation (GLAAD) Web site,

> The current model of treatment for intersexual infants and children, established in the 1950's, asserts that since the human species is sexually dimorphic, all humans must appear to be either exclusively male or female, and that children with visibly intersexual anatomy cannot develop into healthy adults. The model therefore recommends emergency sex assignment and reinforcement in the sex of assignment with early genital surgery. It also encourages care providers to be less than honest with parents and with intersexuals about their true status. This management model has led to profoundly harmful sorts of medical intervention and to neglect of badly needed emotional support.[31]

There is tremendous variety in terms of motivations, goals, methods of achieving personal fulfillment, gender expression, etc., on the part of gender-variant persons. All of these elements fall under the extremely broad umbrella heading of *transgender*. We are discovering that "Contrary to popular opinion, most crossdressers are usually heterosexuals, most drag queens aren't transsexuals, and the majority of the transgender individuals, while having the benefit of an extraordinary experience, have lives similar to those in the general population."[32] Lumping these unique types of people, with their extremely varied incentives, desires, and behaviors, into a single undifferentiated class or category is not only inaccurate and disrespectful but potentially detrimental to everyone involved. Ultimately, it is also disadvantageous to society as a whole. Our social institutions—including educational, medical, psychological, political, and business organizations—can and must do better than that.

INTERLUDE: SO, WHADDYA KNOW?

It can be useful to discover how much (or how little) we actually know about the transgender phenomenon. After taking this short quiz, people sometimes realize that their preconceived notions about transgender may have been inaccurate or misinformed. This little exercise may help you determine your own level of knowledge about the issue of transgender. Answers can be found in the back of the book (the first appendix)—but do not peek until you have completed the quiz.

True or False

1. Transgender has no definitive scientific explanation for its existence.
2. Every transgender person ultimately seeks sexual reassignment surgery.
3. Organizations that hire transgender workers usually regret that decision.
4. Everyone who is transgender is also gay or lesbian.
5. There is no cure for the existence of a transgender identity, nor is there a need for one.
6. Current federal law prohibits discrimination against transgender persons in the areas of employment, housing, and public accommodations.
7. Most transgender persons remain deeply "in the closet."
8. Transgender people are often excellent employees who make valuable contributions to their organizations.
9. Transitioning from one gender to another is a form of immoral sexual behavior.
10. The transgender phenomenon has been documented in cultures worldwide since the dawn of recorded human history.

Multiple Choice

1. Identify at least two types of transgender individuals from the following list:

   a. Prostitutes
   b. Cross-dressers
   c. Child molesters
   d. Intersex persons
   e. Drag queens
   f. Preoperative transsexuals
   g. Transvestites
   h. Hermaphrodites

2. Why would it benefit an organization to include gender identity, gender expression, and gender characteristics in its employee non-discrimination policies?

   a. Doing so can help in avoiding potential discrimination lawsuits.
   b. Doing so can improve an organization's ability to foster a positive workplace environment and provide equal opportunity for every employee, regardless of their gender identity.
   c. Doing so can help an organization meet its quota of diversity hires.

d. Doing so can help the organization promote good public relations within the community.

e. Doing so can help the organization comply with federal nondiscrimination laws.

3. Every transgender person

   a. is some sort of sexual deviant.
   b. is gay or lesbian.
   c. possesses some sort of mental illness.
   d. is a disaster waiting to happen.
   e. None of the above.

4. Transgender is

   a. the latest diversity training flavor-of-the-month.
   b. a manifestation of homosexual tendencies.
   c. a naturally occurring phenomenon that has existed in every culture and in every country in the world throughout history.
   d. a strong indication of immorality and/or perversity.
   e. usually portrayed with accuracy in the media.

5. A good reason for raising your own level of awareness about gender identity issues is because

   a. you may find yourself working with a transgender colleague. If you do, greater awareness of this issue can help you avoid potential obstacles to success for yourself and your team.
   b. transgender is a growing area of business interest throughout corporate America. The more you know, the better you will be equipped to interact effectively with transgender persons in general.
   c. hopefully, your organization expects each employee to abide by the same standards of positive, respectful, productive workplace behavior.
   d. All of the above.
   e. knowing something about this issue will give you a leading-edge topic to discuss at the office holiday party.

CHAPTER 2

Who Are Transgender People?

Accepting and identifying oneself as transgender can be a statement of personal empowerment. Some transpersons may opt to identify themselves as either female-to-male or male-to-female. Others may reject such categories outright, believing our society's binary gender system to be unacceptable, limiting, oppressive, and unworkable, at least for them.[1]

Also, some gender-variant persons may oppose being identified or categorized as transgender at all. Most people would probably agree that self-identification and self-determination are individual rights and liberties that everyone, whether transgender or not, can support and rally behind. No one particularly enjoys being classified according to someone else's decisions or determinations. Autonomy in terms of personal identification and expression is a natural desire for all human beings.

The widely accepted idea that gender is, above all, a cultural construct adds credibility to the premise that an individual need not be limited to or by a birth-designated gender, especially when that gender is based on purely biological factors such as genitalia or chromosomes.[2] Biology is not destiny, or at least it does not have to be. If the prevailing hypothesis about the cultural origins of gender is accurate, it follows that gender is actually an extremely malleable and variable human characteristic that is socially derived, shaped, and sustained. Given this cultural paradigm, gender can presumably take many forms and be manifested in numerous ways—which, as numerous global anthropological studies indicate, is indeed the case in various societies around the world. The issue has broad-based implications for human expression within social contexts, which is precisely why transgender deserves to be recognized and addressed as a human rights/civil rights/social justice issue as well as a practical business issue in our workplaces.

THE TRANSGENDER COMMUNITY

Anyone who self-identifies as transgender may belong to and is, in fact, already and automatically part of the transgender community. Nangeroni has defined this community as a "loose association of people who transgress gender norms in a wide variety of ways. Celebrating a recently born self-awareness, [the transgender] community is growing fast across all lines, including social, economic, political, and philosophical divisions. The central ethic of this community is unconditional acceptance of individual exercise of freedoms, including gender and sexual identity and orientation."[3]

Nangeroni's definition of "transgender community" presumably includes the families, friends, partners, and other non-transgender allies of transpersons. To support and/or identify with the transgender community is also to transgress gender norms in this culture, so supporters of transpeople are part of the community as well. There are many individuals who do not personally identify as transgender but, for various reasons, still care deeply about issues of justice and equality for the gender-variant. They actively support their transgender friends, family members, colleagues, coworkers, and loved ones as well as the philosophies of gender rights and equality in general. These non-transgender supporters and allies deserve to be welcomed, respected, and considered as much a part of the transgender community as anyone else.

Due to the social stigma associated with gender-variant expression, the transgender community has historically been fragmented and disjointed. Until fairly recently, transgender individuals and groups rarely worked together or even knew much about each other. For that reason, the concept of an actual, active, readily identifiable transgender community is still relatively new. Transpeople only began reaching out and finding each other starting in the 1960s, and it has only been in the last couple of decades that the Internet has become a primary source for developing community and sharing information. An even more recent development is the advent of openly transgender advocacy/political lobbying groups and influence on state and national levels. This is still a fledgling movement, though it holds promise in terms of potentially securing civil and legal rights for all transgender persons.

Due to a lack of community cohesion and unity, transgender persons have historically tended to focus on isolated and/or individual concerns of personal interest instead of larger issues—e.g., civil/human rights, changing unjust laws that penalize or oppress transpersons, and working for equality within society and its institutions—that concern the entire transgender community. However, this narrow focus on individualism is slowly beginning to shift as the need for consolidating systemic social and political influence becomes more apparent.

Opposition to social acceptance and respect for transgender people will inevitably necessitate more visibility and active involvement by gender-variant individuals. Society's fears of "difference" and the unknown that transgender represents call for trans individuals to band together, join with other supportive and/or like-minded individuals, create effective coalition, and strive together for the benefit and security of all.

SOME REAL-LIFE TRANSGENDER STORIES

It is often helpful and informative to learn about people who are living unique lives within a certain situational framework. In the next few pages, you will read about the true experiences of several gender-variant people who work for a living, beginning with the story of a college professor who came out as transgender at work.

Jeffrey Dickemann is an emeritus professor at Sonoma State University in Sonoma County, California. He came out in the workplace as a female-to-male transsexual at age 65. Dickemann recalls that from the age of five, he felt that the sex assigned to him at birth did not match his gender identity, though he did not act on that awareness publicly.

Late in his career as an anthropologist, Dickemann began some work that involved research on transgender issues. It was only after an anthropological conference where he presented his research and first met other transsexuals that he began to recognize his own deeply internalized transphobia, i.e., fear of his transgender nature. This discovery is similar to the way in which some gays and lesbians may learn about their own homophobia. Admitting that the fear exists is the first step to overcoming it.

Despite his misgivings, Dickemann started to realize and eventually acknowledge that, though born a biological female, he fundamentally identified himself as a male, at least internally. He began working with a therapist and soon came out as a female-to-male transsexual. Dickemann talks openly about "coming out" at work: "When I transitioned, I asked the chair to announce my new name, which she did. And that was that."

Dickemann apparently did not experience any opposition or discrimination from his fellow council members. In fact, he says, "All of these folks didn't even bat an eye. One guy even started talking to me about his prostate problems!"

"I have had no negative responses from anyone," said Dickemann on his coming out experience. "What I continue to get, with some nervousness and embarrassment, is a lot of praise for my 'courage.'"[4] While certainly courageous, Jeffrey Dickemann is fortunate and perhaps atypical in some respects, for many transpersons who come out at work or transition on the job are not so lucky as to be accepted without question or protestation.

Here is another story about a professional educator. Theresa (not her real name) is a British schoolteacher, a transsexual who transitioned from male to female on the job in 1999. She believed at first that transitioning at her school would be difficult if not impossible. However, she went to the school administration, shared her situation honestly, and was offered much more support than she had dared hope to receive.

The school wisely decided to go about informing everyone of Theresa's impending transition by preparing packets of information for staff, students, parents, and the press. According to Theresa, the staff and students have been incredibly supportive and there have been no disciplinary problems in any classes. Only a small number of parents complained about Theresa's transition on the job. The school's headmaster wrote to those parents, making it clear that Theresa had the full support of the school and bolstering that stance with factual information on transgender that had been previously prepared for such a contingency.

Theresa is a competent, skilled teacher who has now fully transitioned on the job and continues to hold the respect of her employers, peers, and students. She is proof that a successful workplace transition can be accomplished.

Now let us look at another—and not so inspiring—side of transgender employment.

On June 26, 2008, Sabrina Marcus Taraboletti went to Washington, D.C., to testify about transgender workplace discrimination before the House Committee on Education and the Workforce. In her testimony she described the despair she experienced when, six weeks after she announced her intent to transition from male to female, she was dismissed from her job as an aerospace engineer: "I cannot tell you how meaningless life feels when an event like this happens. I didn't know where to turn or what future I had. I was humiliated. I was fired. After 20 years of service, I received no severance pay nor was I allowed to collect unemployment. I have had to tell future potential employers I was dismissed; it has made finding new employment impossible."[5] In her deposition, Taraboletti also shared her thoughts on whether being transgender is a choice or a "lifestyle." She said, "Personally I have lost my wife, most of my assets, and my home in divorce. I have been abandoned by half my family and friends. At the same time, I had to find the $70–90,000 of funding and endure the extreme pain of electrolysis, and the various other surgeries required to complete the transition from male to female. All this while trying to stay employed! Believe me, no one wakes up one morning and thinks, 'Hey, I'm going to change my sex today.'"[6]

Katrina C. Rose is an attorney and transgender legal historian who is a postoperative transsexual woman. Rose candidly shares her viewpoint about what transgender means to her:

> So, what does transgender mean to me?
>
> [Among other things,] transgender means economic ruin. Because I'm transgendered [sic], I was unemployed for over a year after I graduated from law school. A few friends trusted me with their legal work, but it wasn't enough to survive. When I did find a job in the legal profession, it was 1,200 miles away from my home, in a state where I wasn't even licensed to practice law. Because I'm transgendered, in most states that have enacted employment anti-discrimination laws that protect homosexuals, I am still legally excludable even though I may be as qualified or more qualified than the heterosexual, homosexual or bisexual who was hired.[7]

Rose seems to sum up her feelings when she says, "You see, transgender means the ability to be me. Without that, what's the point of all the rest of it?"[8] Indeed, what is the point? Why should those who are transgender be forced to go through life living a lie, remaining legally vulnerable, having their civil rights violated, hiding in shame, and/or keeping their true identity a secret just because some people may not be "comfortable" with them or appreciate their gender situation? These issues are the primary impetus behind the transgender-at-work movement for equality, for when transgender people are respected and treated equally throughout the culture, no transperson will have to live or work in fear of discovery and/or reprisal. Transgender will be accepted as simply one of many authentic, benign, and positive aspects of human expression. That is no "special right," as some have attempted to portray it: it is an unalienable human right that deserves to be respected and valued because it will enhance society and make it a better place for us all.

Unfortunately, not everyone is aware of or cares about the importance of this particular human right. As of this writing, there are no federal statutes that protect transgender persons from discrimination in employment, housing, or public accommodations. According to a recent Human Rights Campaign (HRC) poll, 66 percent of respondents incorrectly believed that it is not legal to fire people because they are transgender.[9] The stark reality is that people are fired all the time because they are or are perceived as being gender-variant. Many in the transgender community are unemployed or underemployed, have experienced job discrimination, or have been exploited by working without any real job security. Some have lost hope altogether, given up, and turned to high-risk methods for finding survival income. Let us consider a few real-life examples of the employment situations of some of these transgender individuals.

Kristine Holt, a Pennsylvania social services agency worker, was fired from her job after she began a medically supervised male-to-female transition. She sued to get her job back, but the Commonwealth Court of Pennsylvania insisted that state law did not protect persons who suffered discrimination because of their transsexual status.[10] Not only is there no state statute protecting the employment rights of transpeople, but, as of this writing, there is still no federal law in place to protect transgender persons from job discrimination.

Peter Oiler, a truck driver for the Winn-Dixie food store chain, was fired when he revealed to his boss that he sometimes cross-dressed at home. Oiler had never cross-dressed at work, but his employment was terminated because his supervisor disapproved of Oiler's off-duty cross-dressing. A federal district court ruled in 2002 that federal employment discrimination law offered Oiler no legal protection since federal law does not prohibit discrimination against transgender people.[11]

Dana Rivers is a male-to-female transsexual who, as a man named David Warfield, was an award-winning teacher at Center High School in the Sacramento area. Rivers worked primarily with difficult and at-risk students, and was very good at it. Consequently, when he announced his impending transition from male to female, she was supported by the principal and staff of her school. The students, too, seemed supportive.

Things appeared to be going well for Rivers in the beginning, but she soon found herself vehemently opposed by a few members of the local school board who felt that her decision to transition publicly was inappropriate. They enlisted the aid of a local watchdog organization in a concerted effort to oust her from her teaching position. Rivers was put on leave pending a hearing to force her exit from the school. After nearly a decade of successful and award-winning work with extremely challenging pupils, she was suddenly pronounced unfit for service as a teacher.

Dana Rivers never again entered a Center High School classroom. She decided to sue for wrongful dismissal and eventually reached a settlement with the school district. Since then she has become a spokesperson for transgender persons, women, and civil rights. She has appeared on several national talk shows, including Oprah Winfrey's, and speaks at universities and conferences nationwide. Her message is the same no matter where she appears: "Human rights are every person's birthright, and this country must face the fact that discrimination based on gender, whether aimed at a butch lesbian, effeminate man, or transsexuals like myself, is wrong."[12]

Here is a happier story of transgender employment. Mary Ann Horton is a married heterosexual cross-dresser with a Ph.D. in computer science. She works as a professional engineer, building and deploying UNIX servers. She formerly worked for what is now Alcatel-Lucent Technologies, a worldwide leader in the information technology field. That organization has a comprehensive nondiscrimination employee policy, which specifically includes transgender employees. Mary Ann came out to her coworkers as a cross-dresser a few years ago and was able to begin cross-dressing occasionally on the job. Her experience was especially interesting in that she was sometimes Mary Ann at work and sometimes Mark, her male self. The key point is that her organization supported her right to dress and/or present herself as the unique person she knows herself to be. This was a powerful recognition of the rights of employees to determine for themselves how they will express their gender identity on the job.

Since cross-dressers often have both a masculine and a feminine persona, Mary Ann/Mark was free to come to the office and get her work done while wearing the clothing that seemed appropriate to her on a given day. Of course, there were corporate expectations that both Mark and Mary Ann would dress professionally and suitably for the office in alignment with the company dress code, but that is a perfectly reasonable expectation for all employees in any organization.

The freedom of personal gender expression that Mary Ann Horton enjoyed in her workplace can be a model for organizations that want their people to be at their best. Not only was Mary Ann more productive for her company because she was able to be her authentic self at work, but she was also able to help educate her coworkers about transgender and human difference in general while benignly exposing them to one of life's more intriguing phenomena. Everyone benefited from her presence and learned from the experience, and her organization became a better place to work because it upheld its nondiscrimination policy for all employees.

The preceding stories of transpersons are all true, and yet they are all different. Each individual had their own unique situation, and each found a way to address that situation. Some had a more difficult time than others, while some are still having difficulties. Others have prospered and been successful in their circumstances. In each case, they found the courage to come out and be their gender-variant selves on the job. Hopefully, many transpersons and their employers will appreciate the examples of bravery and personal integrity illustrated in these real-life stories.

THE IMPACT OF WORDS

Author Veronica Vera says that most of the time "people know just enough to be aware of the [transgender] phenomenon but not enough to know the rules of behavior."[13] To help us become more familiar with those rules, this part of the book will offer some definitions of transgender-related terms along with general ideas and suggestions about how to converse appropriately with and/or about gender-variant persons.

By now you have probably discerned that using the appropriate terminology is important when it comes to transpeople and their situations. That is because words are the ticket windows of thought. They effectively keep us from making intellectual progress until we have paid for that progress by using the acceptable currency, i.e., existing and/or commonly accepted terms and phrases that, by design and unwritten social agreement, limit our thinking to whatever we can articulate. And if our language does not allow for what we may be thinking (or at least considering), we usually do not—or cannot—go there conceptually.

However, if we want to understand transgender and its significance for the modern workplace, we must be able to think and speak clearly about the topic. This implies a need for specific language that can help us frame and articulate our ideas and reasoning. Therefore, we need access to words that permit a shared meaning among their users.

SPEAKING OF LANGUAGE

Whenever we define people we also confine and encapsulate them, at least on a conceptual level. That is why it is so important to use appropriate terminology when discussing or speaking to transgender individuals. If you are like most people, you may have heard or seen a few things about transgender people on television, at the movies, or in the newspaper but do not really know enough to speak about the issue in an informed way. If that is your situation, this chapter will provide a framework for better understanding as well as some tools for transgender-related thoughts and conversations.

We humans seem to have a mysterious but apparently insatiable need to categorize others and ourselves. That is probably because many of us do not handle uncertainty or instability very well. In response to our feelings of distress, we try to impose order. This need for categorization and order is often implied and/or unspoken, but it is no less real for all that. We want to make sense of the world, and we struggle to organize our thoughts and actions. In the process of doing so, we create meaning for ourselves.

It is emotionally important for us as individuals to be able to identify with one group or another. The desire to belong and/or identify ourselves as part of a group is a significant aspect of the human condition. Such a need for belonging and identification may perhaps be useful in helping us find others who may be similar for friendship, but judging and/or imposing categorization on someone else (whether well-intentioned or not) can sometimes be harmful. We all deserve the right to identify and/or categorize ourselves.

Travelers who are preparing to visit another country will often learn a few words and phrases in the native language of that country so they can operate a little more efficiently. If we are going to journey into Transgenderland, we probably ought to learn to speak at least some of the language so we can maneuver without becoming lost or disoriented. This chapter is not intended to be a comprehensive examination of all transgender-related words and phrases, but you should find enough information here to help you converse a bit more readily about the phenomenon that is transgender.

To begin, let us distinguish between the words "transgender" and "transgender*ed*." One online commentator remarked, quite tellingly, "The term 'transgendered' has incorrectly come into widespread usage. This form should be avoided as it is linguistically passive and implies something being conferred [or, in this case, socioculturally imposed] on a person from outside. In terms of gender identity, which comes from within, 'transgendered' is no more appropriate than it would be to talk of a person being 'maled' or 'femaled' or to say that a gay man was 'homosexualed.'"[14]

Furthering this line of thought beyond the notion of mere linguistics and moving into the realm of enhanced social awareness, note that an -ed is often attached to the name of a group of people as long as that group is still being culturally oppressed. Examples might include "The Colored; The Retarded; The Handicapped; The Intersexed; [to this list we can add] The Transgendered."[15] But when the oppression is shifted and eventually lifted by a raising of consciousness and increased acceptance within the larger society, the -ed suffix is dropped and a new phrase is coined, e.g., "People of Color; People with mental challenges; People with Disabilities; Intersex People; Transgender People."[16]

When we place the words Heterosexual, Gay, Lesbian, Bisexual, and Transgendered next to each other in this context, it is obvious that "transgendered" is not equal to the others in status. The implication of an inferior or subordinate condition is why the word "transgender," *not* "transgender-ed," should be used. "Transgender" deserves the same cultural standing, dignity, and respect as other groups.

Removing the -ed from transgender allows transpersons to be more fully perceived as human beings of infinite worth rather than as an afflicted or unequal group. Dropping the -ed thus becomes a distinctive social marker of the group's empowerment. It is a linguistic signal—a verbal indication that the group is beginning to come of age, that it is being taken seriously, and that it is moving beyond victimization and/or inferior status toward a more significant and culturally viable position.[17]

Interesting, isn't it, what a simple -ed suffix can do? It significantly alters the tone, sociocultural implication, and character of the word in question. This is a demonstration of the impact of appropriate terminology when we are talking about complex subjects such as transgender. Behold the power of language to create, continuously inform, and shape our reality.

GENDER, SEX, AND AWARENESS

Now let us take a look at the important distinctions between sex and gender. We touched briefly on this topic in the last chapter and have learned that our culture often confuses the two words, mistakenly classifying them as somehow identical or analogous and using them interchangeably. This is a significant sociocultural blunder, and it creates a pervasively negative public perception of gender and sexual minorities. Despite this seemingly ubiquitous cultural paradigm, it is necessary for us to be aware of the nuances and distinctions between sex and gender if we are to advance in our understanding of these complex human characteristics.

Gender may be defined as the ways in which we perceive individuals to be masculine, feminine, or other within the overall context of social expectations and understandings. In this culture, we tend to associate masculine and feminine meanings with human characteristics that may include

- Genitalia and/or chromosomes, which are the usual definers of physical/biological sex;
- Other physical features such as body shape and size, weight, height, voice, and the lack or presence of body hair;
- Sexual orientation, which is an incomplete determinant for a person's gender since gender and sex exist on different (though occasionally overlapping) spectrums of human possibilities;
- Behavior or dress; for example, a male who cries easily or wears a skirt might be considered "unmanly," while a woman who is aggressive or wears a masculine-tailored suit coat and slacks may be considered "unfeminine."

Our society's notion of gender is subject to all the cultural expectations, preconceptions, and unique possibilities of which human beings are capable. Those possibilities have an extraordinary range in terms of their potential manifestations in people's lives. When social expectations and preconceptions about gender serve to limit those human possibilities, however, everyone is impoverished.

Mike Reynolds states that gender "is a series of behaviors that we learn, and then repeat as we mature. Our understanding of our gender is built through our continuous interaction with others over time and is driven by a basic need for social inclusion. These behavior patterns allow others to easily identify us as male or female, and then behave toward us according to an assumed confidence in our sexual identity."[18]

Persons who are transgender do not always fit nicely or neatly into the expected patterns of behavior and/or appearance that society has designated for all males and females. For transpeople, culturally created gender expectations often do not feel right or sit well emotionally/psychologically. The undeniable presence of internal discomfort can be a compelling motivation for transpersons to explore their gender identity and its many personal ramifications. Therein lies the conundrum—and much of the mystery—that surrounds the existence of transgender as a social phenomenon: it cannot be explained or rationalized, but neither can it be ignored.

Gender identity is about how we individually perceive and understand ourselves. It has to do with recognizing our inner psychological sense of self within the framework of our socialization. Gender identity encompasses our own personal awareness, i.e., our core internal knowledge of who we are as masculine, feminine, or other. Characteristics associated with gender identity may include self-image, physical appearance and biological attributes, behavior, and gender-related conduct/behavior in the context of relationships. However, the most significant elements of gender identity are (1) one's internalized, individual self-perception and identification, and (2) the gender-based perceptions of others with regard to an individual. In the workplace, the phrase "gender identity" is sometimes used when referring to the situations of transsexual (or other transgender) employees, particularly those who transition from one sex to another while remaining on the job.

Reynolds has written,

The key to understanding gender identification lies in an understanding of symbolic interaction. The perceptions of others, if internalized by us, eventually become our reality. If we collectively attach meaning onto all the things that surround us and then treat these objects according to the values that are implied by the meanings we attach, this objectification, when we come to accept it as true and relevant, can form our sense of identity when it is socially reinforced over time. The appearance we present as masculine or feminine directly affects the way we are treated by, and thereby treat, those around us.[19]

Reynolds's premise of gender identification, recognized as an individual understanding acquired over time and as the result of repeated experience, indicates that gender identification is based upon a variety of personal qualities. Those qualities often impact the ways in which we are perceived and treated by others.

Gender characteristics refers to embodied primary and/or secondary physical attributes such as weight, height, body hair (or the lack thereof), eye color, and other factors over which the individual may have little or no control. Examples of gender characteristics might include a male with a high voice, a female with facial hair, or someone with ambiguous genitalia (e.g., an intersex person) or an androgynous appearance. Physical gender markers like these are not always chosen or arbitrarily determined, yet they may become the criteria for social judgments based on an individual's form of gender expression or perceived sexual orientation.

Gender role has to do with society's gender-based expectations for men and women. Interestingly enough, the words "men" and "women" are gender-related terms that refer to persons in social settings and depend exclusively upon cultural context to provide their meanings. After all, what is a "real man" or a "real woman"? People from different cultures may (and probably will) offer a variety of different answers to such questions.

On the other hand, "male" and "female" are biological terms that refer solely to physical distinctions and organic characteristics—and even here we note the potential for variance within the human species, since not all people everywhere have exactly the same naturally supplied equipment. Mother Nature delights in variety, even in matters of human biology.

In this culture, the ubiquitous influence of gender roles begins at or even before birth. That powerful influence often begins its work the moment parents learn the sex of their child. From the choice of the child's name to the way the child is held and treated, and from the colors of the child's nursery to the clothing that is worn to the kinds of toys that are provided, children are both subtly and overtly nudged toward what society considers an appropriate gender role—a role that is almost always determined by a physician's assessment and based upon the child's genitalia and body type at birth. Parents and children who attempt to circumvent or ignore these social norms and expectations relative to gender role may find themselves the victims of surveillance and/or the subject of general confusion by others. The process of socialization, which includes the enforcement of cultural gender roles, is especially meaningful in early childhood development and continues into adolescence and adulthood. The scope and parameters of a child's existence are powerfully influenced by the gender role into which the child is steered in the course of this pervasive, ever-present socialization experience. Educational and career choices as well as the social definition of what is considered "successful" by either gender may be defined well before a child of either sex reaches a significant turning point in life.

Gender roles and their accompanying expectations—as well as the actual words used to refer to them—are extremely subjective and may vary widely from culture to culture. If we take a look at other cultures, we can readily observe that being a "man" or a "woman" in our society is not "normal" or "natural" but learned behavior. We are learning that very few people are found at the extreme ends of the gender scale. Hardly anyone is "100 percent" masculine or "100 percent" feminine, while people who exist near the middle of the gender scale are often considered to be androgynous.

Amy Bloom reminds us of the unique nature of gender roles: "We know that neither the object of desire nor the drinking of beer nor the clenching of fists makes maleness [or femaleness, for that matter]. We don't know what does."[20] That is part of transgender's inherent mystery: we do not really know what makes masculinity or femininity. We only know it (or think we know it) when we see or experience it in ourselves or others.

Gender expression is how we communicate our gender status to others. The term has to do with the manner in which we convey and/or present ourselves externally through our appearance, clothing, carriage, body language, personal mannerisms, and behaviors. It is about how we outwardly manifest our fundamental, internal sense of ourselves as masculine, feminine, or other. Personal gender expression may include varying elements such as dress, accessorization, posture, gestures and other body movements, vocal pitch and inflections, language choices, and personal interests. These physically based presentational aspects offer a variety of social "gender cues" to others, although sometimes such cues may be misread or misinterpreted.

There are many ways to manifest gender, and certain methods of gender expression tend to convey powerful cultural meaning and significance. That is because, as Nangeroni informs us, "Gender expression is a function of behavior, voluntary and involuntary. It includes facial appearance, vocal intonation, as well as general body carriage and movement. While some aspects of expression (smiling, acting nervous, etc.) are not gendered, many (wrist and hip motion, voice pitch and phrasing, use of facial makeup, choice of clothing, etc.) are strongly gendered."[21]

A discussion of gender-based behaviors brings us to the socially complex topic of *gender stereotypes*. These are the idealized and often romanticized patterns, the stylized templates, and the accepted "social forms" that shape our broad cultural expectations of what people ought to be like. For example, gender stereotypes for females in our society include being sensitive, socially oriented, emotional, weaker, and physically smaller than males. Obviously, this kind of generic labeling or categorization for females can be inherently unfair, faulty, and misleading; as we know, some women are strong, large, insensitive, unsociable, and/or may not exhibit overt emotionalism. The feminine cultural stereotype is often inaccurate and has never accurately applied to all females.

Our culture's gender stereotypes for males can be equally inexact. The masculine stereotype includes characteristics such as being muscular, tall, hirsute, and emotionally impassive. In actuality, there are many males who are relatively non-muscular, are short, have little or no body or facial hair, and are highly emotional. (A female-to-male transsexual once jokingly referred to himself in this way: "I'm on the cutting edge of hip—short, fat, and bald is in this year.") Lumping all males and females into generic or stereotypical categories is not only imprecise, it does a disservice to the wide variety of remarkable possibilities that are inherent and available within the human condition.

Despite the unfairness of stereotyping, B. J. Gallagher's book, *A Peacock in the Land of Penguins: A Tale of Diversity and Discovery*, indicates that stereotypes are in fact a significant part of social and organizational life in our culture. In the workplace, common stereotypes may include

- Assumptions about another person based only on their occupation (e.g., "Typical middle management type!");

- Assuming that everyone in a certain category is just like everyone else in that category (e.g., "You know how those mechanics/engineers/administrative assistants/academics/vice presidents are . . . ");
- Assuming that certain types of people are naturally suited to specific jobs or activities (e.g., "That tall guy must have played basketball in high school," or "Women fit so well into social work.").

Sometimes we may arbitrarily categorize a person and then discount their input or personal value based on that categorization (e.g., "What could she possibly know or contribute? She's only a secretary."). We may automatically place career advancement or job change barriers in front of others because we view them as suited for only one kind of position (e.g., "He wants to be a project manager? But he's always worked in shipping!"). Rather than learn about someone's skills, abilities, and interests, we may make assumptions based solely on physical appearance (e.g., "That transgender person looks a little 'different'—obviously not a candidate for upper management."). And sometimes we may attribute certain characteristics to individuals based on only one piece of information about them (e.g., "He's from France; I bet he smokes like a chimney—all French people do," or "She's got such a short haircut—she has to be a lesbian").

Gender stereotyping in a workplace setting is inaccurate at best, fantasy much of the time, and potentially detrimental to the organization and/or the individual(s) in question. Few of us, regardless of our gender status, can realistically live up to the improbable cultural stereotypes we are expected to achieve. Trying to force individuals into narrow, unyielding gender stereotypes is often a root cause of discrimination stemming from unmet (or unreasonable) expectations about gender expression, identity, or characteristics.

WHY THE WORDS MATTER

Workplace oppression sometimes occurs through harmful "discriminatory semantics," or verbalized negative attitudes toward others. Verbal discrimination may be overt or implied. Sometimes subtle, cleverly worded discrimination can be the most psychologically subversive and damaging (as well as the most difficult to prove). This can be especially dangerous for transpersons, who may feel powerless and/or unequipped to counter the effects of such understated, though no less devastating, discrimination.

Many scholars and researchers have affirmed that language is the primary shaper of a culture. The Sapir-Whorf hypothesis of linguistics indicates that the language we use molds the very form and texture of thought itself. Much of our current workplace language is a holdover from the old, "mechanized" days of the Industrial Revolution, a time when workers were considered to be interchangeable cogs in a corporate machine instead of unique, special, valuable human beings with remarkable potential to bring to their organizations and the world. Continued use of Industrial Era language in business settings may impose antiquated limitations on our thinking, which is precisely why we need to develop a more helpful and relevant workplace vocabulary.

> *Words are the bugles of social change. When our language changes, behaviour will not be far behind.*
>
> —Charles Handy

Handy's implication is that if we change the way we speak, we will change the way we think. Following this line of reasoning, if we change the way we think, then we will inevitably begin to change how we act—and if we change the way we act, imagine what might be accomplished in terms of making our organizations more just and equitable places for everyone. Whenever organizational leaders choose to model an "emerging" mind-set (i.e., a newer, more inclusive, and socially relevant business paradigm to replace the outmoded Industrial Era ways of speaking, thinking, and acting), then positive change—a beneficial transformation that includes respect and acceptance for human diversity in all its forms, including gender variance—in the workplace often results. In an affirming, respectful work culture, positive language will thrive, and so will the people who regularly speak that language.

NAMES, DESIGNATIONS, AND PRONOUNS

Like all human beings, transpersons prefer to be addressed respectfully. When speaking or referring to a transgender individual, it is customary to use the correct name or pronoun for the gender in which the person is presenting at that time. Using "she," "her," "Ma'am," "Ms.," "he," "him," "Sir," or "Mr." in an appropriate manner can help bring about the following:

- It will demonstrate to the transgender person that you respect them enough to use accurate terms when speaking to or about them.
- It can help defuse or de-escalate a potentially difficult or embarrassing social situation.
- It will set a tone of respect and acceptance, which can be a model for other people who may be observing or engaged in the conversation.
- It will demonstrate that you are reasonably knowledgeable about the expectations and guidelines for interacting with a transperson, and that you are a culturally aware individual who understands how to converse respectfully with a gender-variant human being.

One of our fundamental cultural markers for recognizing other people is gender. Because our society is so obsessively gender-oriented, we may become anxious and/or irritated when we cannot immediately recognize the gender of another person, whether child or adult. Transperson Jessie Gilliam, who presents as androgynous and identifies as gender neutral, uses feminine personal pronouns but is sometimes perceived as male in public. Gilliam tells of a startling encounter with someone who was not sure of Jessie's gender. That indecision led the other person to behave in a way that was not overly polite or respectful. "The other day, a stranger on the street asked, 'Girl, right?' I told him it was none of his business and he followed me for almost two blocks trying to figure it out. That was really scary," Gilliam recalls.[22] "People feel it's their right to confront strangers about their gender in ways they would never question other aspects of your identity."[23]

Jessie Gilliam's situation is an example of how important it is for some persons to be able to instantly recognize the gender of another. When they cannot make an immediate gender determination, people sometimes become obsessive and cannot rest until the uncertainty is settled in their minds. Jessie Gilliam lives in a rather androgynous place on the gender spectrum, and her personal method of gender identification/presentation seems to push some people's buttons to a substantial degree.

Admittedly, it may sometimes be difficult to immediately discern a person's gender. Everyone's gender identity is not always clear and overt at first glance. When in doubt and/or if necessary, you can always politely ask how that person wishes to be addressed. Common sense, courtesy, respect, and honesty can work wonders in such situations. Keep in mind that potential confusion or ambiguity about someone's gender status does not convey the right to be purposely crass, rude, or demeaning toward another individual.

Sometimes it is not even the words themselves that suggest an intent to be disrespectful or dehumanizing. Negative, degrading intentions can also be communicated through the attitude and vocal tone of the speaker. Referring to less-than-positive interactions with others, transgender stage and television actress Alexandra Billings has remarked, "It's not about what you say to me, it's about how you say it. There's a tonality about it, an ownership that's insulting." Tone and demeanor can reveal much about a person's intentions toward someone else.

Defamation of an individual or a group is often a precursor to persecution. Denigration can quickly turn to social marginalization, which fosters a climate that is ripe for overt discrimination. The danger of a discriminatory climate is that such environments have historically led to a systematic movement designed to minimize—and in some extreme cases, eliminate—the targeted person or group. Just ask the Jews of Hitler's Germany. The holocaust began with defamatory rhetoric.

Transgender author Monica F. Helms has written, "It took African-Americans decades to make white America understand how hurtful the 'N' word is to them, and they had more people to deliver the message. [It sometimes feels as though] the transgender community may have to wait until the 22nd century before non-trans people finally get the message about improper pronouns."[24] Hopefully, it will not take another hundred years to help non-transpersons understand the significance of this issue in terms of its cultural implications.

Correct uses of appropriate pronouns for transfolk are verbal signals that indicate whether the person who is speaking "gets" it. If the signal is not a positive one, it may be an indicator that the transgender person is potentially in for some difficulty. The other individual may not understand the importance of using the correct words; even worse, he or she may have grasped the idea but is not happy about it and has decided to attack, ridicule, or annoy the transperson by purposely using incorrect gender terms. When a negative situation like this occurs, there are usually three options for the transperson:

1. Ignore or overlook the misuse of the name, designation, or pronoun and hope that things will improve over time.

2. Gently attempt to correct the person in good faith, with the hope that they will be open to learning and change.

3. Confront the offending person directly by challenging their inappropriate speech.

The option chosen by the transgender individual may be pivotal in establishing the atmosphere that will emerge in that workplace. Ignoring rude or purposely disrespectful verbiage will usually not make the problem go away. In fact, doing so may potentially be interpreted as a sign of weakness or an implied acceptance of inappropriate behavior—and then other people may start believing they, too, are free to be disrespectful toward the transperson. If the transgender individual chooses to gently but firmly correct the other person, it demonstrates that the transperson "caught" what they did and is trying to help them. This approach may or may not be successful, depending upon the attitude and response of the other person involved. Finally, the transgender individual may decide to openly confront the other person's inappropriate behavior by calling them on it and insisting that proper terminology be used. If the latter approach is chosen, the transperson should know their rights and be prepared to go to management and/or file a complaint if necessary.

Keeping a written record of any negative encounters, hurtful language, and/or inappropriate treatment while on the job is strongly advised for transgender workers. Transpersons are urged to document such occurrences to the fullest extent possible. Write down all the specific details of each incident, including names, dates, times, locations, witnesses, and the effects on your frame of mind and ability to work. (And do not do it on your work computer—do it in longhand, on your own paper. That way you can protect yourself from charges of inappropriate use of company property. You can type your notes up later at home.) If legal action should ever be required, there will be appropriate documentation of those incidents. Such documentation can demonstrate an established pattern of improper behavior on the part of detractors and may potentially lead to a judgment in the transperson's favor.

As noted previously, names and pronouns can sometimes be confusing when a transgender worker begins the coming out process on the job. For this reason, transgender individuals who are transitioning or presenting in another gender at work are encouraged to be patient with others. Remember, this is new for everyone. Coworkers and team members are adapting to change, too. An adjustment to a new situation does not always happen immediately or automatically. However, no one should be forced to become a doormat just to try to please someone else or to avoid conflict at all costs. Personal dignity should never be compromised.

The Web site www.tgender.net tells us:

> If you follow the transgender community customs, you should be addressed by your femme name when presenting as a woman, and your masculine name when presenting as a man, with the appropriate pronouns [she/her/hers, or he/him/his] to match the presentation. However, it is important that you [be realistic and] not impose a burden on your co-workers. Answer to both names [at first, if necessary]. If your co-workers are supportive, it's OK to gently correct them if they get the pronoun or name wrong, if they are trying to get it right.[25]

People's genuine intentions make a difference. Even if they slip up, most people are considerate and will try to get it right next time. An honest mistake is certainly no cause for anger or hurt feelings, but purposely continuing the mistake over an extended period of time may be perceived as a direct insult and/or a lack of respect, and should be treated accordingly.

The appropriate use of terminology for transpersons is a symbolic act indicating respect for them as individuals and for the transgender community of which they are a part. Correct names, designations, and pronouns are a sign that progress is being made, respect is being shown, and acceptance is occurring—but if words are not used appropriately, there may be a problem. That negative situation may quickly turn into the organizational status quo if left unchecked, which is why it is necessary to deal with such issues early on before they can become larger, more pervasive problems. The words we use matter, and no one should be forced to work in an environment of verbal or behavioral disrespect.

CHAPTER 3

Why Transgender Inclusion Matters to Your Business (Even If You Didn't Know It)

> *Work is a mysterious thing; many of us claim to hate it, but it takes a grip on us that is so fierce that it captures emotions and loyalties we never knew were there.*
>
> —Bob Greene

Most successful business organizations today are active users of technology and digital information. No great surprise there, right? We are swamped with data and barraged with messages all day, every day. Some people have begun calling this "the age of too much information." According to Richard Saul Wurman's book, *Information Anxiety* (Doubleday), "The information explosion has backfired, leaving us inundated with facts but starving for understanding."[1]

Despite the seemingly ubiquitous technological advances that we see all around us, human potential will remain "the primary source of competitive advantage in almost every industry."[2] Besides, "the success of any organization is based on the individual success of each person in that organization."[3] Presumably, "each person in that organization" includes transgender employees.

The significance of transgender in the workplace is this: transgender is corporate America's last great human rights issue. Although the situation is improving in certain organizations and areas of business, transgender is the last major inclusion topic that has yet to be confronted in most of our workplaces today.

Unfortunately, our knowledge of this unique subject may be incorrect or misinformed. If you are like most people, you probably do not know a great deal about the transgender phenomenon. You may not think you know any transgender individuals, either. (Just so you are aware, the odds are high that you are acquainted with at least one or more transgender persons. However, because most transpeople keep their gender-variant identities hidden from the general public for fear of rejection or recrimination, you probably do not know that you know them.) Despite this lack of overall social awareness, transgender is increasingly becoming a specific area of interest for business leaders and organizations across the United States and around the world. The topic deserves to be examined from the varied perspectives of management, ownership, employees, and customers.

THE INTRINSIC, BUSINESS-RELATED VALUE OF HUMAN DIVERSITY AND INCLUSIONARY STRATEGIES

The late business management guru Peter Drucker once indicated that the only legitimate functions of a business are to create customer (value) and to innovate.[4] Jeffrey R. Immelt, CEO of General Electric, has stated, "Most people inside GE learn from the past but have a healthy disrespect for history. They have an ability to live in the moment and not be burdened by the past."[5] Looking to the future and innovatively imagining their way toward it is how organizations create customer value. The fact is, "Innovative companies have innovative cultures."[6] Continuous innovation that leads to lasting customer value has proven to be the optimum way to achieve business success over time.

Unfortunately, not every organization's leadership understands (and some may have forgotten) what it takes for a company to create customer value and be innovative in this modern economy: finding, hiring, and retaining the best people to do the job, then providing a work environment that is conducive to innovation and the creation of value. Smart, skilled, imaginative, hardworking people are the most important determinant for any winning business endeavor. They are the ones who drive innovation through their ideas and efforts, and the success of any organization is always directly proportionate to the success of its individual members.

Many businesses have discovered that an increasingly significant aspect of attracting and retaining the best people involves a proactive pursuit of pluralism. It is no longer a stretch to say that for many companies, an inclusive workforce has become a business imperative. Today's primary business currency is ideas, and the most creative ideas do not arise from a rigid similarity in thought, appearance, attitude, and human experience. Such conformity leads only to stagnation, not innovation. The best, most groundbreaking ideas tend to emerge from a wealth of human differences, which comprise a unique pool of talents, skills, knowledge, and abilities. A surplus of creative new ideas can only reside in a workforce that is intentionally diverse and inclusive.

Marketing and hiring demographics are changing, and business studies indicate that companies seeking only orthodox conventionality in their employees will limit their ability to become high performance organizations. In an increasingly global market, the "same old same old" hiring approaches cannot meet the constant challenges of that market. The active, intentional pursuit of inclusivity in the workforce is an insurance policy against stagnation and a corporate similarity of thought, both of which are virtual death in today's complex, ever-changing business arena. As "Organizations compete for human resources and as the workforce becomes more heterogeneous, organizations will have to serve the diverse needs of this workforce or they will lose them to their competitors."[7]

If everyone in a company thinks alike and adheres to the same worldview, from where will the new, original, and/or breakthrough ideas arise? Recognizing the dangers inherent in a sameness of thought, many organizations are discovering that "In the context of the workplace, valuing diversity means creating a workplace that respects and includes differences, recognizing the unique contributions that individuals with many types of differences can make, and creating a work environment that maximizes the potential of all employees."[8] It is all about developing a welcoming, accepting, intentionally inclusive business culture where people can do their best, most creative work.

Developing a shared vision that includes pluralism is a way for organizations to move forward more effectively in today's ever-shifting world of commerce. Part of such a vision will hopefully involve a healthy respect for the many benign differences that exist within the human race. However, it is important to clarify what is meant by "respect."

Educator Alan Horowitz has said, "We throw these words around, especially words like 'respect'... But if you had a roomful of 10 people, and asked them what respect was ... you'd get different answers. I think the trick in a ... corporate environment or any type of institution is to develop a shared vision and move forward from there."[9] Significant, ongoing conversations about the meaning and implications of respect are recommended as an important tool for developing that shared vision within a workplace community.

A common misconception in business organizations is that diversity and inclusion is only about gender or race, or that it is structured solely around affirmative action or Equal Employment Opportunity (EEO) efforts. In actuality, pluralism in the business world takes many forms and can come in a variety of packages. Successful initiatives are always accompanied by an organizational mind-set that is committed to continuously and purposefully developing an inclusive company made up of many different kinds of people—a place where everyone is allowed, encouraged, and liberated by management to live into their potential and do their best thinking.

The American Heritage Dictionary says that pluralism is "A condition in which numerous distinct ethnic, religious, or cultural groups are present and tolerated within a society," and "The belief that such a condition is desirable or socially beneficial."[10] In the words of the American Society of Mechanical Engineers Professional Practice Curriculum, to value human diversity implies an acknowledgment

> that other people, other races, other voices, and other cultures have as much integrity and as much claim on the world as you do. It is the recognition that there are other ways of seeing the world, solving problems, and working together. Managing diversity means promoting inclusion, creating an environment where all differences are valued [and where] each employee can develop to her or his full potential. From a business perspective, managing diversity is valuable because it means an organization gets the most from its employees. Companies that effectively manage diversity recognize that it is not enough to hire employees from underrepresented groups; they must also provide an environment where all employees are supported and valued.[11]

Inclusion in an organization can become a key to a positive work environment which is conducive to productive, professional working relationships. When implemented effectively, inclusion is a purposeful long-term business strategy that includes and influences all systems and processes of the organization. Affirmative action and EEO initiatives, on the other hand, usually have more to do with legal issues and eliminating discrimination in hiring based on race and gender concerns. While removing racial and gender-based discrimination are certainly worthwhile endeavors for any company, there is a great deal more to organizational diversity than merely those two elements.

Pierre Loewe and Jennifer Dominiqui of Strategos, an innovation consultancy, are convinced that pluralism is a key to creativity and to the imaginative ideas that are necessary to keep organizations competitive. They say,

> Though companies often pay lip service to the need to harness innovation talent throughout their organizations, in practice they restrict innovation to a few areas or departments. Diversity matters too. Too many companies view innovation as the domain of R&D only, or perhaps R&D and marketing. But people in manufacturing, supply chain, human resources, finance, service and other functional areas can be creative too—if given an opportunity. Creativity and imagination are unevenly and somewhat randomly distributed, and one never knows where the next big idea might come from.[12]

Hiring and retaining the best people is a prerequisite to getting any organization to effectively do what it is supposed to do. If businesses do not support their people by encouraging the development and expression of their full human potential, Maslow says, "our successes will be short lived, our plans nothing more than short-term, and our ability to continue to compete in a global world severely restrained."[13] A nonnegotiable commitment to the continued development of its people always adds to an organization's competitive advantage.

It does not matter how powerful your technology or how much capital you have at your disposal: no organization can remain consistently competitive in today's marketplace without competent, capable people to run it and help it grow on every level. This places a significant responsibility on employers and hiring managers to hire the best people to help their organizations succeed. People are more important than technology, machines, business processes, or even extreme profitability, which is why employers must make work fulfilling and fair.

Long-term business success comes from hiring workers for their skills, talents, and abilities, then liberating those individuals to do their jobs and live into their full capacity as human beings. It takes great people doing great work in fair, just, and rewarding workplaces to make great companies. Today, more than ever, leading organizations are recognizing the value of transgender employees in the quest for business success.

"NORMAL": A STATISTICAL AVERAGE, NOT A VALUE JUDGMENT

"It is abnormal. It is un-natural. And it is an act against God the almighty." This quote was taken directly from an excerpt of the Congressional Record and refers to women who sought the right to vote.

It may be difficult for most of us to imagine today, but women who were courageous enough to stand up and be counted—women who spoke out for equality, justice, and their inalienable right and franchise to vote—were once labeled as "abnormal" and "un-natural." Many of the males in positions of sociopolitical power at that time considered women's suffrage efforts to be an affront to the Deity, to the structure of society, and to the "natural order of things." President Grover Cleveland, presumably not a feminist, pontificated that "Sensible and responsible women do not want to vote." Women have only been permitted to cast ballots in the United States since 1920. The lesson of history is that full equality for minorities, no matter what the group or the issue, does not come without struggle.

Women who sought the right to vote were not the only ones subjected to charges of abnormality. For example, there was very deep prejudice against Irish-Americans during the nineteenth century. Miscegenation, i.e., marriage between persons of different races, was considered unnatural and aberrant (not to mention illegal in many states until a 1967 Supreme Court ruling permitted such marriages throughout the country). The ongoing struggles of gay and lesbian citizens for social acceptance and civil equality have been well documented over the past few decades. Inequality and injustice are still alive and well in various aspects of American life, as certain groups of minority citizens can readily attest. Today, the words "abnormal" and "unnatural" are often directed toward transgender persons.

Transpeople are individuals

who want to live their lives true to their [internal gender] identities—at home, in public, and yes, at the workplace. Transgendered [sic] people suffer tremendous discrimination in
employment. Indeed, it's part of our culture that if you admit to
crossdressing, or plan to change your sex, you'll be automatically
fired. But all that is changing. Increasing numbers of companies
are understanding of transgendered [sic] people. White collar
employers, universities, and government branches large enough
to have a Human Resources department are often understanding
of a transsexual who must transition. In many cases, the transition
can take place while keeping the same job. Crossdressers can
often be open about who they are.[14]

THE BUSINESS SIGNIFICANCE OF TRANSGENDER AWARENESS

> *Don't be afraid of change. Be afraid of not changing.*
>
> —Anonymous

Why is it important for today's business organizations to be aware of
the transgender phenomenon? Mostly it is because growing numbers of
successful companies are beginning to realize the value of an increasingly pluralistic workforce. They want to hire people that are used to
dealing with others who are different. Many of today's organizations
are international in scope and will actively seek to hire workers who
are culturally adaptable and comfortable with pluralism and human
difference. "Adding gender identity to company non-discrimination
policies makes good business sense. Maryella Gockel of Ernst & Young
says, 'It's all a part of our inclusiveness strategy to help people believe
and feel they are valued.' "[15]

"Proponents see the trend as a natural progression from the protections for women and gays against harassment. 'Gender identity and
expression was the next step,' adds Maria Campbell, director of diversity
at S. C. Johnson."[16] (S. C. Johnson has consistently been rated in the
top 10 of "100 Best Companies to Work For" by *Fortune* magazine's
annual survey.)

There were few transgender-related Human Resources policies at U.S. employers until the late 1990s, and practically none at large employers. However, in 1997, transgender HR policy adoption began to appear, and began to rapidly increase in 2001.[17] The number of organizations of all sizes with transgender-inclusive HR/EEO policies continues to grow steadily with each passing year. As of this writing, over 175 *Fortune* 500 companies have adopted policies that prohibit discrimination based on gender identity.

In addition to the business community, escalating numbers of cities and states as well as large, midsize, and small business organizations are moving definitively in the direction of justice and human rights for transpeople as the social awareness level surrounding the transgender phenomenon continues to rise. Enlightened jurisdictions are on the rise: as of this writing, 14 state governments, the District of Columbia, and over 100 city and county governments in the United States have implemented some form of antidiscrimination protection that includes gender identity. "More municipalities are slowly including gender diversity under the human rights umbrella, and many more personnel departments are equipped to deal with sex and gender change."[18] It is a notable cultural shift toward an acceptance of greater pluralism, further indicating that transgender is a valid public issue that today's organizations can no longer afford to ignore or dismiss as socially, politically, legally, or financially irrelevant. This remarkable trend is building momentum in workplaces because businesspeople are realizing that it is a practical thing to do to help ensure the ongoing success and growth of their organizations.

The word "practice" implies engaging in some type of action or behavior—and that is exactly what we are talking about in terms of workplace best practices: behaviors. Terry Howard, Diversity Director for Texas Instruments, has written, "[The transgender] workplace issue is about behaviors and *not* about beliefs. Everyone has a right to his or her opinions, and *no one* should be telling others what to think or believe. Beliefs are ours, and ours alone. The behaviors we each exhibit at work, however, are dictated to us and are non-negotiable. Treating others with respect is an example of a non-negotiable behavior."[19] In other words, believe whatever you want to believe and think whatever you want to think. No one is stopping you, and no one has the right or ability to do so anyway. We do not live in a "thought police" state. However, when it comes to specific behaviors at work, everyone should be expected to abide by the same set of just and fair standards. It is the right—and most intelligent—thing to do for business.

Despite the unfounded fears of some detractors, the movement for gender-based integrity and equality in the workplace is not part of some coldly calculated or well-financed sociopolitical "transgender agenda" to corrupt and undermine society as we know it. Paranoid conspiracy theorists will doubtless be disappointed, but transgender cabals are not holding secret meetings about overthrowing Western civilization. Transpersons do not collaborate with their cronies to conjure nefarious plots about stealthily infiltrating our nation's business organizations or subverting the social order to create cultural chaos, thereby intentionally precipitating the collapse of the economy or the moral infrastructure of society.

Frankly, the concept of a tightly organized, moneyed, and strategically implemented "transgender agenda" is laughable. There is no such animal. The transgender community is not yet cohesive enough to accomplish anything like that even if it wanted to. Instead, the transgender movement for equality is, with relatively few exceptions, happening on its own and so far has remained mostly amorphic. It is still very much a grassroots initiative that is occurring only because people innately sense that there is a hole in the fabric of justice and a need to make a change for the sake of human rights and personal dignity. It is a raw, basically unplanned, mostly impromptu, and often messy movement rooted in principles of integrity and fairness for everyone. It includes both transgender and non-transgender people of good will from all walks of life. It is an honest manifestation of the human desire to seek justice and gender-based fairness for everyone.

The fact is that gender identity is immaterial and irrelevant when evaluating how well an employee does his or her job. Fairness mandates that gender identity or any other benign and/or immutable personal characteristic should not be an issue when it comes to performing the work. Either you can do the job or you cannot, and if you can, then you deserve to be hired, compensated appropriately and commensurately, and afforded the same dignity and respect in the workplace as any other worker.

No one should have to live in fear that, regardless of how well they perform their work or how qualified they may be for a job, they are subject to an employer's arbitrary decision to refuse to hire or fire them because they may be (or may be perceived as being) gender-variant. The desire to be hired for your qualifications, to be paid a fair wage for your work, and to receive equal treatment in the workplace is not an extremist position. It does not constitute a radical social experiment or revolutionary political "agenda."

FINDING (AND KEEPING) THE BEST AND THE BRIGHTEST

Astute business leaders know that the recruitment and retention of talent are major concerns for many organizations today. Workplace research performed by Jillian Todd Weiss, J.D., Ph.D., indicates that "there will be more jobs than candidates in the next decade, particularly jobs requiring a college education. This will cause severe competition among employers for talent. Employers that can attract top minority candidates will win the talent war, and that may mean the difference between profitability and bankruptcy."[20]

"A high score on the [Human Rights Campaign's] Corporate Equality Index has become a recruiting tool for companies," says reporter Julie Forster of the *St. Paul Pioneer Press*.[21] "The index rates employers on a scale from 0 to 100 percent on treatment of gay, lesbian, bisexual and transgender (GLBT) employees, consumers, and investors."[22] In other words, increasing numbers of employers are paying attention to sexual and gender minorities and are choosing to treat them fairly in the workplace because they are perceived as business assets. "In a market where top-notch prospects have their choice of employers, corporate culture is joining pay and career track as a key competitive issue. For a significant number of prospects, inclusiveness is viewed as a cultural asset."[23]

Today's successful organizations strive to minimize one of the major hidden costs of doing business: employee turnover. By the time an organization adds up the direct and indirect costs and lost opportunities associated with replacing an employee, the total figure can equal anywhere from half to twice the employee's annual salary. That is a steep price to pay for someone who is not producing a thing for your organization. The business lesson here is simple: lower turnover means lower costs. Therefore, it is in an organization's best interest to retain talented employees rather than spend time and money replacing them.

The recruiting, interviewing, hiring, and training process is expensive and time-consuming. It costs a lot of money to replace talented, capable workers. With many top employees restless in their jobs these days, organizations must develop strategies to keep their most creative and productive people from moving on to greener pastures. "The best employees are often the first to leave," says Reesa Staten, Accountemps director of research.[24] That business concern is why Susan R. Meisinger, president and CEO of the Society for Human Resource Management (SHRM), has emphasized, "Employers need to be keyed into what's important to employees in order to implement practices that will keep valuable employees satisfied and productive in the workplace."[25]

How a worker feels about his or her workplace culture is often a key element in determining whether that person stays or goes. Many companies are discovering that good people tend to remain in organizations that care about them personally, offer opportunities for growth, and demonstrate a commitment to treating their people fairly. Terry Howard reminds us, "This is about attracting and retaining talented and productive people, regardless of their differences. And that, after all, is a core reason for embracing diversity. Viewed in this context, [transgender] matters."[26]

Today, "Companies are recognizing the business imperative of being first in their industry to ensure equal treatment for all of their gay, lesbian, bisexual and transgender employees," said Emily Jones, co-chair of the HRC's Business Council.[27] Additionally, laws and social expectations regarding corporate America's " 'diversity paradox' require employers to increase minority hiring, but without calling much attention to minority differences. When minorities with top marks in college go looking for employers that they feel comfortable with, other things will start to loom large. One of these is transgender policy, which … [stands] as a symbol of minority-friendliness without racial or ethnic overtones."[28]

> The main reason why companies should consider changing their policies [to be transgender-inclusive] is due to the new trend that is developing amongst the youth and young adults. University research has shown individuals are starting to identify as gay, lesbian, bisexual, and/or transgender (GLBT) much earlier in their lives than only five years ago; many of them "come out" as early as middle school and high school. These students are selecting higher education institutions based on the GLBT "friendliness". These students will, upon their graduation, decide to find employment in the companies that meet and/or exceed the college or university they attended.[29]

A third of the *Fortune* 500 have already discovered that creating respectful working environments for all employees (including those who are gender-variant) translates into stronger productivity, enhancement of the bottom line, and more efficient alignment of business/cultural strategies with the organization's mission and vision statements.

Business authors Harvey Robbins and Michael Finley have written, "In the work world, we could generally give two hoots about what a person's insides are like. That is their business, after all. But how they act—and interact—is essential to their value to the enterprise. You don't have to like one another to produce together. You do have to 'get along.'"[30] The idea of "getting along" and working side-by-side with transgender persons is a new idea for many in our workplaces, admittedly, but it is an idea whose time has arrived. If a company wants to promote and encourage the value of effective teamwork in an inclusive workforce, employees must learn to accept and respect the benign human differences that may exist among their coworkers.

MAKING A POSITIVE DIFFERENCE THROUGH TRANSGENDER INCLUSION

Target Corporation's Web site states, "Diversity is any attribute that makes an individual unique and does not interfere with effective job performance."[31] A desire to be evaluated on one's work ethic, talent, skills, abilities, and experience rather than on gender identity or expression is not an "agenda."

When questioned about the readiness of corporate America to deal with gender variance and transgender persons in the workplace, Ford Motor Company's Vice Chairman Allan Gilmour (now retired) said, "I think it is moving to deal with those situations, as it has with other diversity-related situations. Ford is committed to diversity as good business and the right thing to do ... If corporate America wants the best employees, who produce the best products and services for the wide-ranging tastes and backgrounds of its consumers, then it is smart to attract all types of good employees into its organizations."[32] When asked what companies can do to acknowledge employees with different sexual or gender orientations, Gilmour responded, "I think the best answer is to not treat them differently ... All people should be valued for their abilities and for the contributions they make to an organization—not for their sexual [or gender] orientation, their race, their religion or any other reason that doesn't affect the way they do their jobs."

Human possibility and potential in the form of a transgender identity is increasingly being manifested and expressed in a variety of ways throughout society. Because workplaces are important institutions with powerful social influence, organizations and their employees are learning to adapt to this growing cultural shift toward greater gender-variant expression on the job.

Julie Goodridge, president of NorthStar Asset Management, Inc., a Boston-based wealth management firm specializing in socially responsible investing, has said, "Including gender identity in the company's non-discrimination policy is the first signal a company gives employees, and potential employees, that it values all its workers equally."[33] Goodridge adds, "We believe that an open and inclusive workplace nurtures the creativity necessary to build a successful company."[34]

Growing numbers of organizations are progressing beyond a minimalist response of merely complying with antidiscriminatory policies and are now fully embracing the concept of workplace pluralism as a core business value. This significant development is supported by empirical studies, which indicate that advocating such pluralistic efforts makes excellent business sense.

Forcing transgender workers to remain hidden or secretive about their gender identity on the job can have harmful consequences, including a measurably negative impact on an organization's bottom line in terms of lost or diminished productivity and low employee retention rates. Transgender employees who must operate in constant fear of being discovered by intolerant or abusive management, supervisors, or coworkers cannot work at peak efficiency or high energy, nor will they want to stick around for long. Absenteeism rates are higher when people are forced to operate in a hostile work environment. Think about it this way: how well would *you* be able to function if you had to work in an isolating, prejudiced workplace setting that required you to look over your shoulder with apprehension at every moment? Would you be energized to give your best effort or be motivated to plan for a long career with that organization?

> *Without diversity, there can be no innovation; without innovation, there can be no new wealth. In other words, diversity is not just the right thing to do, it's your source of greatest potential.*
>
> —Joel Barker

The ability to trust one's organizational management, direct supervisors, and coworkers has a significant bearing on the well-being and performance of every employee. An atmosphere of nonjudgmental acceptance, good faith, mutual respect, and trust within teams and/ or work groups is almost always found in healthy, successful companies. The opposite, of course, is often true in businesses that do not adequately support or affirm all of their employees.

Bottom-line considerations have historically been the primary impetus for adopting diversity policies for business organizations. However, many advocates of workplace pluralism now view issues of inclusion to be every bit as relevant as issues of business ethics, production, public relations, and revenue generation. The conscientious alignment of a comprehensive and inclusive cultural strategy, involving an intentional emphasis on developing a pluralistic workforce, with an organization's business strategy is often a sign of a successful company.

Some business executives or managers may balk at taking action in a newer inclusion area such as transgender in the workplace, possibly fearing the negative effect that such actions could have on their organizations and their bottom line. It is only natural to have some concerns about how such a new and/or different initiative might impact an organization, and a dose of healthy skepticism can sometimes be a strategic approach that keeps companies from making big mistakes. However, there is a growing body of quantitative evidence indicating that companies can improve their revenue streams, enhance their organizational cultures, and gain business advantages by intelligently addressing sociocultural issues like transgender in the workplace. The overriding principle is not to be held back or limited by fears of what might be but to proceed in an affirming, productive manner that will augment the organization's overall effectiveness, business performance, public profile, and work environment.

Business authors John Weiser and Simon Zadek tell us,

Convincing business people [about inclusion initiatives] is not a matter of evading their skepticism. Rather, it is a matter of understanding the corporate imperatives and cultures that make such skepticism a core survival technique, and working to ensure that [corporate engagement in a just and fair inclusion initiative] can demonstrably be consistent with, and relevant to, these operating realities. The key is not simply to show business people that [such corporate involvement] can be financially rewarding. This is an important but insufficient piece of the puzzle. When a business person is already over-stretched in meeting the challenges of the complex and highly competitive corporate environment, it is critical to demonstrate that [appropriate corporate engagement in social issues] improves their ability to meet *existing* objectives. The key is to show not only that it can generate black on the bottom line, but that it does so in strategically important areas of business performance.[35]

Pluralism should be more than just a policy: for many organizations, it is a key driver for success. These companies leverage the plurality of their employees, clients, shareholders, vendors/suppliers, and communities to build a competitive advantage in the markets they serve. They take the initiative to recognize and affirm the unique qualities, characteristics, and contributions that each person can make to a company's overall success. In turn, these intentionally inclusive initiatives help create a positive work environment that is conducive to the development of productive and professional teamwork, collaboration, and effective working relationships.

Here are some documented examples of the improvements that can occur when organizations commit to transgender inclusivity as part of a pluralistic, nondiscriminatory workplace strategy for all employees.

- By making a commitment to inclusion, you improve your company's image and reputation . . .
- You minimize complaints and legal liability . . .
- It becomes easier for you to attract and hold on to employees who share this value . . .
- Most importantly, your ability to deliver products and services will be enhanced with a pluralistic staff that will reflect the diversity of your customers . . .[36]

It is really all about inviting people to

- create a workplace spirit that invokes justice and fair treatment;
- heighten their awareness regarding the beneficial differences that exist within the human community; and
- from a purely business-oriented perspective, find practical solutions to business problems by implementing best practices that involve fairness and inclusion for everyone.

These combined elements translate into an enhancement of a company's operating strategy, organizational culture, work environment, and business success.

A dedicated inclusionary initiative that includes awareness, respect, and acceptance for transgender persons in our workplaces will be more than worth whatever temporary struggles may arise as a result. It is an opportunity for growth and learning that all employees, regardless of gender, deserve on the job.

EXPERIENCING THE BENEFITS, OR "WHAT'S IN IT FOR YOU?"

Perhaps you may be wondering why you should be thinking about all this transgender-in-the-workplace stuff anyway. Why choose to become involved in welcoming and affirming the unique human differences in others? Why make the decision to struggle with such issues? Why confront any potential concerns that the open presence of transgender individuals might introduce to the workplace? Why rock the organizational boat? Why push the envelope? Why take the risk?

Here is why:

- because there is so much to be learned and to be gained by everyone involved;
- because respect for and acceptance of human difference is a key to increased business success in today's global marketplace of ideas;
- because including transpeople in the fabric of your organization's culture can augment the potential pool of new ideas and fresh concepts, which are the currency of the modern marketplace;
- because the taking of intelligent, strategic risks is how organizations and individuals move toward success.

Hopefully, you will agree that these possibilities are meaningful in their implications for the future of the human race, not to mention the world of work. Here, listed in no particular order, are only a few of the business advantages that can accrue to organizations choosing to implement an employee policy of transgender inclusion:

- Attracting the best and brightest employees. Qualified, creative candidates are drawn to organizations that demonstrate a commitment to hiring, developing, and promoting an inclusive workforce.
- Retaining good people. Excellent employees are more likely to remain in organizations that value difference, appreciate human uniqueness, and reward positive workplace contributions.

- Improving your organization's productivity and profitability, thereby increasing the overall value for shareholders.
- Complying with federal, state, and local government regulations to avoid potential legal entanglements. Compliance will diminish the potential for complaints, legal liability, and/or costly discrimination litigation.
- Creating a more respectful and positive workplace environment, i.e., an organizational "culture of affirmation" where every person's humanity and intrinsic worth is confirmed and validated.
- Developing a happier, healthier, more engaged, and better-informed workforce. People who are happy and well adjusted while at work tend to be physically and psychologically healthier. This translates into more energy, which means more productivity on the job. It also means fewer work days missed due to illness and/or depression, which saves money in terms of avoiding lost work hours and increased insurance/medical costs for the organization.
- Enhancing workplace creativity and innovation. This often occurs in workplaces where people are encouraged to stretch their minds and pursue new ideas. Creativity is a powerful and commercially viable force. A company that invites innovation through pluralism in its workforce also invites business breakthroughs.
- Promoting feelings of inclusivity, greater confidence, trust, and hope within the people of your organization. These desirable qualities serve to undergird and encourage a work environment of commitment, motivation, justice, and fairness. In places like those, good and profitable work gets done.
- Developing a clearer understanding of the organization's commitment to equality for every associate. This means everyone will know exactly where they stand and what is expected from them in terms of nonnegotiable behavior under the organization's nondiscrimination policy. It may also mean changing or updating company policies, providing expanded new guidelines for management and employees, and offering training opportunities that can allow for greater understanding of human difference in all its forms, including transgender.
- Fostering better teamwork and trust building, which leads to improved employee morale. Employees who trust management

and each other can achieve more together. There is immense social capital to be gained through building trust that flows freely between team members, other associates, and management.

- Respecting the human value embodied in pluralism, including gender identity/characteristics/expression and sexual orientation. Continued affirmation of each individual's intrinsic human worth helps to lift up everyone in the entire organization, resulting in an upward spiral of energy, commitment, and productivity.

- Creating powerful opportunities for meaningful dialogue about gender-related issues that impact your organization and customer base. Never underestimate the power of significant, mutually based conversations about issues of substance in our workplaces. Those conversations can literally change the course of people's lives.

- Improving internal branding—i.e., creating a stronger sense of personal identification and pride within the organization for all stakeholders.

- Enhancing PR and generating more widespread public recognition as a forward-thinking, just, and socially aware organization. Why not be widely known and respected as a company that affirms and values its people—*all* of them?

- Generating a greater individual and organizational ability to adapt to workplace change in its many forms. Adaptability and a readiness to change are absolute requirements for growth and sustainable success in the modern business climate.

- Developing an organizational culture where every person is respected for his or her contributions and innate human value. In such stimulating workplaces, limitations tend to fall away and become a thing of the past. Once artificial barriers are removed, anything becomes possible.

- Improving productivity due to increased personal freedom of expression and the liberated psycho-emotional energy that accompanies such freedom.

- Enhancing your competitive business edge by improving employee retention, morale, and teamwork. Transgender inclusion can be part of an overall corporate strategy that will generate lasting value for the organization.

- Strengthening profitability, which translates into greater business stability, more personal and professional rewards, increased organizational longevity, stronger sales, and the ability to continue or expand what you do.

If women are from Venus and men from Mars, transgender people travel the cosmos in ways most of us never dream about.

—Patrick Letellier

CHAPTER 4
The Great Restroom Debate

Emotional discomfort with gender-based ambiguity can sometimes lead to irrational responses toward transgender individuals. Some of these reactions have been prompted by public restroom concerns—a topic that, for fairly obvious reasons, has become important to many transpersons. It is certainly a visceral issue, one that can quickly conjure up all sorts of responses from different quarters. The subject has become a point of contention in some workplaces, and therefore, deserves attention in these pages.

Restroom usage may appear to be a frivolous issue at first glance, but it is no joking matter to a transgender human being who needs to answer nature's call while in public. In fact, it can quickly become a potentially difficult and dangerous situation. To understand why, ask yourself this question: "If I were a transgender person and needed to use a public restroom right away, what would I do?" Think about how you (the hypothetical transgender person) might respond, given the cultural misunderstandings that so often accompany a transgender individual's presentation in public.

For many transpeople, the stark reality is this: "If your presentation does not rigidly conform to the gender binary, you may be harassed if you attempt to use either the men's or the ladies' bathroom. Self-deputized gender police (and sometimes, the actual law-enforcement kind) stand ready to protect these sacred spaces."[1] Restroom accessibility for transpersons in the workplace is a serious matter of business practicality that merits attention and consideration. Organizational decisions on restroom usage have significant implications for transgender individuals and the companies that employ them.

Female-to-male transsexual Matt Kailey has said, "There are actually those who believe that trans people use the restroom in order to spy on others or to get some kind of sexual thrill. How many sexy bathrooms have you been in lately? . . . [We transpeople] are there for one reason only, just like you, and . . . we have no ulterior motives."[2]

Sometimes "there's this absurd fear there will be men who cross-dress to go into bathrooms and rape women," says Dr. Paisley Currah, a Brooklyn College political science professor, author, and gender advocate who is affiliated with the Transgender Law and Policy Institute.[3] On the other hand, and particularly from a personal safety standpoint, males who cross-dress and/or otherwise present an externally feminine persona cannot enter a men's restroom without confronting the very real possibility of being verbally harassed, physically threatened, or even attacked. The same situation is true, only in reverse, for masculine-appearing females who may enter a women's restroom.

Restroom usage is an issue of privacy and personal modesty for many. These are legitimate concerns that should be respected and taken seriously, perhaps especially in our places of work. Everyone deserves to be treated with dignity in such matters, which means that facilities must be made available for everyone. Seclusion in women's restrooms is usually provided by the use of stalls with doors, and most men's restrooms have at least one stall as well. Privacy and personal modesty are usually not compromised to any major extent. Also, increasing numbers of organizations are now providing private or unisex restrooms with locking doors.

One workable and proven solution is for everyone to use the restroom facilities that are designated for the gender in which a person is presenting at any given time. Some organizations are already achieving successful results with this commonsense approach. Another strategy is for business organizations to provide more restrooms that are unisex in nature so that any potential privacy concerns can be easily avoided. Unisex restrooms circumvent the gender issue altogether and make the necessary facilities available to everyone in a nonthreatening manner. Yet another solution can involve making single-user and/or unisex restrooms available so that there is no simultaneous sharing of facilities. New York attorney Tamara Lange has said, "This question about bathrooms is socially complicated, but there are many ways to accommodate transgendered [sic] people without infringing on others."[4]

In a Manhattan courtroom on January 16, 2003, a New York Supreme Court judge ruled in the case of *Hispanic AIDS Forum v. Estate of Joseph Bruno* that a transgender person's anatomy is not relevant to gender identity. Based on that legal precedent, the public restroom debate with regard to transpeople should be a nonissue. If gender identity is not relevant to one's anatomy, as the New York Supreme Court has seen fit to interpret, then why the ongoing fuss about who is using which restroom?

Here is a suggestion: just use the facility that is designated for the gender identity in which you are presenting. It is eminently logical, yet some people remain paranoid about the perceived gender of another individual who may be using the restroom at the same time. Really, why should you care as long as they are not purposely bothering or harassing you? (And if they are behaving in an obviously inappropriate manner, it is an issue for management or the authorities. Report it and move on.)

Dan Woog reports, "One transsexual employee was forbidden to use any bathroom at work for two years. Saddled with concerns about transitioning from male to female, she chose to use the restroom at a nearby gas station rather than fight."[5] That is a ridiculous and dehumanizing situation to which no worker should be subjected. No one deserves to be put in such an untenable position, especially in a place where people come together to earn an honest living. Restrooms are for relieving one's body, and workplaces have a responsibility to take the legitimate human needs of their employees—including those who may be transgender—seriously.

Let us all grow up, use the restroom that is most congruent with our gender presentation, and allow others to do the same without hassling them. Public restrooms are intended to facilitate bodily functions, not to create psychosexual disturbances or traumatize anyone. Most of us understand, believe in, and can readily accept that reasonable premise. Transpeople use washrooms, restrooms, and locker rooms for the same reasons as everyone else, not for spying on or having sex with others. In short, we are all human, we all have bodily needs, and we all have to use the restroom from time to time.

There are many ways to deal effectively with restroom concerns in the workplace. For example, organizations can set aside a designated restroom if one is available. Then, if someone in the organization objects to a transgender employee using the restroom that has been assigned to their expressed gender, invite the resistant employee to use the separate restroom. This should immediately provide a fair solution to their concern. Why make a transgender worker suffer or be inconvenienced if they are not purposely making waves? After all, transgender employees only seek to use the restroom for its intended purpose. Let the person who is voicing objections use the designated restroom if they are so upset.

Lisa M. Hartley, ACSW-DCSW, has written,

> It [the restroom issue] is the most foolish issue that culture has ever come up with to say that it doesn't like adjusting to the transgendered [*sic*] person. If a worker has an "issue" with the transgendered person using the bathroom appropriate to his or her "new" sex and gender, then let that worker find another place to go. Forcing the transgendered person to make an accommodation is the same thing as saying that the transgendered person is the one with the problem, when in fact, he or she is not the one with the problem at all.[6]

As with most workplace diversity issues, the keys to success are clear communication, a desire to institute fair, respectful policies for all employees, and common sense.

Interestingly enough, it is usually not complaints or objections by coworkers that create problems around the restroom topic. More often, difficulties begin among the organization's decision-makers due to fears and/or confusion that someone might become offended or upset and sue the company. Apprehension about potential lawsuits or negative publicity can strongly influence organizational thinking. While management must always be legitimately concerned about an organization's legal status, transgender restroom issues can be resolved without resorting to hysteria or giving in to misplaced fears on the part of a few. Many successful organizations have already discovered how to make the situation work for everyone. With a little thought and attention to detail, your organization can do it, too.

Having frank and open conversations within departments can work wonders in terms of helping employees recognize the legitimacy of the issue and developing practical strategies that will work for everyone. The Society for Human Resource Management has said this about policies that involve transgender persons: "The simplest answers are the easiest. We don't have a lot of complicated rules and expectations. Simplicity is good: we don't discriminate, we cover medically necessary procedures, use the bathroom that matches how you present... It just works."[7]

The employee policy of Alcatel-Lucent Technologies can be a model for other businesses to emulate when it comes to transgender policies on the job. This successful IT organization has created a sensible workplace policy that says, in part, "At this time, [Alcatel-] Lucent recommends that transgendered [sic] employees use the restroom for the gender they are presenting (unless a state law prevents an employee from doing so)."[8] See how easy and uncomplicated it can be if everyone will just calm down, set their fears aside, and do the sensible, feasible thing that is fair for everyone?

It may be helpful to know that the restroom issue as it applies to transpersons has already been specifically addressed at least once in federal court. "In landmark case *Cruzan v. Davis*, a ruling was made in June 2002 by a federal appeals court in Minnesota that an employer is within its rights to instruct a transgendered [sic] employee to use the restroom matching their new presentation, and that if another employee complains, the company may offer the complaining employee an accommodation (such as the use of a different restroom by the complaining employee)."[9]

It is a simple premise: if an employee presents herself in a recognizably feminine manner, she should be accepted as such and use the women's restroom facilities accordingly. The same concept should hold true for an employee who presents himself in a masculine-identified manner: he should use the men's restroom, which is only fair and logical. Restroom usage ought to be a matter of common sense and practicality for everyone, and management should make that stance clear from the beginning.

"A human being's gender identity is a function of self-discovery and personal understanding. Therefore, business organizations must find ways to respect and uphold the right of an individual to be self-determining in this regard." It is probably unwise, not to mention discriminatory and/or potentially illegal, for organizations to place themselves in the position of arbitrating or demanding proof of anyone's "real" sex or gender by examining medical records, doctors' letters, etc. Since most employers will understandably not want to police the genitals of every employee, many have concluded that it is better not to do so for anybody. Besides, as we have already learned, gender is not about what is between one's legs, anyway: it is about what is between the ears.

Speaking of examining genitals, it seems rather ludicrous (not to mention rude, embarrassing, certainly discriminatory, and probably illegal) for an employer to implement a policy of verifying the genitals of *only* transgender employees, or those perceived to be transgender, but not others. The potential for sexual harassment lawsuits and/or charges of invasion of privacy is hardly worth the risk of subjecting transgender employees to such indignities and unwarranted scrutiny. OutFront Minnesota's Web site tells us, "The bottom line is this— we all make assumptions about the gender of people around us without remotely considering requiring genital verification. We look to such cues as clothing, hair, make-up, jewelry, name, and voice— all of which can be changed—and go from there. Common sense suggests [that business organizations] should reflect this everyday reality."[10] That reasonable premise holds true for transgender employees who need to use the restroom, too.

The important thing to keep in mind is that workable options can always be developed and put into practice as the need arises. One quick and easy solution is that of providing "reasonable accommodations," which might include designating and labeling at least one or more restroom facilities as gender-neutral or unisex in a particular building or location. Good judgment and common sense should always prevail, and the simplest answers are often the best.

Another consideration may involve restroom signs. Most workplaces have restrooms with signs that say either "Women" or "Men." This does not help transgender people very much, since the signs indicate that the organization has not completely thought through the social gender-based messages that their restroom door signs convey. "Women" and "Men" are culturally derived terms that are often arbitrary and/or vague enough so that they do not apply to everyone across the board. If someone is in transition or in an ambiguous/ androgynous place on the gender spectrum, they may not be readily perceived as either a man or a woman. However, they still need to know that safe restroom facilities are available for them, too. After all, they are still human and have bodily needs, no matter what their gender status may be. Not everyone fits neatly into a predetermined gender category at every moment. That is why it can be helpful to post a "Unisex" sign on specific restroom doors. Doing so can help avoid discrimination issues and provide useful alternatives for those who need them.

Each organization's situation may be somewhat different or unique, depending on the circumstances and individuals involved, but the idea is to think about these concerns in advance and develop some practical ways to respect everyone while avoiding potential problems. It is not that difficult to do, but it does require a little thought and planning. Justin Tanis of the National Center for Transgender Equality (NCTE) has written, "When agencies, schools and groups make it clear that their restrooms are safe places for transpeople, they send a message that they are genuinely welcoming to trans people, they've considered our needs and planned ahead for our participation."[11]

In the midst of all this talk about restrooms and bodily functions, transgender workers are strongly encouraged to never compromise their dignity or self-respect in these matters. We are all human and have bodily functions. Transgender individuals have as much right to use the restroom as anyone else. If you are a transgender person, never be ashamed or afraid to ask for (and demand, if necessary) what you legitimately need and deserve. Workplaces should always be safe environments for everyone, but they should also be places where common sense, sound judgment, respect, consideration, and courtesy toward each individual are fundamental, inviolable principles.

CHAPTER 5

Benefits of Transgender-Specific Awareness Training

If an organization's expectation is that all employees are to be supported and valued, then transgender employees should logically be included within the scope of that expectation. If they are not, then the employer is failing to meet the responsibilities of effectively managing diversity and employee relations. This, in turn, implies that the organization's people are being denied the opportunity to function to their maximum effectiveness due to management's negligence and/or incompetence. For this reason, awareness training and education for employees are critical for a transgender inclusion initiative to be successful.

Today's businesses need transgender awareness training to help in developing more respectful, accepting, equitable, and productive workplace environments for all workers. Nondiscrimination laws that affect workplaces are expanding in a number of states and municipalities to include various combinations of gender identity, gender characteristics, and gender expression. The Human Rights Campaign Web site (www.hrc.org) offers updated information about states, cities, and organizations that legally protect the rights of transgender individuals. Companies that plan strategically for success will want to be equipped to deal with the business ramifications of such statutes. Organizational leaders, in particular, will want to have at least some awareness of transgender issues and relevant laws so that all workers and/or organizational stakeholders can be treated with the respect and dignity they deserve.

TRANSGENDER CONSULTANTS

Encouraging workforce pluralism as a method for increasing productivity and profitability has become standard practice in many major corporations, and inclusion experts are needed to help make it happen. That is why organizations will usually want to contract with an expert transgender inclusion consultant who can offer unbiased opinions and share diversity information from an experienced, objective perspective. Input from an outsider can be extremely valuable, for it is usually less subjective, biased, and/or opinionated than contributions from an in-house person might be.

However, please note this caveat: an effective inclusion consultant must live it, know and understand it, and have a passion for the subject. If they do not, they will probably be ineffective and people will see right through them. While many individuals bill themselves as diversity consultants, relatively few are informed enough about transgender issues to provide the insights, accurate information, tools, and resources that are necessary for organizations to initiate lasting change in this particular area of workplace interest. Organizations are encouraged to be judicious in contracting with transgender inclusion consultants. Keep in mind that just because someone may be transgender, it does not necessarily make them an expert on the subject. It can be helpful if the diversity consultant is a transgender person, but make sure they are a knowledgeable and experienced professional as well.

PLACING TRANSGENDER AWARENESS TRAINING IN CONTEXT

Awareness training on transgender issues is an efficient way for large corporations, medium-size organizations, and small businesses to receive low-cost, high-return, lasting value for their training dollar. Such training helps generate legal, ethical, and practical solutions to the challenges that employers may confront when working with transgender employees. (It can be especially effective when the transgender awareness training is presented as part of a more comprehensive, overall organizational pluralism initiative.)

When an employee is seen, recognized, and appreciated within the organization, she/he tends to feel more valued. This often results in the employee expending greater effort and generating more productivity in his or her work. It is about more than token "inclusion" or paying lip service to the notion of pluralism—it is a responsible, practical way to foster and encourage a satisfactory, safe, and efficient workplace environment in which people can succeed. The "intangible" perception of personal value and individual worth by an employee may result in a strong return on the organization's investment in that employee.

Transgender awareness training is an issue that deserves to be part of a company's overall response to the legitimate concerns of gender-variant employees. Optimally, the trainer's approach will include extensive discussion/dialogue, strategizing and collaboration, education/training, and advocacy—not necessarily activism, which is sometimes overtly political in nature—in terms of recognizing the inherent business value and benefits of ensuring equality for everyone, including transgender workers, throughout the organization.

Understanding how to deal intelligently and effectively with transgender-related issues can help organizations achieve a number of preferred business objectives. Those objectives may include, but are not necessarily limited to, the following:

- Transgender-specific awareness training can help in avoiding complaints and/or costly discrimination litigation that may result if/when employees believe their workplace has become a hostile or intimidating environment. Offering transgender-specific awareness training opportunities for all employees provides powerful evidence that the organization takes these issues seriously and is striving to provide a fair workplace setting for everyone. When management chooses to spend money on training employees about transgender issues, it sends a clear signal that the organization cares and is trying to do what is right by promoting a positive, inclusive workplace environment for everyone.

- Transgender-specific awareness training can help ease the potential difficulties of coming out and/or transitioning on the job for transgender workers. This, in turn, allows these employees to contribute more productively to the organization. That happens because transgender employees are no longer constrained or intimidated in terms of their intrinsic need for personal gender expression while at work.

- Transgender-specific awareness training will increase the overall knowledge level while helping to minimize levels of potential discomfort and/or misunderstanding that may occur among non-transgender employees. Such training allows people to address their fears and discuss them in a safe, respectful environment. Employees are free to ask questions and have their concerns addressed in healthy, productive ways. It is all about establishing a positive, productive work environment for everyone, regardless of gender status.

- Transgender-specific awareness training will help organizations create and implement effective transgender nondiscrimination guidelines and best business practices that can be communicated and understood throughout the entire company, thus keeping distraction and speculation to a minimum while enhancing employee morale and productivity.

- Transgender-specific awareness training will provide important tools and resources for dealing more effectively with organizational changes that may occur as the result of an openly transgender employee's presence. Such tools may include specific questions to ask, dialogues to have, policies and guidelines to discuss, biases to consider, behavioral expectations, restroom issues, appropriate names and pronouns, and appropriate documentation. This, in turn, will result in an opportunity for constructive personal growth and learning on the part of everyone.

- Transgender-specific awareness training will help management teams develop effective organizational strategies designed to plan for, address, and successfully resolve gender-variant workplace concerns.

- Transgender-specific awareness training will help organizations review and decide upon a variety of options and procedures relative to the specific issues of transgender workers. This may include such topics as coming out on the job, changing organizational policies and guidelines, communicating with management and coworkers during transition, use of restroom facilities, eliminating workplace discrimination, the business and cultural expectations of the organization, and other potentially sensitive areas.

- Transgender-specific awareness training can supply practical infor-mation and answer questions about legal, medical, insurance, or other issues that may pertain to transpersons in the workplace.

An organization that seeks to attract top talent will probably find it easier to do so if the company demonstrates that it values diversity and embraces human differences. Some business leaders believe that the most effective way to accomplish these goals is to hire an outside consultant. However, it is strongly suggested that organizational leaders not waste their time or money hiring transgender consultants if a strategic and comprehensive business case for pluralism in your company is not a priority.

Transgender-specific awareness training affords everyone the opportunity to voice fears, ask questions, have access to accurate information, and be better equipped to deal with change as it impacts the workplace environment. Cumulatively, and over time, these actions will create a meaningful difference and improve the organizational culture for each member of the company.

CHAPTER 6

Coming Out as Transgender at Work

> You are not here merely to make a living. You are here in order to enable the world to live more amply, with greater vision, with a finer spirit of hope and achievement. You are here to enrich the world, and you impoverish yourself if you forget the errand.
>
> —Woodrow Wilson

People should not be forced to sacrifice their self-esteem or their gender identity to be successful in their work or to gain access to workplace opportunities. Nevertheless, "With no federal laws prohibiting discrimination based on gender identity or expression, the [job site] can be an uncertain place for transgender [workers]. Transitioning and even coming out can often jeopardize their relationships with co-workers and management. The result can be an isolating experience where transgender employees avoid coming out, fearing that to do so could cost them their jobs."[1]

Given this reality, it seems reasonable to ask a few questions about coming out as a transgender person in the workplace. For instance, why would a transgender employee seek to come out at all? What is to be gained or lost by doing so? Why go through all the aggravation, anxiety, and complexities that coming out in the workplace may potentially generate? Why put oneself and/or others through that experience?

If you are a transgender worker, there are two primary reasons for undertaking such an important step. The first reason is personal: you will be a better, happier, more productive and healthier individual and employee if and/or when you are able to live your life openly and without fear of discovery. Anxiety about potential blackmail at work will no longer be an issue. You will not have to pretend anymore. You will have peace of mind and new opportunities to live a fuller and more satisfying life. You will be free to do your job and make your best contributions in a way that demonstrates wholeness and integrity.

Human Rights Campaign Education Director Kim Mills has said, "Those who feel safe enough to come out at work often experience a more integrated and honest identity. The stress of living a dual life— sometimes in, sometimes out—can be exhausting."[2] There is a remarkable liberation of the spirit that occurs whenever someone comes out and begins to live life as a complete human being. Coming out as transgender will enable you to honestly be the person that you want and need to be at work. You will be liberated to be who you truly are, not who others may think you are or should be.

A second reason for coming out on the job is that you will enrich not only your own life but the life of your organization and those around you as well. Honesty about your gender situation can lead to strengthened relationships and greater trust among friends and coworkers. By coming out you will gift others with an opportunity to learn, to become more aware, to have their boundaries stretched, and to have the experience of working with someone who may be "different" but who is equally valid in terms of his or her human worth and professional abilities. Mary Ann Horton's story in a previous chapter is an example of such an enriching workplace experience.

Your presence as an openly transgender person in the workplace can be a strong statement about the human ability to "be" in the world in uniquely different ways. When people discover that they personally know an openly transgender person, they are far more likely to respect him or her and support his or her struggle for equality in the workplace and in every other area of society.

Transgender people are metaphorical mirrors: they reflect our culture's expectations about what it means to be masculine, feminine, both, or neither. You—i.e., the transgender worker—can be a real-life example of that concept for your teammates/coworkers. What a meaningful contribution you can make to your organization, to its culture, and to the world by coming out!

The other side of the coming out coin involves certain risks of which you should be aware before making a decision about coming out on the job. Consider this: once you have come out, you cannot go back in the closet. People will know about you and they are not going to forget. The door will have been opened and there is no shutting it again. Mark Shields, director of the HRC's Coming Out Project, has said, "Coming out includes a unique set of challenges for those who identify as transgender—particularly when it comes to coming out at work, and managing identification documents and medical privacy issues." Those are significant concerns for transgender workers, and they should be carefully considered by gender-variant employees.

Coming out risks may involve experiencing discrimination, bigotry, and intolerance from others. While increasing numbers of workplaces have adopted transgender nondiscrimination policies, it is possible that harassment, gossip, hurtful jokes, unseemly comments, and exclusion may still occur.

Some individuals may have problems with the presence of an openly transgender coworker, perhaps stemming from religious teachings or other personal beliefs. While all individuals are entitled to their religious views, and no one has to unconditionally like someone else, it is unacceptable to behave in ways that are detrimental or destructive toward others on the job. Secular workplaces are not appropriate venues for espousing religious beliefs at the expense of others. The right to individual religious views and beliefs should be respected, of course, but those views and beliefs must not be mandated or offensively imposed into a work environment. To do so is the antithesis of the religious freedom guaranteed by the Constitution.

Others may believe that you, the transperson, are doing something that is socially unacceptable. They may feel that by expressing yourself in a gender-variant manner you are somehow weakening the status of male authority and/or masculine privilege within society. Some males may even perceive you as a threat to their own manhood, although how or why anyone should feel personally threatened by another individual's form of gender expression remains unclear. An overtly hostile reaction to the mere presence of a transgender individual probably says a good deal more about the emotional security of the defensive person than the gender-variant one.

Some people do not like gay individuals and may think you, the transperson, are gay. (Since most transgender persons are heterosexual, this can be—and often is—a point of contention and confusion for the general public.) Some people may find themselves sexually attracted to you. Unfortunately, they may also fear that such an attraction might indicate that they are gay. That possibility may scare them to death, so they might overreact in a hostile manner. As we can see, there are many different reasons why individuals may respond negatively toward transgender persons.

The important thing to remember is that the focus should always remain on workplace *behaviors*, not on personal beliefs or values. Behaviors are at the center of workplace nondiscrimination policies. Such policies are not intended to demean or attack people's individual beliefs but are designed to protect everyone's rights and prevent improper or nonproductive workplace actions. Organizational employee policies must carry certain expectations for behaviors, and those expectations must apply uniformly and equitably to everyone regardless of his or her religious or personal belief systems.

Each individual has a personal and inviolable right to his or her own beliefs and values. However, and while the honest concerns of individuals always deserve to be heard and taken seriously, most successful organizations have adopted specific policies and/or guidelines that require everyone to behave and be treated in a respectful manner. (This book's appendix contains examples of such policies. Readers may wish to consider developing and adopting similar policies in their own organizations.) At work, everyone is expected to speak and act with respect toward everyone else—and, hopefully, everyone else includes transgender employees. If you are drawing a paycheck from a company, that company is renting your behavior (along with your skills, talents, and abilities) while you are on the job. Consequently, the organization has a right to expect its people to act in accordance with its stated policies, mission, guidelines, goals, and values on a day-to-day basis. If you do not want to behave in such a manner and/or comply with the organization's behavioral expectations, perhaps you should consider working elsewhere.

People react in different ways to the presence of human difference. A transgender individual may experience rejection or the loss of a relationship upon coming out. Not everyone is always going to be welcoming, accepting, or affirming of a person's gender-variant status. Sometimes transgender persons lose the support of their family, friends, or coworkers when they make their gender identity known.

Unfortunately, coming out on the job may precipitate confrontations, physical attacks, or property damage. Though regrettable, it has been known to happen. It is best to be aware, be prepared for possible hostile reactions, and try to avoid potential situations in which physical altercations might occur. That is not being cowardly—it is being intelligent and safe.

Sometimes the greatest challenges transpersons confront in the workplace may not come from extremist or quarrelsome individuals. Instead, obstacles to workplace equality may stem directly from the silence, ignorance, and lack of confidence that transpeople sometimes impose upon themselves. Nevertheless, we must not minimize or understate the antipathy and/or overt antagonism that are often intentionally directed by others toward people who are transgender. Denigrators may insist that transgender employees are "extremists" who are somehow trying to force a "transgender agenda" down the throats of everyone else in the company. Nothing could be further from the truth, but that is their emotionally based argument. (History proves that if you repeat a lie long enough and loud enough, people will start to believe it.) Business organizations should be aware of the potential dangers of such divisive, diversionary tactics and be prepared to act swiftly to counter them.

Transgender employees can contribute significantly to their organizations by demonstrating courage, integrity, and personal honesty whenever they let others know they are gender-variant. The following words from Margaret Wheatley seem to apply to this situation:

> What happens when we claim our right to be fully human? Everyone benefits. Even those who feel superior, who demean and discount us, benefit when we claim our full humanity. When we refuse to accept degrading conditions and behaviors, those in power no longer have a target for their oppressive acts. Even if they want to continue in their old ways, we don't let them. Our refusal gives them the opportunity to explore new, more humane behaviors. They may not choose to change, but as we stand up for ourselves, we give them the chance to be more fully human as well. When we are courageous enough to honor ourselves, we offer everyone else their humanity.[3]

By offering everyone else their humanity, transpeople make powerful contributions to their workplaces and to society.

GOING ABOUT IT FOR THE RIGHT REASONS

In a just and equitable world, coming out as transgender would be a "nonevent" in the workplace. Unfortunately the world is not always just, nor is it equitable. Not everyone is a friend of benign human difference, and that regrettable reality will continue to exist for some time to come.

If someone says they are transgender, what does that tell us about them? Not much, really, other than perhaps offering a minimal insight into their personal gender status. It indicates that they may perhaps be "different," but it says nothing about whether they are smart or slow, professional or amateurish, capable or incompetent, interesting or boring, and ethical or unethical. That is why it is important to treat each person as a unique individual, not as a stereotype. A personal transgender status says nothing about that individual's character, skills, abilities, talents, intelligence, or his or her innate ability to function well in the workplace or in society.

Pam Branahan of Minnesota-based Supervalu, Inc.—a company that recently scored 100 percent on the HRC Corporate Equality Index—has said, "It is important to show employers the workplace needs to be all-inclusive. This means employees need to come out, if it is physically safe to do so. Only when the workplace community realizes there are all types of people working to make the business successful will diversity be embraced."[4] Supervalu's organizational philosophy led the company to create a diversity and inclusion department, launch a diversity council, and expand its support system for personal and professional development.[5] These advances occurred because GLBT and other interested employees successfully made the business case for treating everyone equally by demonstrating that fair and equal treatment for all employees results in significant benefits for the organization. Once again we see that common sense, intelligent strategy, and meaningful initiatives are keys to successful transgender inclusion on the job.

Coming out at work can uniquely demonstrate the intrinsic value of human difference, including gender variance, in making organizations more successful. People who remain in the closet cannot be fully honest about who they are, nor can they share openly about the important aspects of their personal life. Such sharing is significant, for these human interactions bring a team together, helping them to function effectively during stressful, demanding moments. One thing is for certain: the coming out journey is "a psychological as well as a [physical] odyssey, a journey of self-discovery and self-realization."[6] Whenever a transgender employee comes out at work, the people of his or her organization usually end up going on a remarkable, affirming journey of discovery and realization right along with him or her.

When transpeople first come out on the job, they begin the process of what Ruthann Rudel has called "negotiating our own visibility."[7] Rudel says that "by coming out, we allow others to see us, to understand us, and to empathize with us. We move away from the feeling of alienation and invisibility that most of us are so familiar with and toward the small but significant level of openness with our peers that most straight people take for granted."[8]

The act of coming out on the job can vary widely and distinctively from person to person, organization to organization, and situation to situation. Referring to people who have come out at work, Lourdes Rodríguez-Nogués writes,

> Not only are our work situations and circumstances different, but so are our styles of becoming visible and the challenges and consequences that we each have had to face. For some, it was important to make themselves known in the job interview, risking the possibility of not getting a job. Others have had to deal with the reality of having the choice taken out of their hands by being outed at work. For some the decision to come out had to do with finding the gap between the personal and the professional. For them, that gap had become so wide that it became unmanageable. For still others the choice has been between a real self and a false self, with the consequences of silence ultimately being too much for their souls to bear. Then there are those who have come face-to-face with injustice and unequal work situations that they can't help but challenge with their coming-out. And for some the search for an identity has brought them, inevitably, to a coming-out moment.[9]

Ed Gray, a sportswriter for the *Boston Herald*, reached such a "coming-out moment" in his life when he revealed himself as an openly gay man, telling the Associated Press in a 2003 interview, "I can't come up with a single logical reason why I should have denied myself the right to live and work as openly and freely as everyone else."[10] What is true for a gay man like Ed Gray is also true, at least in principle, for transgender workers: there are no logical reasons why gender-variant individuals should deny themselves the right to live and work as openly and freely as everyone else.

When considering coming out on the job, transgender workers must choose between doing nothing, continuing to settle for second-class status on the job, and allowing the real or perceived obstacles to workplace equality to remain in place—because not to choose *is* to choose—or, conversely, looking deep within, finding the courage to be honest, to dialogue with and educate coworkers and teammates, and moving forward openly and with integrity by seeking the acceptance and respect and dignity that everyone wants and deserves. In most cases, no one can make that choice for anyone else. It is a very personal decision that can generate far-reaching, life-changing consequences.

The act of coming out at work has been viewed and/or described in many different ways. Some consider it foolhardy, a mistake, or a gross error in judgment to disclose something so uniquely personal and so culturally misunderstood. Some believe that coming out as often as possible (yet as safely and wisely as possible, too) is a powerful, sacred action. Coming out is an absolute necessity if progress is to be made in terms of generalized workplace acceptance for transpersons throughout society. Whatever else one may think of it, revealing one's transgender identity to others in a work environment is a remarkable act of raw courage.

Being a pioneer is not always easy or comfortable, but it means that you get to be the leader. You get to push the envelope and explore new territory. You get to breathe the rarefied atmosphere that only trailblazers experience. It takes bravery, individual confidence, inner strength, commitment, and dedication to come out publicly as transgender, especially if you are the first one in your organization to take such a step, but it can also be exhilarating and worthwhile in ways you never imagined.

It is not only about courage, either. Perhaps even more, and deep down where it really counts, it is about candor, brutal honesty, clarity of vision, and personal integrity. It is about being whole and healthy. It is about being who you are and choosing not to hide any longer for the sake of your own convenience or so that others might be appeased. It is about no longer pretending you are not gender-variant just to placate someone else's tender sensibilities. After all, what about *your* personal comfort level? What about *your* feelings, needs, and sensibilities—do they not matter just as much as anyone else's? Where do someone else's rights to be comfortable end and where do yours begin? Why should you continue to deny or hide your true self because of what someone else might think or say about you? Since when are any of us here to live up to someone else's expectations about how we ought to live our lives? Why should you be forced to deny your own integrity and personal truth merely to pacify someone else or make him or her feel more comfortable?

In the workplace, it is all about appropriate behaviors. As long as you are in alignment with your organization's policies for workplace behavior and treatment of others, you should have nothing to fear. (Please note: I said *should*. The reality may be very different, especially in organizations that do not have transgender-inclusive employee policies.)

You can begin by making a decision. You can refuse to apologize for being who and what you are just because someone else may or may not like it, or because another person may disapprove of you for being transgender. If you are not hurting that person—and, frankly, it is difficult to understand how living a life of honesty and integrity is going to legitimately damage someone else—does not the problem really reside with him or her and his or her own apparent inability to cope with some new knowledge and/or adjust to a new situation? At some point, you deserve to think about your personal peace of mind, your own validity and wholeness, your own needs, your own mental/physical health, and let others take care of theirs in their own way. We should all try to be considerate and respectful of others as much as possible, to be sure, and it is important to be kind and patient with people, but keep in mind that you are not personally responsible for the ways in which someone else may deal with or respond to the important truths and realities of your life.

Of course, there are certain intimate, personal things that any transperson should keep to himself or herself and not share with people at work, and maybe not even with friends. We all have our private secrets that we do not share, for any number of perfectly legitimate reasons. Boundary issues necessitate developing a sense of what is appropriate in a given context. For example, speaking and/or behaving in a sexually gratuitous or salacious manner is unacceptable in a professional work environment, no matter what one's gender status situation may be. However, a core transgender identity is not one of those personal issues that an individual should be forced or required to keep hidden. A person's essential identity should not have to remain clandestine. Being transgender permeates *everything* about an individual, including the way they view the world, the way they perform their work, the way they interact with other people, and the ways in which they think about and identify and express themselves.

Being transgender is about the fundamental nature of who one truly is—and who we are, we are 24 hours a day. And no, we should not have to hide that or keep it to ourselves.[11] It is not fair to expect an individual to keep a secret about something so vital to his or her own sense of self. No one deserves to be forced into an untenable position like that. Besides, there is nothing wrong, immoral, or criminal about being transgender. If you have done nothing wrong, you have no reason to hide.

Consider this: if you are happily married or live with a significant other, how would you feel if you were forced to keep that most important of relationships a secret at work? How do you think it might affect you if you had to hide such a central aspect of your life every day? Do you think you or your work might suffer from having to hide it? If you are in a marriage or a primary relationship, your connection with your spouse/partner is a large part of what defines you and makes you the person that you are, isn't it? Chances are you would not tolerate having to hide something so momentous in your life, and rightfully so. You should not have to be subjected to something like that. In the same manner, having to keep one's gender identity—which is an integral aspect of a person's core individuality and a major factor in determining who that person is—a secret on the job is unfair, unjust, degrading, inhumane, and unacceptable. A person's gender identity is simply too important to have to keep it hidden. People deserve the right to be open about such a central part of life.

Coming out as transgender at work is certainly a significant and potentially life-changing act. This key decision may have all sorts of consequences, some good and some bad, and many times those consequences will depend upon how you go about the process of revealing your gender-variant self. Your relationships at work and perhaps even your job itself may hinge on your actions and attitudes about coming out. However, as mentioned previously in these pages, in January of 2003 a New York Supreme Court judge ruled that a transgender person's anatomy is not relevant to his or her gender identity. Transgender workers can take heart: if the New York Supreme Court can comprehend enough about transgender to rule that one's anatomy and gender identity are not necessarily identical, then surely there is hope for other organizations to eventually come around as well.

Inequity based on gender stereotypes has been widely considered to be illegal, based upon interpretation of the Civil Rights Act of 1964. That notion was reinforced by the U.S. Supreme Court's landmark ruling, *Price Waterhouse v. Hopkins*, which found that an employer who has allowed a discriminatory motive to play a part in an employment decision must prove by clear and convincing evidence that it would have made the same decision in the absence of discrimination. The court determined that Price Waterhouse, the petitioning employer, had not carried this burden of proof. There is, however, still much conjecture regarding how broadly the Court's 1989 ruling may be applied. Many states are waiting for further clarification of the ruling, apparently choosing to discern what the ramifications might be before instituting legislation that protects gender minorities from harassment or discrimination. Meanwhile, and as the elected officials are waiting to see which way the political wind blows, many transpersons remain the unfortunate legal victims of ongoing discrimination and social bigotry.

Nondiscriminatory workplace policies that protect employees regardless of sexual orientation are important and necessary. They deserve to be supported and affirmed. However, and despite the insistence of some who fail to understand the nuances or the scope of the issue, sexual orientation policies alone are not enough to ensure protection for everyone. Many organizations confine their employee nondiscrimination policies to gender, race, religion, age, and/or sexual orientation but do not include specific protection in the areas of gender identity, gender characteristics, and/or gender expression. Unfortunately, this means that even heterosexual and/or married employees whose form of personal expression may differ from traditional gender stereotypes and social expectations are potentially exposed to workplace discrimination.

Male-to-female transsexual Donna Rose, who has successfully transitioned in the workplace, says,

> I can't think of anything that's similar to the work that a transgender person has to do when they come out at the workplace. But it's a necessary process. It's not as if you have a choice. From a sexuality standpoint, people can choose to share or not share in the workplace, but for us [i.e., the transgender employee] we don't have that option. This secret is going to be shared with a bunch of people who basically are strangers.[12]

Perhaps we can take encouragement from the words of Peter Nee (of the then Bank of Boston), who has said: "Attitudes change in the workplace. Segregation changed in the workplace, and when companies started to do the right thing society changed. Today, when industry leaders do the right thing they are going to change the way America thinks and acts for the better. But if we don't come out, they will never have the chance."[13] That is why it is so important for business leaders to recognize and respond appropriately to the critical role they play in helping to influence workplace attitudes and social change.

Most people want to do the right and fair thing. Studies indicate that once people know someone who is openly transgender, they come to understand there is nothing to fear. At that point, their acceptance level increases dramatically. The more often a human face is placed on the issue of transgender, the greater the opportunity for learning and then for acceptance by others. When gender-variant workers come out on the job, others will see the truth of transgender lives for themselves. They will learn that transfolk are simply human beings who pose no threat to anyone. They will find that transgender individuals are their friends and coworkers and team members. They will discover that they have known transgender persons all along and that they are good people. And, in the end, most will respond to transgender individuals with respect and acceptance because it is the right, fair, and logical thing to do.

REACTIONS AND RESPONSES

Let us consider some ways to deal with the various challenges of coming out as transgender in the workplace, and look at what sort of reaction a transgender worker might potentially expect from other people in his or her organization. We will examine how others may respond, how they may address and/or treat transpersons at work, and where things might go from there.

Unfortunately, the first thing a transgender worker needs to be aware of is the potential for *transphobia*, or "fear of and discrimination against transgender people [or people thought to be transgender, regardless of their actual gender identity]. Transphobia leads to violence and bias that can make coming out as transgender even harder."[14] A transperson would be wise to thoroughly reflect on all the ramifications of coming out in the workplace before taking the important step of coming out. You may be the most courageous transgender person in the world, but that will not help you much if you are lying comatose in a hospital bed or on a slab in the morgue.[15] If it is really that dangerous to come out where you work, you might want to seriously consider looking for a new job in a safer and more accepting work environment.

Chances are, however, that if you are intelligent about it and plan strategically, you may be able to come out in your organization with a relative minimum of aggravation. Of course, there is no foolproof way to determine how every individual will react to the news of your coming out. Some may be delighted, others might be angry or upset, and some will probably be confused. Some may object to your disclosure on religious or other grounds. Most people probably will not care too much one way or the other as long as you do not bother them. Expect a variety of reactions and think about how you might respond to them appropriately.

It is especially important to remember that a transgender employee's attitude can be pivotal in influencing and/or determining how they are treated by others. If you offer respect and treat other people with patience and compassion, you will likely discover that they will do the same for you in return. If you present yourself as a capable, professional person with a sense of humor—but with no tolerance or patience for bigotry and/or discrimination—your transgender status will likely cease to be an issue at work within a reasonable period of time.

Try to set a tone that says, "This is not a spectacle for anyone's entertainment. I'm here to work and make contributions, not to be a clown or a sideshow. Let's pull together, act as a team, and get the job done." By behaving in a dignified yet personable and friendly manner, as though you assume your transgender situation is normal (which it is, at least for you), you also silently demand and serve notice that you expect to be treated respectfully by others. In the end, "the workplace is not the playground: nobody cares who likes whom—so long as employees work in a professional manner, the job gets done. For all employers, this is the bottom line."[16] Remember: it is about appropriate behaviors, not personally held values or beliefs, on the job.

> *Courage is not the absence of fear, but rather the judgment that something else is more important than fear.*
>
> —Ambrose Redmoon

People who come out as transgender at work are almost always a little nervous and apprehensive. That is to be expected. Who would not be somewhat concerned about how things will go in such a new and unique situation? You would not be human if you did not have a few butterflies. But nervousness in a new and unique situation is one thing, while guilt or embarrassment about actually being transgender is quite another. Being gender-variant is no cause for humiliation or apology. There is no shame in being who you truly are.

You have the right to be yourself, to work for a living, and to exist and operate on this planet as a transgender individual. Please do not undermine or diminish your rightful status by running away, hiding, avoiding people, or cowering in fear of others. Keep your head up and your shoulders back, walk tall, smile, be approachable, and demonstrate confidence in your own human worth. Almost always, others will respond to you in the same manner that you behave toward yourself.

Transgender individuals can take quiet pride in being gender-variant, but please do not be vain, obnoxious, or overbearing about it. Also, try not to overcompensate for any anxieties you may be experiencing. Trying too hard can be annoying and off-putting, so avoid being shrill or overbearing about your situation. The people in your organization certainly do not need or want to see a manic, unduly frenetic person or a frightened, whimpering, irritating weakling who is wracked with guilt and confusion. Instead, they deserve to see a strong, calm, confident, and competent transgender role model who is there to work in a professional manner.

If you feel ashamed or confused about being transgender, you definitely are not emotionally equipped to come out in the workplace and will probably do more harm than good for yourself and others. Professional counseling is probably in order to help you learn to deal with confusion or feelings of gender-based inadequacy before you should even consider disclosing your transgender status at work. Personal shame and gender-related confusion are issues to be sorted through over time and in a therapeutic environment, not on the job. You need to present a competent, professional, productive, and cooperative persona when you are at work. Your employer surely does not want a scatterbrained, disorganized, inept, gender-confused, or shame-filled employee.

> In a 2002 study led by Barry Goldman, Ph.D., J.D., professor of management and policy at the University of Arizona, people with a strong sense of their own identity not only had greater work satisfaction, but also higher levels of personal well-being and overall life satisfaction. The study by Goldman and his colleagues defined personal identity as "a psychological state reflecting self-knowledge and a firm consistent sense of personal values and of one's ability to sustain one's conclusions in the face of opposition from others."[17]

Thus, greater self-knowledge was associated with confidence in one's own judgment. This understanding is particularly significant for transgender workers, who will be dependent upon their own inner resources as they struggle to be their true selves in extraordinary circumstances. A keen sense of self-awareness and personal confidence is vital to success in coming out on the job.

Remember, too, that your work should speak for itself. If it does not, perhaps you ought to consider addressing that issue before you take on the additional task of coming out on the job. You were hired to do a job, not to focus on your personal concerns when you are at work. Your organization expects you to work hard, perform well, and follow through on your responsibilities. Do your best to make strong, solid contributions through your work. No matter what your gender situation might be, your company deserves and has the right to expect a capable, willing, competent worker, not a slacker or a bungling employee. No one appreciates a lazy or incompetent team member, so be sure you are not one of those. Do not give potential detractors any additional ammunition to use against you. Be a member of the "able family" when you are on the job: be dependable, reliable, accountable, and available. Let your professionalism and productivity shine so brightly in your organization that any potential negatives will quickly fade into obscurity.

It is possible that you may encounter difficulty with an uncaring or unsympathetic manager or supervisor. You may even have to file a grievance if the situation warrants it. Andrew Stone, senior editor at *Gotham*, *Hamptons*, and *Los Angeles Confidential* magazines, says, " 'Sometimes a boss won't care about shared values or anything else you say. In that case, investigate your company's workplace grievance policy. Most firms have standard procedures for resolving disputes.' However, Stone warns: 'Don't compromise yourself. Your work should speak for itself. And if an employer discriminates against you and you don't want to go the route of pressing charges, then leave your job. Life is too short to work for a jerk.' "[18]

Before you reveal yourself as transgender at work, understand what you are doing and know exactly why you are doing it. Be prepared to articulate your reasons for coming out, because you will surely be asked about them. Coming out in the workplace means you are no longer willing to accept the role of silent victim but that you desire to be an active participant in your organization. It means you are making the conscious choice to do so openly, with authenticity and integrity, as your transgender self. You need to be able to speak intelligently about that decision.

Coming out on the job should be one of several logical and well-considered steps in a Personal Development Plan, i.e., a comprehensive, individualized strategy prepared in conjunction with a therapist or support group and your organization's management team. That action plan should be pursued with a desire to help minimize disruptions and difficulties for all the people of your organization (and especially for yourself).

If you are going to come out at work, please do it wisely. Do it when you are ready, and not before. Plan. Strategize. Think it through and cover all your bases. Be smart about it. Read. Do your homework. Have a support team in place. Talk to your organization's management. Have a Personal Development Plan prepared. Be psychologically equipped and mentally prepared to get through the initial coming-out moments of insecurity or awkwardness. Be aware of what the potential problems might be so you can address them logically and intelligently. Let your behavior on the job be professional, productive, and beyond reproach at all times. Become the best and most conscientious worker in the entire organization. Make your company proud that you are their employee.

Thousands of transgender individuals have already come out successfully at work, and more are doing so all the time. They have become full and equal participants in the life of their organizations and communities. Take courage from their example, and never give up the quest to be renewed every day as your authentic gender-variant self.

CHAPTER 7

Tools for Organizational Leaders

> *There are three principles in a man's [sic] being and life: the principle of thought, the principle of speech, and the principle of action. The origin of all conflict between me and my fellow-men is that I do not say what I mean and that I do not do what I say.*
>
> —Martin Buber, *The Way of Man*

An organization's leaders must be concerned with generating measurable results. For the organization to be successful, its workers must produce as efficiently and effectively as possible. Study after study indicates that productivity improves as people are professionally and personally empowered by leadership to live and work in truth.

Successful organizational leaders must also be concerned with the principles, practices, values, and future of their companies. Business author Tim McGuire says, "Leaders and managers have a fundamental responsibility to allow, encourage and motivate each worker to develop and grow to be their best. Growing individuals is as important as growing the business."[1]

Additionally, it is management's responsibility to establish a positive work environment. That responsibility necessitates reflecting on some relevant questions. How can you, as a leader in your organization, support and encourage the release of the immense human possibilities that each of your people possesses? Will you accomplish that by removing obstacles to their personal growth? By inspiring and motivating those individuals? By insisting upon a more just and fair place in which to work, and by instituting policies and guidelines that ensure such a work environment? By modeling appropriate behaviors, speech, and attitudes? All of the above? Other?

In many cases, the most effective way to remove obstacles and inspire people involves the intentional development of an affirming work environment that builds relationships, encourages teamwork, and invites people to be and do their best. The opportunity of leading people into that kind of affirming organizational culture can be an intricate but deeply rewarding challenge. William Isaacs has written,

> One of the most fundamental struggles for any leader—in business, in organizations, or in public life—stems directly from the separation that most of us feel between who we are as people and what we do as practical professionals. . . . These things cannot in the end be separated. What we do in private *does* impact how we perform in public. How we think *does* affect how we talk. And how we talk together definitely determines our effectiveness.[2]

According to author and corporate diversity consultant Liz Winfeld, formulating company policy or modeling desired behaviors around any aspect of human resources will be impossible if leaders are not equipped with information that enables them to take appropriate action. Winfeld indicates that the three primary message points for senior leaders include

1. Making the business case.
2. Creating or improving leaders' vocabulary and overall communication about this aspect of diversity.
3. Enabling accountability.[3]

To change an organization's culture, we must evaluate the ways we speak about it, the ways we think and feel about it, and the ways we behave within the context of that culture. These moment-to-moment decisions about language, thoughts, and actions will profoundly affect the company's success. That is why it is critical for business leaders to become more educated and informed about transgender issues: leaders cannot truly act with confidence in this new area of business interest until they know something about the phenomenon that is transgender.

"Leadership is usually discussed in the abstract. But leadership is composed of three elements: a sense of strategy; the ability to inspire confidence; and seeing farther ahead than others."[4] A leader cannot set forth a genuinely imaginative vision of respect and affirmation for all of their people—a comprehensive vision that is transgender-inclusive—if that leader knows little or nothing about transgender-related workplace issues.

It is not enough to say, "We are not transphobic in this organization." Leadership must be proactive in developing a long-range plan for transgender inclusion and committing to it for the long haul. Success or failure of the plan will rest squarely on the shoulders of leadership. The owner, CEO, president, managers, and other leadership team members must get on board first, and they must be able to articulate the business case for doing so. This will demonstrate that the company's leadership is fully behind the transgender inclusion initiative and is prepared to ensure its lasting success.

In addition, organizational leaders must initiate, model, and encourage the important workplace conversations that will bring people together and produce successful, measurable results. First, however, they must have access to the tools, resources, and accurate information that are necessary to achieve those objectives. Education and training are the keys, and this is particularly true when it comes to workplace issues such as those of the transgender employee. "The point is not to say to company leadership, 'You don't understand and you're bad.' The point is to say, 'Look, you have these employees that you probably don't know much about, so let's educate you about what they need.' "[5] When business leaders become more informed about the issues of transgender workers, they will be better positioned to make wise, effective decisions on behalf of the entire organization and its people.

> *Leadership: The capacity to influence oneself and others in the pursuit of meaningful individual, team, organizational or societal objectives within one's meaningful life areas.*
>
> —Bruce H. Jackson

As a leader, i.e., a person presumably in a position of influence within your organization, you are extremely fortunate. Because of the legitimate business need to be fair and equitable toward transgender employees, you are being gifted with a tremendous opportunity to demonstrate your leadership abilities by supporting an important workplace diversity initiative that will benefit your company in numerous ways over time. Leaders have an ethical obligation and commensurate responsibility to be the conscience of their organizations. The manner in which you deal with transgender employees and customers will send a powerful message to everyone in your organization about the quality of your leadership, not to mention the content of your character. Dealing honestly and fairly with transgender people is not only good for business, it is an ethical imperative for leadership. Treat transgender persons with integrity, always affording them the human dignity and respect that every person, transgender or otherwise, deserves.

You are embarking on a remarkable new leadership journey that can help your organization become more successful. If you will take action to ensure fairness and a work environment free of harassment, bullying, and discrimination, every person in your company will benefit. Please do not be discouraged if you make some mistakes as you learn—try to grow from the experience, address the problems head-on, and keep working to do the right thing for all of your people. Other leaders and organizations have successfully achieved this, and you can do it, too.

Acknowledging the existence and relevance of transgender as a legitimate organizational issue must be the first item of business. This means fully accepting the fact that transgender persons are part of the fabric of society and, thus, of the organization. Not everyone is traditionally gendered, and the company needs to realize and understand this critically important concept. Also, be aware that inclusively addressing the needs of transgender workers may necessitate accommodation by the organization. In any case, acknowledgment and affirmation must come directly from (and be modeled by) senior leadership in order for such workplace accommodation to successfully occur.

In addition, organizational leaders must become more aware of the potential for generating revenue from the transgender market, which has traditionally been misunderstood and/or ignored by the business community. An increased awareness in this area by leadership may result in increased opportunities for pursuing and profiting from that particular market group.

It is important to realize that without at least a basic knowledge of transgender-related terminology, business leaders will be at a distinct disadvantage. An awareness of appropriate verbiage is particularly significant in terms of generating the significant conversations that need to be held within the organization about transgender inclusion issues.

Most people, including leaders, would not feel comfortable discussing unique issues such as transgender until or unless they have an adequate, relevant vocabulary that can enable such conversations. Unless leaders are equipped with appropriate language to convey symbolic meaning and practical application, consequential discussions of transgender in the workplace will be limited or nonexistent.

Finally, leadership should be prepared to be accountable for organizational changes that may occur as the result of implementing a transgender-inclusive policy. Addressing relevant questions and concerns in a calm, reasonable, and businesslike manner will be critical if this issue is to achieve credibility within the company.

TRYING SOMETHING NEW

> *Change and risk are inextricably linked. One is not possible without the other. The more innovative the change, the greater the risk that comes with it. Yet, the risk must be taken—for without risk, the changes that propel humankind forward will not occur and we will begin to stagnate and wither away.*
>
> —Unknown

Have you ever learned a new game or a new sport? Were you perfect the first time you tried it? Probably not, and you should not be expected to. Anticipating perfection from the beginning is unrealistic, arrogant, or naïve.

Transgender is a new topic for most people, and the journey toward respect and acceptance of transgender workers will doubtless be one of many new experiences. You may occasionally lose your balance and fall over, but so what? As long as you keep getting up and trying again, you will eventually get to where you need to go and, if nothing else, you will have discovered what to avoid next time. The keys are to commit to the transgender inclusion process, keep moving forward, and resolve to never stop improving.

Try to be patient, understanding, and forgiving of yourself and others as you learn and grow. This is most likely a new situation for everyone involved, so do not worry if you occasionally stumble or fall. Besides, it is not about how many times you fall down: it is about how many times you get back up and keep moving ahead. Transgender workplace inclusion is an adventure, a journey of change, newness, and growth, not a canned or predetermined exercise in "business as usual."

LEARNING MORE ABOUT TRANSGENDER IN THE WORKPLACE

Although it has often been misunderstood by the general public, gender-based nonconformity has been a naturally occurring element of the human experience in every society. And, "just as many gay, lesbian and bisexual people come out about their sexual orientations, some people examine, redefine and acknowledge their gender identities, or how they understand their gender as a man, woman or somewhere in between."[6] This may be the case for some of the people in your own organization. If you are part of a large company, you can practically count on that eventuality.

Individuals do not get to choose who will be transgender: nature does. However, society can have a difficult time accepting nature's decisions when it comes to something new and/or foreign. We tend to look askance at almost anyone or anything that shakes up our comfortable views, especially when that person or thing may involve questions of gender and/or sexual identity. We all have the tendency to quickly reject or condemn whatever may be outside the comfort zone of our own personal or communal frame of reference. That is a problem that will need to be addressed and overcome if we are to make progress regarding the treatment of transgender workers.

Due to rapid advances in modern medicine—e.g., innovative surgical techniques, hormone therapies, psychological treatment modalities, and widespread availability of new gender-variant information—opportunities for personal choice in transgender expression have expanded considerably in recent years. This means that transgender people are becoming more publicly observable today than ever before. The resultant visibility is helping transgender become an increasingly significant human rights issue in our society and its institutions, including our business organizations. Still, many in leadership positions do not realize the extent to which transgender people are already present in their companies. These leaders are often unaware of the disproportionate rates of discrimination faced by transpersons whose gender situations may become publicly known.

As a leader in your organization, you now have an opportunity to deal with the transgender phenomenon in a pragmatic, humane, and businesslike manner that can positively impact your organization's bottom line.

No one is saying that dealing with transgender issues in your organization will necessarily be simple or easy, but you are encouraged to move forward and institute the appropriate changes anyway. Be aware that adopting new nondiscrimination policies supporting respect and acceptance for transgender workers may not necessarily be a popular thing to do at first. However, trepidation about potential complexities or possible resistance does not relieve leaders of the responsibility to take appropriate action on behalf of all their people.

You are not in a leadership position to win a popularity contest or to make everyone like you, but to help your organization be successful. That is why they pay you more than other employees, and it is why you are accountable for doing what is best for the organization.

It is no secret that doing something new and different can present its own risks as well as rewards. In *The Prince*, Niccolò Machiavelli wrote, "There is nothing more difficult to take in hand, more perilous to conduct, or more uncertain in its success, than to take the lead in the introduction of a new order of things." While it is true that being a pioneer is not always easy, there are few experiences more exciting and rewarding than being part of a new initiative that succeeds in improving the lives of others. Despite the risks, introducing a powerful new idea to your organization can be the one of the most exhilarating and potentially beneficial things you can do, especially if that idea is rooted in justice, equality, and fairness for all concerned. Ina Fried, National Lesbian & Gay Journalists Association Board Member and Trans and Allies Co-Chair, has said, "Without a clear statement from an employer, it can be hard for transgender workers to know where they stand. Adding gender [identity, characteristics, and] expression to a company's diversity policy is a step that enhances the workplace for all employees."[7]

We all know that in business, knowledge is power. That is why equipping yourself with tools, resources, and accurate information about transgender concerns as they affect and influence the workplace can allow you to make informed decisions that will benefit not only the transgender worker but all the people of your organization, both now and in the future.

MODELING WISE, COURAGEOUS, AND EXEMPLARY LEADERSHIP

> *Our success depends on having a workforce that is as diverse as our customers*
> *—and on working together in a way that taps all of that diversity.*
>
> —Steven Ballmer, CEO, Microsoft

The ways in which people perceive your leadership can be as important as the reality of that leadership itself. Mahatma Gandhi referred to this principle when he said: "Leadership by example is not only the most pervasive but also the most enduring form of leadership." It is a leader's responsibility to model professional behaviors that will inspire and help others to realize their full individual potential. "Do as I say, not as I do," simply will not cut it if you want to be a successful leader: you have to walk the walk in addition to talking the talk.

An effective transgender-inclusive policy should articulate, in simple, straightforward terms, what the organization expects and what is promised in return by the company. If you want your organization to successfully implement employee policies that are meaningful and relevant, you must lead by your own example of fairness and justice-oriented decision-making. Leaders are encouraged to be unequivocal and consistent in their messages. People deserve to know where they stand. Clear communication and decisive, informed action from management are significant aspects of creating the necessary cultural changes in any organization. Such an approach serves two purposes: (1) it will make the organization's objectives better understood, and (2) it will build increased confidence in the structure and culture of the company and its leadership. The importance of setting a respectful, equitable organizational tone through effective modeling on the part of leadership cannot be overemphasized.

KEYS TO RESULTS

Robbins and Finley propose three keys that leaders can use to create positive outcomes and desired results for their organizations. To make them easy to remember, they all begin with the letter "a."

The first key is *attitude*, which helps set the stage as the leader attempts to energize and inspire others into change. The demonstrated attitude and consistent behavior modeling of the leader are essential in creating an expectation for change as the norm for all employees. The second key, *analysis*, has to do with assessing the situation objectively, observing and noting progress (or the lack thereof) as it occurs, and generating feedback from those who are involved. *Action* is the third key. This involves taking on leadership responsibility, developing successful initiatives, and assuming personal accountability for progress and success. Steady and measurable steps toward a specific goal keep will help people remain energized and moving forward.[8]

An invitation to personal ownership and support of management's decisions can be especially important when introducing a nondiscrimination workplace policy for transgender employees. There may be some in the organization who resent the policy decision for any number of reasons. They may not understand or admit the need for such a policy. This is where trust and respect for leadership become critical, for if employees do not believe in their leaders, how can they be expected to wholeheartedly trust, respect, or support a leader's new transgender inclusion initiative?

We cannot logically expect people to robotically buy into a decision with which they may disagree. Alternative viewpoints deserve to be encouraged and courteously considered. In fact, it should be any person's right to respectfully express an opinion about something they may genuinely believe to be incorrect, inappropriate, or unfair. Listening to others and respecting an individual's right to a different opinion are hallmarks of an open, respectful organization that values the input of its employees. When people choose to listen to others in good faith and with respect, trust is built.

While honest dissent is one thing, willful disobedience to a reasonable organizational policy, especially a policy about workplace behaviors involving justice and human rights for all employees, is quite another. When the Xerox Corporation chose to recognize transgender employees in its company policy, Christa Carone, a Xerox spokeswoman in Rochester, New York, said, "It's the right thing to do . . . It's a no-brainer."[9] It is management's responsibility to make it clear to everyone in the organization that there is now a specific zero-tolerance policy regarding discrimination, harassment, bullying, or inequitable treatment of transgender employees. If your organization does not have such a zero-tolerance policy, consider developing one and implementing it immediately. Your people need and deserve to have that protection, and leaders have a responsibility to provide it for them.

It may be helpful to know that you will not have to reinvent the wheel in terms of dealing with workplace discrimination toward transgender workers. Transgender activist and educator Debra Davis says, "Absolutely every company knows how to deal with discrimination. They've been doing it for years. [Transgender in the workplace is] exactly the same thing; if there is discrimination going on, you deal with it the same way. They have those skills, they just have to use them and apply them to this particular issue."

The support of the organization's top management and Human Resources/Diversity professionals will be essential if a transgender-inclusive policy is to be effective. Acquiring at least a rudimentary knowledge of transgender issues will be necessary for organizational leaders, as illustrated by the following true story. Author and transgender rights activist Jamison Green tells about a diversity training session at PlanetOut Partners, where Green serves as a contributing editor:

> After the diversity trainer went through all of the basic categories of different groups, a member of the PlanetOut staff asked why the diversity trainer excluded mentioning transgender people. To the amazement of the PlanetOut staff, the diversity trainer said that transgender people in the workplace is a non-issue "because all transgender people are prostitutes." I was stunned, but at the same time I wasn't stunned because these are the kinds of preconceived notions that even well-meaning, well-educated diversity trainers have about transgender people.[10]

Green agrees that "the challenge faced by transgender activists and educators is parsing out sexual orientation from the discussion of gender identity before it can be reincorporated again."[11] In other words, a basic and accurate understanding of transgender-related terms, concepts, and meanings—as opposed to terminology that refers specifically to sex or sexual orientation—is essential to deal with these issues effectively in our workplaces.

Ultimately, it is management's responsibility to make the workplace environment as safe, functional, and productive as possible for everyone. Among other duties, organizational leaders are charged with

- ensuring an inclusive and caring work environment;
- ensuring equality of opportunity for everyone;
- ensuring equality in workplace practices;
- supporting the empowerment of every employee;
- facilitating the professional growth and well-being of every employee.

To effectively achieve these goals, leaders must embrace and model the values of inclusion and pluralism while encouraging their people to respect the full humanity of each employee, vendor, and customer. "A work environment in which all employees are treated with dignity and respect is a more productive environment. Yet fair and equal treatment of all employees rarely happens without clear and consistent guidance from corporate management."[12] This implies a need for specific transgender inclusion policies and guidelines from management if the quality of work life in the organization is to improve. It is not enough to merely preach pluralism in an organization: you must actively practice and promote antidiscrimination awareness throughout the entire company if you want to prove that you are serious.

More than ever, today's organizations require leaders with courage and wisdom to cope with an area of organizational life such as transgender in the workplace. Business guru Peter Koestenbaum says, "Aristotle believed, correctly, that courage is the first of the human virtues, because it makes the others possible."[13] Both Koestenbaum and Aristotle were correct: unless one can summon the courage to take the necessary action, all the other virtues do not really matter. Leaders must be determined to look deep down inside, find their courage, and use it as an ethical platform for acting in the best interests of the organization's people. Koestenbaum goes on to say, "Courage involves both advocacy—the ability to take a stand—and the internalization of personal responsibility and accountability."[14] Taking a resolute stand for transgender inclusion may not always be politically expedient or convenient in the short run, and it may not make you very popular in some circles, but it is definitely the right thing to do for your company. Doing what is right is not always easy, admittedly, but you will sleep better at night and your organization will surely benefit from your actions in the long run.

PRACTICAL SUGGESTIONS FOR LEADERS

> *Character is the most important of the three qualities I look for when considering someone for a key job. The other two, intelligence and energy, can actually be liabilities if strong character is lacking.*
>
> —Warren Buffet, from an address to the Harvard Business School

There are thousands of people who have changed their sex, changed their gender, come out as gender-variant, or otherwise identified themselves as transgender in the workplace. More and more transpeople are finding the courage to take such steps every day. Previously, gender-variant employees were told to leave their jobs and start over as members of the opposite sex, preferably in some other organization where they might not "make waves" or "create problems." However, today many transpersons are courageously choosing to stay on in their jobs and transition openly while continuing to work hard and contribute strongly to the success of their organizations.

This type of corporate sea change can admittedly create some initial challenges for employers and managers, but it can also offer powerful opportunities for learning, growth, and business improvement that will transcend any short-term struggles. All successful businesses want to preserve good relations with their customers, create a satisfying working environment, and maintain a strong level of productivity and profitability. Most employers are people of good will who want to do the right thing and would presumably choose to support their transgender employees. However, until now there has been relatively little accurate information available to help employers and managers learn about the transgender phenomenon or to deal effectively with the issues related to a transgender employee who comes out in the workplace.

It may come as a surprise for an employer to learn that a transgender person is already working in his or her organization. Often the transgender employee appears to be no different from any other worker, at least on the outside, and they are typically valuable contributors in the workplace. If employers will take action to support the transgender employee who comes out at work, they will almost surely be rewarded with strong contributions and increased productivity from that individual. They will also demonstrate leadership and a commitment to fairness and equality for everyone in the organization. There is potentially much to be gained by employing transpersons, by providing a supportive work environment for them where they can be open about themselves, and by affirming them as they move forward in their process of becoming healthier, happier, more productive workers.

The following paragraphs contain some ideas that can be helpful for employers and other business leaders when addressing the issues of transgender workers who come out and/or transition on the job. Obviously, it is impossible to cover every potential situation or workplace scenario, but these are sound general guidelines. Please allow common sense, factual information (as opposed to emotionally based responses), and your own good judgment to guide you in making appropriate decisions that will benefit your organization.

First, *do not worry if you find much about transgender to be confusing: you are not alone*. Many people have little or no experience with transgender issues, and most do not even have a language for talking about transgender with any real clarity. You certainly do not have to become an expert on the subject of transgender, but you should care enough about your employees to learn some of the basic information so you can speak intelligently to and about the topic. Educate yourself on at least a fundamental level. (The suggested reading and Web site lists included in this book's appendices can be convenient resources.) Talk to the transgender employee(s) in your organization and/or other transpersons in your community and learn their stories. Work with a knowledgeable transgender business consultant as necessary. Do not remain ignorant of the basic facts, and do not depend on hearsay, the opinions of others, or secondhand information. Do some research, learn the truth for yourself, and apply it accordingly.

There is no substitute for strong leaders who model exemplary behaviors for their people. As a leader, your personal attitude toward the transgender worker's situation can potentially make or break the success of your company's response to an openly transgender presence. Management has a responsibility to set a tone of respect and dignity for every employee. It will not be helpful or productive to view a transgender worker's situation as something to be endured or as a major organizational problem that may disappear if you wish hard enough or ignore it. Negative attitudes about change and new ideas are like rotten apples: sooner or later the rot of pessimism will spread throughout the company. Please do not allow toxic attitudes and negative energy to ruin a golden opportunity to improve your organization's culture.

Referring to business decisions about diverse workplaces, Steven Ballmer, Microsoft's CEO, has said, "It all boils down to trust. Even when people disagree with something that we do, they need to have confidence that we based our action on thoughtful principles, because that is how we run our business."[15] Choose consciously to be supportive and enthusiastic about this chance to help your organization improve. A leader's job is to inspire his or her people to change for the better, and transgender in the workplace is a unique opportunity for you to help provide that inspiration in a new way.

Strive to avoid discrimination complaints and/or potential costly legal entanglements for your company. When interviewing and hiring new people, make it clear that your organization does not discriminate based on personal characteristics such as age, race, physical ability, sex, gender, gender identity, gender expression, and sexual orientation. This should help alleviate any anxiety that may exist on the part of the interviewee or new hire about these legitimate concerns. Also, make it clear to all employees that performance reviews, promotions, raises, bonuses, etc., are not to be affected or influenced by discrimination in any form, including gender-based discrimination.

Hopefully, the transgender employee who makes a decision to come out on the job will want to talk to management first, allowing you to converse privately with him or her about his or her individual situation. It will also provide an opportunity for you to hear his or her story, express your concern and respect for that employee, ask your questions, voice your fears, and collaborate in making some initial decisions about how best to proceed. If you hear about the transgender worker's coming out from someone else, you will want to meet with the transgender employee and your HR director as soon as possible to discuss what steps should be considered.

Organizations rarely hire people for no apparent reason, so it might be a questionable business decision for you to immediately terminate, lay off, or otherwise casually discard the investment your company has already made in an employee who comes out as transgender at work. That employee was almost certainly hired because you or someone else in the organization believed he or she could perform the responsibilities of his or her position. Have his or her skills and ability to do the job somehow magically diminished or disappeared because he or she made a decision to be honest about his or her gender status while at work? Has he or she mysteriously lost the expertise and proficiency that made him or her right for the job before you knew about the transgender situation?

When making a decision about retaining or terminating a transgender employee, it is logical to carefully consider the employee's history, experience, skill set, job performance, overall record, and previous contributions to the organization. If the transgender employee is able to come out in a supportive atmosphere, the quality of his or her work will likely improve due to the increased personal liberation and affirmation they will experience. Discarding a heavy load of psychological baggage can free up significant amounts of energy. This contributes to an improved mental attitude, which in turn enables more on-the-job productivity. It is remarkable how much a person can accomplish when he or she do not have to hide his or her true identity and can simply be who he or she is at work.

You will probably want to have several conversations with the transgender employee to assess his or her specific needs and work-related concerns. You will also want to collaborate closely with your HR department to guarantee that everyone's rights are protected, including the rights of non-transgender employees. Workplace expectations, standards, and appropriate behaviors should be made clear to everyone concerned, including the transgender employee(s). Also, it might be wise to contract with a transgender diversity consultant or a reputable organization that offers professional awareness training on transgender issues. Making educational opportunities available for your employees will surely be in your organization's best interests.

Your employee is not mentally ill because he or she is transgender. Gender variance is not a disease, it is not communicable, and it is nothing to fear or avoid. The transperson is probably not gay or lesbian either, though that may be the case for some. In any event, their sexual orientation should not be an issue either way. They are not coming to work to have sex or otherwise disrupt the organization—they come there to do their job, just like you.

Make it clear to the transgender employee that he or she will be expected to be professional and businesslike in his or her conduct while at work. For example, a transperson who has recently come out may feel emotionally needy and/or overly vulnerable, and thus may potentially overreact to gestures of friendship. You will want to address that concern together beforehand to avoid potential problems.

A male-to-female transgender person's IQ does not suddenly drop 30 points just because he is now working as a woman. Stereotypes about women can be highly inaccurate, and they have no place in a professional organization. In the same manner, a female-to-male transgender employee's IQ does not automatically go up by 30 points, either. Typecasting is counterproductive: valued employees are valued employees, regardless of their gender.

Creating a safe environment for transgender workers does not mean you have to eliminate or ignore your organization's dress code. Your organization has the right to develop and enforce a reasonable dress code that is appropriate for your business.[16] It has long been established that employers have a right to determine and enforce standards of dress in the workplace. Take this opportunity to clarify and reinforce the organization's expectations around the dress code. Keep in mind that appropriate clothing for work relative to one's gender identity, gender characteristics, or gender expression should be no cause for alarm as long as reasonable taste and common sense hold sway.

It is unlikely that your employee will choose to come to work dressed like a drag queen, a hooker, a bum or bag lady, or a clueless vagabond, but if they should actually have the dubious taste and questionable judgment to do so, invite them to go home and make themselves presentable before they come back. An inappropriate or unprofessional presentation reflects poorly on the organization and should be unacceptable from any employee.

Company dress codes exist to make clients and coworkers comfortable, to establish organizational expectations, and to encourage a workplace atmosphere of respect and professionalism. Make it clear that appropriate professional attire and behavior are always the expectation for everyone in the company, no matter what an employee's gender identity or gender expression may be. You are running a business—not a nightclub, a bordello, or a home for vagrants—and your workplace dress code should reflect that reality and expectation.

Most people have at least a general idea of what attire is acceptable on the job. Professional standards and businesslike expectations are always appropriate in the workplace. If someone is dressed in an unsuitable manner, you always have the option of requesting that they go home and put on something more suitable before returning to work. That is not unreasonable at all: it is simply good business practice.

Want loyalty and commitment from your employees? Here is a tip: value them, talk with them (not at *them), listen to them, and share your appreciation for their contributions.* Treat each employee, transgender and non-transgender alike, with respect and understanding. You will build trust, loyalty, and a sense of pride in ownership (i.e., internal branding) within your organization's employees. Morale will escalate, productivity will increase, and everyone will benefit.

As a leader, you lead by example. The integrity of your personal leadership will be carefully scrutinized and assessed every day. "When there is a lack of alignment between what you say as a leader and what you do, the results are often confusion, frustration, demoralization, even anger and sabotage."[17] Other employees will be watching closely to see how you deal with a transgender worker who comes out on the job. Some may make personal decisions about continuing loyalty and commitment to the organization based upon the way you treat a transgender employee. People are not stupid: they know that treating any employee unjustly means that similar treatment could also be visited upon them sometime in the future. Therefore, be scrupulous and purposeful in your application of fairness toward everyone. That is how you can cultivate loyalty and trust among your people.

"Transition is the term used to identify the period of time required by the transgender person to change over from their birth gender to their preferred gender. [This description usually refers to transsexual employees who choose to transition while remaining in their job.] From a workplace perspective, it will probably be perceived as the day on which the staff member informs management and other staff that they will be presenting in a new gender role."[18]

Transition can be an important time of growth and learning, both for the transgender employee and for your organization as a whole. Try to give this experience the respect and the "breathing room" it deserves. "Where management becomes aware of an individual's intention to transition, they should take all appropriate action, in consultation with the transitioning person, to provide a safe and supportive environment for the individual concerned and for all other staff members."[19] In a very real sense, the transgender worker is not the only one making a change: your organization is transitioning as well. Try to encourage everyone to appreciate and learn from this unique opportunity for enhanced success.

There is an existing, well-established medical protocol for treating and assisting persons who have been diagnosed as transsexual. It is known as the World Professional Association for Transgender Health (formerly the Harry Benjamin Standards of Care) Standards of Care and has been adopted by the American Psychiatric Association and other health professionals as the primary method for helping transsexual persons transition into their new lives. This rigorous process includes a meticulously defined set of parameters and supervised procedures designed to ensure that the transsexual individual is an appropriate candidate for medically approved gender transition. The transition protocol includes various forms of assessment and diagnosis, psychotherapy/counseling, hormone therapy, a "cross-living" period of time (also known as the "real life test," which usually involves one to two years of living full-time in the role of the desired sex), and eventually one or more sexual reassignment surgeries.

A cursory knowledge and/or at least a minimal overview of this medically supervised protocol can be helpful to leaders in dealing with a transsexual employee who seeks to transition on the job. However, please keep in mind that the protocol is designed only for transsexual persons who are actively pursuing transition. It does not necessarily apply to cross-dressers, intersex persons, or other transgender individuals who are not transsexual. Such persons often have their own unique transgender issues and concerns that may differ considerably from those of transsexual individuals, and they should be taken seriously as well.

It is important for your organization's people to understand that there is an extremely wide scope of transgender persons and associated behaviors. The spectrum of gender encompasses a far-ranging variety. Gender-variant persons originate from every race, ethnic group, education level, geographical location, class/social strata, etc. The transgender community is amazingly diverse and unique, so just because you may have hired or served one individual or group of transpersons, it does not mean you have found or now understand the entire transgender community. Try to keep the bigger picture in mind. Transgender human beings are not all alike: they are far too complex to dismiss and/or lump them all into a singular category.

Some in management may be concerned that a transgender employee's presence within the organization could potentially create insurmountable difficulties and/or engender chaos for the company. However, "there is no evidence that allowing an employee to transition will open the floodgates to nonconformity. Developing an appropriate management process, however, will make it easier next time, if there is a next time."[20] Setting a strong precedent by instituting transgender-inclusive policies and procedures will serve your business well. Also, it will actively demonstrate your commitment to justice and fairness for everyone in the organization.

A transgender employee's coming out experience in the workplace must not be permitted to become a circus or a freak show. The transperson almost certainly does not want that (they will probably be apprehensive enough as it is), and your organization definitely does not need that kind of counterproductive distraction. Given adequate time and preparation, any transgender-related issues that may perhaps seem thorny at first will usually resolve themselves fairly quickly, especially if the organization's leaders are consistently communicating and modeling an enlightened, professional example of acceptance and respect for the transgender employee.

Most workplace concerns about the presence of a transgender worker tend to fade with the passage of time. "Experience has shown that backlash is usually brief and, if the company holds firm in its commitment to true equality of opportunity, quickly dissipates."[21] People soon come to the realization that a transgender person in the workplace is no big deal, which is exactly as it should be. Any concerns about potentially negative coworker and/or customer reactions should be carefully considered from this long-range perspective. Initial knee-jerk overreactions to the presence of an openly transgender worker should be looked upon as precisely that: initial knee-jerk overreactions that will diminish and probably disappear within a reasonable time frame. Refuse to waver from your stated commitment toward justice and fairness for all team members. Fully and firmly support the transgender employee (and the rights of all employees), uphold the policies regarding appearance and behavior for everyone in your organization, and things will almost always work themselves out. Thoroughness, responsiveness, adaptability, professionalism, and consistency are the hallmarks of successful transgender employee initiatives for organizations.

Transgender awareness training and education for your organization's people can help enhance business success. Such training will give your people the facts—and, if introduced appropriately, the inspiration and motivation—they need to cope successfully with this new situation. Transgender awareness training can help produce a more unified employee team, which translates into more work done better in a positive, affirming workplace environment. "And a word of caution to executives with the red pencils. In these challenging times when we're faced with the need to innovate, don't cut the training budget!"[22] If anything, employers should consider offering even more opportunities for awareness training to their people so they can be more productive in their work. This will provide employees with the knowledge and skills they need to do their jobs efficiently in a positive, supportive workplace culture.

When a transgender employee changes his or her name, title, or sex, the company should immediately revise the personnel records to reflect that change. Organizational accuracy requires responding to these important change(s) with an appropriately documented records update. This action may also help in avoiding potential legal difficulties.

Additionally, these record changes will further affirm the institutional validity and authenticity of the transgender employee's status within your organization. Make sure your company's human resources director is aware of the legal and cultural significance of this important step. For everyone's benefit, check to ensure that all employee records are being maintained and updated accurately.

It is okay to demonstrate a sense of humor and laugh with—but not at—the transgender worker. After all, this is admittedly a new and somewhat unusual situation, and you may as well carry a light heart as you meet your leadership responsibilities. Laughing together can help ease tension, create a friendlier atmosphere, and strengthen relationships in the workplace. Respectful humor, laughter, and wit can be helpful tools during the time of change and growth. However, it is definitely *not* okay to make transgender persons the butt of cruel jokes or the target of inordinate teasing and insensitive comments. Such behaviors have no place in a professional workplace environment. This is a culturally sensitive situation that should be handled with understanding and professionalism.

The most powerful and lasting change processes tend to happen at the individual level. That is where relationships, interactions, and simple rules uniquely come together to shape the emerging patterns of personal human behavior within organizations. When you positively influence how people relate to each other on a one-to-one basis, you begin to change the organization's culture for the better.

Your help, involvement, and active cooperation as a leader matter to an incalculable degree. The transgender employee needs your leadership and support, as do all the people of your organization. Decisive, intelligent, compassionate leadership and strong decision-making on your part can set a pivotal example of affirmation and acceptance for gender-variant employees within the company's work environment.[23]

THE SIGNIFICANCE OF ORGANIZATIONAL CULTURAL CHANGE

> *You don't have to be great to start, but you have to start to be great.*
> —Zig Ziglar

In order to make a transgender inclusion initiative a lasting success, changes need to be introduced and take root within the organization's culture. It has been said that successful change in a company involves about 20 percent tools and tactics and 80 percent culture. Almost always, the challenge for an organization lies in convincing people to voluntarily change their behavior. Fortunately, there are ways to take the fear out of impending cultural changes and persuade employees to accept the desired changes in a professionally beneficial manner.

A lack of understanding about the issue is often one of the first impediments to implementing transgender-related cultural changes in a workplace environment. Since a dearth of knowledge about the transgender phenomenon is common throughout society, some resistance is probably to be expected. After all, transgender as an organizational initiative is at least somewhat counterintuitive. Some people will probably say, "It won't work here. It's stupid. It's crazy. It's not right." Others may dig in their heels because of territorialism, personal pride, religious beliefs, moral objections, or simple obstinacy about change in general. People who have worked in a certain way all their lives may look at the new situation and say, "You want me to do *what*? You want me to accept *what*?" Frankly, and unless the business case for change is made clear to every employee, it is difficult to blame people for questioning the desired changes. Meanwhile, some managers may worry that they will look bad or lose face with certain employees. For these managers, workplace change is a major problem and they would rather not deal with it. That may perhaps be understandable, but it is not acceptable. Change is a way of life for successful organizations, so a refusal to accept the reality and/or the necessity of change is not going to benefit the organization or the individual. Everyone has to get on board so the organization can continue to grow and evolve. Part of growth and evolution involves learning to adapt to beneficial changes.

Some company leaders may resist cultural change in their organization, especially when the company is making profits. They rationalize their resistance by insisting, "If it ain't broke, don't fix it." Sometimes, too, leaders fail to understand that if they introduce the cultural change, they must also change along with it. Beau Keyte, a trainer with the Lean Enterprise Institute and President/Founder of Branson Inc., says, "[Management] often doesn't understand that you can't just throw tools at a problem and expect it to be fixed. Unless management is willing to stand up and understand its role . . . the transformation will have no success."[24] Management must be invested in the change and be prepared to change along with everyone else if the initiative is to succeed on an organization-wide basis.

Just because you have not tried something previously does not mean it cannot, will not, or should not work. Actually, all indications are that a transgender awareness initiative in the workplace *does* work if it is introduced and implemented in a reasonable and logical manner that focuses on behaviors (as opposed to personal thoughts and/or beliefs) that will improve the business.

It is also important to recognize that an organization's culture will probably not change on its own. Support and decisive leadership from senior management are critical. The more managers understand what the process of cultural change is about, the more they will be able to apply appropriate attitudes and problem-solving techniques to the change process. In addition, managers must present clear goals and communicate the business-related importance of the change initiative to their people.

It can be very helpful to have designated Gender Transition Leaders (GTLs) or Diversity Champions assigned within the organization's various departments to help foster interactions, encourage meaningful discussions, ensure the free flow of communication about the issue, and monitor progress. These in-house leaders can serve a valuable function by acting as liaisons between management and employees.

LEADERSHIP THAT WORKS

We have only touched on a few principles of leadership in this chapter, but there are other important elements to consider as you begin to deal with transgender workplace issues. For additional information, please see the chapter on practical suggestions.

You are being presented with the gift of an exciting new learning opportunity. That is something to be celebrated and embraced, not feared or rejected. The ways in which you respond to this opportunity will have a direct impact on you, the transgender employee(s), and all the people of your organization. Therefore, personally develop and apply a strong ethical compass, a personal quality that author Timothy White has called "an unanswerable belief in the enduring power of one's better self."[25] Through wise and courageous choices you can profoundly influence the development of that "better self" in your people and in your own life.

Business heroes are leaders who envision the bigger picture and pursue magnificent goals. They seek the greatest good for the greatest number of people, and they take decisive action to make that good become a reality for their organizations. They care passionately about doing the right thing even when it may not necessarily be the most popular or politically expedient thing to do. Business heroes are insightful leaders who understand the benefits of doing what is necessary and important for their company over the long haul. They recognize that it is not about assessing blame when or if things go wrong: it is about accepting and encouraging shared responsibility to get the organization on track and keep it moving forward. Business heroes intuitively grasp that doing the right thing brings its own rewards, and they commit to doing what is right regardless of the consequences. They make that commitment because they are able to envision the rewards that will ultimately come for doing the right and ethical thing.

You can be a business hero. You can make the choice to strategically lead your organization by developing and enforcing an organizational policy that prohibits discrimination against employees based on gender identity, gender characteristics, and gender expression. However, keep in mind that this will be a continuous learning experience. The opportunity for growth and change never ends. It takes courage and integrity to do the right thing with regard to transgender inclusion, and it is not always easy to be a strong leader in such circumstances. Doing the right thing does not always make for a smooth or unruffled journey, but it can bring tangible and intangible rewards that are infinitely satisfying. Leaders who do what is right make a positive difference for their people by leading them in the best direction.

Please do not settle for being mediocre or wishy-washy, and do not hide your head in the sand hoping that the issue of transgender in the workplace will simply go away. Cam Lindquist has written, "Mediocrity is not a fertile ground for change."[26] Refuse to settle for mediocrity. The organizational boat may perhaps be briefly rocked to some degree, but if you do the ethical thing with firmness and compassion, then the rocking should be relatively minimal. You can weather any temporary concerns and come through intact to create a stronger, better, more just and fair organization for all of your people.

The transgender movement for workplace equality is about an uncompromising alignment and integration of inclusive, affirming values with sound business principles, practices, and behaviors. It is not some obscure or irrelevant vision: it is a call to decisive action for today's business leaders who operate in the real world. The ways in which you answer that call will say a great deal about the quality and integrity of your leadership.

CHAPTER 8

Help for Human Resources Professionals

In many organizations, the Human Resources department is charged with a wide-ranging variety of duties. HR responsibilities may include (but are certainly not limited to) employment/staffing and recruiting, training and development, compensation, benefits, employee services, retirement, promotion, personnel records, legal issues, health and safety, and strategic planning. Due to the extensive nature of these many areas of organizational interest, practically every employee is touched in some way by the HR department.

This chapter is not intended to tell HR professionals how to do their jobs. Instead, the goal is to help provide some tools, resources, and information about transgender issues in the workplace with the intent of equipping HR professionals to meet their organizational responsibilities more effectively.

When a transgender employee makes the decision to come out and/or transition in the workplace, the HR department should immediately become involved. Since an employee's work life is so intertwined with the functions of the HR department, it seems reasonable to provide some guidelines, basic information, and assistance for HR professionals who may deal with transgender employee issues. In this way, everyone—the transgender worker, the HR department, management, coworkers, and the entire organization—will be prepared to successfully address the new situation.

Speaking at a Human Resources conference, Dr. Richard Rasi stated,

More than ever, the state of GLBT issues at the workplace is changing dramatically. Of primary importance are the individual workplaces, no matter how many employees they have, committing to a policy of inclusion of this particular segment of the workforce ... If you are a Human Resources professional, you can be the best ally a GLBT person has. You, along with the Diversity Professionals you work with, have an obligation to include GLBT individuals in Diversity training and initiatives.[1]

Many organizations and their HR departments have not yet considered how they might deal with transgender issues in their work environment, but sooner or later they will probably be required to do so either by law or due to the pressures of increasing social expectations. "It's a reality of employment now," says Syl Booth, affirmative action director for Minnesota's Hennepin County employees, "and sometimes you've got to break new ground."[2]

According to Jillian Todd Weiss, J.D., Ph.D., "The real 'cutting edge' of workplace diversity is the question of what is required on an organizational level to combat discriminatory norms so that diversity policies can support the needs of covered employees, as well as the needs of employers."[3] Human Resources and other organizational training professionals have a meaningful opportunity to help the people of their organizations become more aware of transgender issues in the work environment. (Dr. Bruce Tuckman's team-building model of "forming, storming, norming, and performing" may be a useful tool for strategizing how to develop an organizational concept of acceptable behavior with regard to transgender workers.)

HR professionals are encouraged to become informed about transgender issues and consider how they might become involved in training/ informing the people of their organization. It will be helpful to view this endeavor not as a burden or a distasteful chore but as an exciting new learning adventure and a legitimate professional growth opportunity.

HR LEADERSHIP OPPORTUNITIES

Some organizations have chosen to identify and train certain HR, Diversity, or other designated employees as Gender Transition Leaders (GTLs). A GTL's function is to help provide clear, professional leadership that aligns with the organization's transgender-based employee nondiscrimination policy. Many companies are discovering that GTLs can help to bridge the gap between the organization's policies/expectations and employee concerns in the work environment.

Resistance and conflict around a new idea such as transgender in the workplace can be a harsh reality in some organizations, sometimes creating barriers to workplace efficiency and team building. For this reason, it can be helpful to know something about the nature of resistance and to possess some tools for addressing a potential conflict situation.

Some people just naturally resist change. They do not like it, do not want anything to do with it, and are probably going to consciously or subconsciously undermine any change initiative. From where does that kind of resistant mind-set originate? What causes certain persons to resist a change so adamantly, even if it is a positive change that will benefit them?

Resistance to a new idea is a condition that is usually based on individual or group perceptions. Human nature being what it is, not everyone will view an issue in the same way. Some persons may have a vested interest in maintaining the status quo and will oppose any alterations or new concepts that may threaten to change the existing framework, structure, or paradigm.

Such resistance-based conflicts are frequently rooted in emotion. They can be heavily influenced by factors such as goals, individual experiences and interests, values and beliefs, one's stage of life (e.g., people of generations X, Y, and Z may all have differing perspectives than those of senior citizens or baby boomers), allegiances, opinions, and thought processes. Personal differences are often at the core of a resistance to change. The good news is that we all make choices that can take us toward or away from conflict. We can always choose to work through resistance in a healthy manner, thereby moving from conflict to collaboration that can eventually lead to success.

The key to overcoming resistance to a new idea may be found in adopting a three-step approach.[4] The first step involves the development of an ever-increasing awareness of oneself and others. The more we learn about the human condition, the more likely we are to be less fearful and therefore more accepting of the uniqueness we discover in ourselves and other people. People who do not know much about another person or group tend to be frightened of them because they do not understand them. With familiarity comes knowledge; with knowledge comes understanding; with understanding comes confidence in one's ability to cope; and with confidence, people become more willing to accept change and new situations.

The second step has to do with a search for accurate and/or appropriate responses to the issues that have created the resistance. Tools for the search may include replacing dead-end phrases with more affirming alternatives. For example, "How might we ... ?" should become a preferred question. The goal is to establish honest connections between people, open up communication channels, and focus on mutual understandings that can generate consensus and agreement instead of dwelling on petty issues that create division.

The third step in confronting resistance is an invitation to engage in conversations that can help to develop new and deeper meaning. Fomenting a heated or highly emotional debate around a complex topic such as transgender probably is not going to help resolve a conflict, but having a series of respectful, thoughtful discussions just might. HR professionals should be prepared to explain why the organization's transgender-inclusive policy is important and why appropriate workplace behaviors around this issue are essential from a business perspective. Also, it helps to try to find a balance between advocacy and inquiry. In other words, be an advocate for the organization's policy but also be open to exploring questions, concerns, and new ideas as they arise. When resistant or combative individuals see that you are willing to listen to them and hear them out even though you may not agree with them, you may be able to defuse a good deal of the anger and defensiveness that so often accompanies resistance. Sometimes all people want is to be heard.

KEY CONSIDERATIONS FOR HR PROFESSIONALS

Most HR professionals are capable people who want to do the right thing for their organizations. Some may be apprehensive about not wanting to offend transgender employees with inappropriate questions or comments, while others may cling to unflattering stereotypical notions about transgender individuals that can negatively influence their thinking, behaviors, feelings, and beliefs. Here are a few important concerns that HR professionals who deal with transgender issues should be prepared to address.

Invisibility in the workplace is a problem for transgender employees, which means it is also a problem for the organization. Historically, the message for transpersons has been, "Don't come out at work. It isn't safe." When transpeople follow this advice, they remain invisible and, as might be expected, their organizations usually have trouble recognizing or dealing effectively with the situations and needs of transgender employees. The larger corporate culture is essentially unaware of the presence of transgender workers and therefore remains unmotivated to do anything to address the issue on a meaningful level. For this reason, an awareness of transgender-related policies, guidelines, procedures, and training opportunities should be promoted and encouraged within organizations. The workplace climate cannot improve for transgender employees until such actions are intentionally undertaken by the company.

Employee retention and workplace productivity are negatively impacted whenever transgender workers are constrained to hide their gender-variant identity on the job. An individual's self-esteem is diminished when they are forced to conceal or guard their identity closely for fear of discovery. Stress, apprehension, anxiety, and even depression may result. These circumstances take a heavy toll, functioning in a depressing way to sap the person's psychic/physical energy and potentially lessen the quality of their work. The possibility of losing the transgender employee also increases, which can potentially cost the organization significant dollars in terms of replacement expenses and training of new employees. Creating a workplace environment that is safe and accepting for transgender workers can do a great deal to alleviate the problems and costs associated with employee retention and productivity.

Just because a workplace policy may be changed by management, it does not automatically follow that the organization's culture will immediately change as well. Transgender-inclusive policy updates, though symbolic and definitely important for any organization, are not enough to change a workplace culture by themselves. If real, lasting change is desired by the organization, additional active steps must be taken toward inclusion and acceptance for transgender workers. Such steps might include (but do not need to be limited to) transgender awareness training and educational efforts that are made available to all employees; the intentional inclusion of transgender workers in marketing, hiring, and diversity initiatives; the encouragement and establishment of transgender-inclusive resource or affinity groups within the organization; and the institution of appropriate benefits for the partners of transgender employees.

The organization must recognize and affirm that transgender rights are not special rights: they are human *rights.* As such, they deserve protection and support from the company. What, exactly, is so special about wanting to have a job that pays a living wage? What is so special about wanting to work in a safe, nondiscriminatory environment? What is so special about wanting to be judged for the quality of your performance on the job, not for your gender identity or expression? Transgender workers do not ask for or expect more rights than other employees—they only desire the same rights as everyone else, along with policy-related protection to make sure those rights are guaranteed. HR professionals are in a unique position to reinforce this concept and to be affirming and supportive of equal rights and fair treatment for transgender employees.

In order for an employee to qualify for a workplace accommodation due to a personal transgender status, some organizations require that the employee must clearly state an intent to transition to a new social gender on a permanent basis. Additionally, the employee must live full-time in the new social gender, and must change his or her name if appropriate. This means that cross-dressers and intersex employees might not qualify for workplace accommodations under an organization's specific policy if that policy only accommodates transsexual persons who wish to transition on the job. While it is important to recognize the needs of transsexual employees who wish to transition fully at work and to address those needs, it is equally important to acknowledge and accommodate the unique needs of other, non-transsexual employees who are transgender. These are issues that will need to be discussed and worked through by the organization's leadership. Some companies allow flexibility in terms of gender expression for all employees. Some do not. Hopefully, progress and accommodations in the areas of gender identity, characteristics, and expression can be made for all who need them.

HR AND TRANSGENDER HEALTH BENEFITS

HR professionals are usually tasked with administering, explaining, and/or facilitating employee health benefits. Though increasing numbers of businesses are including transgender issues as part of their employee nondiscrimination policies, the relationship between such policies and health benefits for transgender employees is often poorly understood.

Most insurance health benefit plans specifically exclude treatment for transsexualism. Therefore, transgender-related mental health counseling, hormone replacement therapies, and transsexual-related surgical procedures will probably not be covered by the employer's insurance carrier. Due to the increasing number of transsexual employees who seek such coverage, it may be useful and appropriate to review and potentially revisit that particular issue with your company's insurance carrier.

Ideally, medically necessary procedures that are consistent with the World Professional Association for Transgender Health Standards of Care (http://www.wpath.org) will be covered in company-designed medical, mental health, and pharmacy plans. Such coverage should be offered at a level comparable to that of other employees. If your organization wants to be a transgender-inclusive business that values its people and treats them fairly, it would be reasonable to consider making necessary health coverages available for transgender workers.

A primary reason for considering these important changes in health care coverage is that transitioning employees are usually required to be involved in a variety of different medical treatments to support their transition process.[5] In addition to medications and surgeries, such treatments may include, but are not limited to,

- visits to therapists, which may vary in frequency from weekly to quarterly depending upon the needs of the individual;
- other doctors' office visits as required;
- laser hair removal treatments (these treatments are usually accomplished in four visits, and may be anywhere from 4 to 12 weeks apart);
- medical leave/time off for major surgeries (this can mean up to six weeks away from work depending upon the surgery and estimated recovery time).

A number of ancillary medical treatments and support programs are also available to assist transitioning persons in adapting to their new social gender role. "These include speech therapy and facial hair electrolysis for [transsexual] women, since hormone therapy has no effect on voice pitch nor does it deplete facial hair. Other surgical techniques for [transsexual] women include augmentation mammoplasty, voice-box surgery, and facial feminization surgery."[6] Female-to-male transsexuals may require hormone replacement therapy, breast reduction surgeries and/or mastectomies, and penile construction surgery. HR professionals should at least be aware of these various treatments and be able to inform transitioning employees as to whether they are covered under the organization's health insurance policy.

Kodak is one example of an organization that is leading the way in providing health care benefits to transgender employees. As of July 1, 2006, Kodak Worldwide Benefits updated their health plan coverage to include procedures, services, and supplies for gender reassignment. The updated health plan coverage applies to expenses for transition procedures, services, and supplies (including therapy, sex hormones, and transsexual surgery) that are provided to any person participating in a self-insured option under Kodak's U.S. medical plans.

UPDATING EMPLOYEE GENDER IDENTITY RECORDS

A formal recognition of an individual's core gender identity, as reflected in a company's employee records, is significant for both the transgender employee and the organization. This is especially true for transsexual workers who may transition while retaining their employment with their original company. Updating their employee records will be a vital part of the transition process.

When an employee transitions on the job, he or she should have employee records revised to reflect the new name and/or gender identity. This should be done on the date that the transition is formally announced to the organization. This step is important for legal, corporate, and personal reasons. HR professionals can ask for an official document to confirm the name change, which the transgender employee should be able to provide once the change has been legally recognized by the state.

All written or other documentation relevant to a transitioning employee should immediately be changed to reflect the new identity. This may include name and security tags or badges, e-mail, health insurance records, organizational charts, photo ID, computer account names, HR records, payroll records, company directory information, employee contact information, and business cards. In short, any relevant documentation that refers to the transitioning employee's gender in any way should be updated to be congruent with the new identity. This step can help the organization avoid potential confusion and/or legal entanglements in the future.

TIPS FOR HR PROFESSIONALS

The following is a brief list of suggested actions that can be taken by HR professionals to ensure that transgender employees are treated with respect and fairness in your organization:

- Check to see that gender identity, gender characteristics, and gender expression are written into your company's employee nondiscrimination policy and are appropriately enforced.

- Become informed and educated about transgender issues by reading, researching, and seeking out dialogue with transgender persons. The list of suggested transgender-related reading materials and Web sites in this book can be helpful.

- Work with transgender employees and management to develop a specific plan for transgender inclusion in your organization. Encourage buy-in and ongoing support from top management so that the plan will be successful on every level of the company.

- Be aware that transitioning employees will be changing their appearance, attire, mannerisms, and some behaviors to be more in alignment with the new social gender role.

- Assist in the formation, establishment, and promotion of employee affirmation/resource groups that include transgender workers.

- Ensure that the partners/spouses of transgender employees are included in relevant activities and are provided with company benefits in the same manner as the spouses/partners of other employees.

- Ensure that all employees have the opportunity to experience transgender-specific awareness training. Such learning events will help to demystify the transgender phenomenon and raise the overall level of transgender-related knowledge within the organization.

- Never assume that you know another person's gender identity (or sexual orientation). What you see on the outside might not correlate at all to what is happening on the inside. People have a right to self-determination in these matters, so it is always best to respectfully ask how an individual wishes to be identified and/or addressed.

- Avoid using the terms "preference" and "lifestyle" when referring to transgender persons. Gender-variant individuals do not "prefer" to be transgender: they *are* transgender, and there is no choice about the existence of a transgender identity. Also, and of equal importance, transpeople do not have a "lifestyle": they live a *life*. There is no "transgender lifestyle." There is only the transgender phenomenon, which is experienced in many different ways by a highly diverse group of gender-variant people. Those persons deserve to be treated with respect and fairness in the workplace, and HR professionals have a responsibility to ensure this is the case.
- Here are some potential expectations for HR professionals with regard to transgender employee situations:

  ○ Act in accordance with and support organizational policies.
  ○ Understand and support the business case for transgender inclusion. Be prepared to defend that business case as necessary.
  ○ Always use the appropriate name and pronouns for an employee, especially if they are transitioning on the job.
  ○ Support and affirm the organization's commitment to all employees, including those who may transition to another social gender.
  ○ Be prepared to deal appropriately with concerns or complaints about gender transitions or gender expression from other, non-transgender employees or customers.

The active involvement and continued support of HR professionals will be pivotal in determining the ultimate success of any transgender-related initiatives in the organization. As a Human Resources professional, equip yourself to effectively address any challenges that a transgender-inclusive workplace may present.

CHAPTER 9
Practical Ideas for Organizations

Speaking about fairness in the workplace, Rob Sheehan, director of executive education for the University of Maryland's James MacGregor Burns Academy of Leadership, has said, "You need to create an environment of integrity, trust and respect to make absolutely certain that everyone is treated fairly, regardless of the differences they may have. It's essential to be inclusive, because that keeps everyone on the same page when it comes to the business's long-term goals."[1]

In a perfect world, all businesses would take their corporate responsibilities to their employees seriously. Unfortunately, our world is far from perfect. In some organizations, the leaders know little about transgender in the workplace, nor do they have a nondiscrimination policy to specifically protect their gender-variant employees. Even some organizations that do have such a policy are transgender-inclusive in name only. Their transgender workers are often merely an afterthought or a peripheral blip on the radar. While changes are occurring within corporate America, there is still a long way to go before all business organizations are up to speed on this unique workplace inclusion issue.

Paying only lip service to transpersons in the workplace is counterproductive to true organizational inclusion, and therefore, to best business practices. Talking about it but doing nothing of substance to help transgender employees become an equal part of the fabric of an organization is disingenuous. An organization may include the word "transgender" in its employee nondiscrimination policy, but if there is no specifically trans-related content in its programs, publications, or guidelines, there is a disconnect. A lack of such transgender-based content might well create scenarios like the following:

- Employees may be misled into thinking there are no transgender information or transgender-related resources available to the organization at all.
- Employees may think that everyone is simply expected to already know about transgender or is able to easily access whatever information they need to deal with transgender issues in the organization.
- Employees may believe that transpeople are the same as gays, lesbians, and bisexuals, and therefore, transpersons do not really exist in the workplace or have their own specific trans-related needs and concerns.
- Even worse, and perhaps like the misinformed PlanetOut diversity trainer we met earlier in this book, employees may be laboring under the misconception that all transgender people are prostitutes, perverts, predators, child molesters, or something equally undesirable. People deserve the opportunity to learn the truth about the transgender phenomenon.

CODES OF CONDUCT, EMPLOYEE POLICIES, AND DEALING WITH MANAGEMENT

A code of conduct is a moral document articulating an organization's standards for the behavior of its employees or members. Learn whether your organization has a specific, fully inclusive antidiscrimination policy with regard to transgender employees. Many major corporations have already adopted such policies and made them available to the public. You can use those documents as models to help craft a transgender-inclusive policy for your own company. A few of these leading organizations and their policies will be discussed in this chapter.

A variety of different corporate antidiscrimination employee policies contain affirming concepts that enhance the quality of life for the people of their organizations, helping all workers in those organizations perform to their fullest potential. For example, Jim Jenkins of AT&T says that "each year, every employee must review AT&T's Code of Conduct, which clearly states that AT&T does not discriminate based on race, creed, color, gender, or sexual orientation ... Knowing that my workplace rights are protected gives me the freedom to always be myself."[2] Edgar J. Whiteacre, Jr., Chairman and CEO of

AT&T, has said, "Diversity makes AT&T a better company. It helps make us an employer of choice, a preferred business partner and an important contributor to the communities we serve."[3]

American Airlines has expanded its EEO policy, adding "gender identity" to sex, gender, and sexual orientation as a protected category. The organization has created an entire set of employee guidelines to deal with the issue of transgender workers at American.

In 2000, JPMorgan Chase amended its organizational code of conduct by adding language that specifically protects its employees from being stereotyped by gender. In essence, this means that the workplace is safe for all employees regardless of an individual's gender identity or gender expression. Should that identity or expression happen to be somewhat more feminine or masculine than would be considered socially normative, such identities and expression are still accepted.

One approach might involve asking your organization's top management to engage in some dialogue about transgender-related diversity issues. Then you can specifically ask them to affirm that your company does not discriminate based on gender identity, gender characteristics, and/or gender expression. If your organization does not have a written transgender-inclusive policy, politely request that your management explain the company's absence of such a policy. Articulate the need for a policy that protects and accommodates the needs of transgender employees. Be prepared to offer some specific examples of organizations that have successfully adopted transgender-inclusive policies and to demonstrate how those policies have benefited the organizations from a business perspective.

Some top managers may be unaware of the need for protecting transgender workers against discrimination. (Sadly, that is not unusual since most people in our society do not know a great deal about the nature of gender variance.) This can be your opportunity to respectfully inform, enlighten, and encourage them to take swift, appropriate action on the necessary employee policy updates. Some in management may think that while transgender discrimination is probably wrong and should not be tolerated, it is not necessary to include such specific wording in their employee policies. They may believe that transgender persons are already covered under a "sexual orientation" clause. Disabuse your management of that notion if necessary, but have your explanations and reasons prepared in advance so you will be able to present them effectively. Keep in mind that if management does not put a transgender nondiscrimination policy in writing and make it known to everyone, it is not an official organizational policy.

This is your opportunity to share how you might feel as a transgender employee whose human rights are not protected through your own organization's workplace policies. (By the way, fearing a backlash or reprisal from management for merely expressing legitimate concerns about discrimination and harassment toward transgender employees is an indicator that such fears may be justified. This awareness can potentially become a powerful part of your discussion and of the overall effort to help the organization become transgender-inclusive.)

If management supports your position of justice, fairness, and equality for all employees, you may want to offer to help your organization craft a transgender-inclusive workplace policy. It is not difficult to do. For example, if your company's policy mentions "sexual orientation," simply expand the wording to include "sexual orientation, gender identity, gender characteristics, and gender expression." Doing so will formally institute organizational protections for transgender workers.

ADDITIONAL IDEAS

You may find the following suggestions to be useful for your organization as well:[4]

Encourage your organization to adopt the position that basic rights—including the rights to freedom of gender identity, gender characteristics, and gender expression on the job—deserve to be extended to all stakeholders in the organization. The issue is not that transpersons are part of the workplace community (for, almost certainly, they are already there), but that they may freely choose to become a visible and vocal part of the company without fear of reprisal due to their gender-variant status. Acting upon this premise will, of necessity, involve eradicating certain negative misconceptions as well as creating newer, more positive expectations about the transgender phenomenon. (Nondiscrimination policies and procedures as well as effective transgender awareness training and education may be in order to assist in the organization's journey toward greater understanding and acceptance.)

Organizations should not confuse the just and fair demands of transgender persons for their human rights with proselytizing or any form of hostility. This is not about lobbying or political maneuvering for "special rights." Transgender workers do not deserve—nor should they ask for, receive, or expect—any more rights and/or privileges than anyone else.

Instead, this issue is about fairness and respect for all employees, including a reasonable accommodation of legitimate needs. Desiring equality and human rights for everyone across the board is not antithetical to a healthy, successful organization, nor does advocating for these rights promote special or preferential treatment for any certain group. Organizations have a responsibility to respond positively and decisively when transgender employees request to participate fully and openly in the life of the organization. Such honesty and integrity on the part of transgender workers should be applauded and affirmed, not disregarded, dismissed, or unfairly criticized.

A person's gender status, gender identity, gender characteristics, or gender expression/presentation should not be eligible criteria for employment decisions. Rather, demonstrated professional competence as well as applicable skills, abilities, and achievement deserve to be the fundamental standards for such determinations.

All employees, regardless of gender identity, characteristics, or expression, are entitled to a work environment that is physically and emotionally safe and non-oppressive. Harassment or bullying based on someone's transgender identity, expression, or appearance is never acceptable. Such inappropriate behaviors should be addressed through specific organizational channels and transgender education/awareness training. A transgender worker's personal status or gender identity need not be a divisive or disruptive issue unless others choose to make it so. (And if others choose to make it so, then *they* are the troublemakers, not the transgender employee. Do not fall into the trap of blaming the victim.) It is management's responsibility to provide a discrimination-free workplace environment for all employees and to respond quickly and appropriately to unacceptable workplace behaviors.

The organization should conscientiously seek out, welcome, accept, and integrate a diversified population—including transgender individuals—into its culture in ways that are responsibly conducive to the overall health and growth of the organization, its stakeholders, and its community. Organizational employee policies should clearly articulate that all opportunities and positions in the company must be open to everyone, including transgender persons. Like all other employees, transgender workers deserve to be evaluated on their merits and measured against the specific criteria for a particular job. Equitable treatment for everyone in the company necessitates such specific organizational measures.

The vital importance of respecting the rights of all people in the organization, not only those of transgender workers, should be strongly reinforced.

Fairness and justice for everyone, not favoritism or special treatment for some, should be the rule and the expectation. Transgender workers deserve all rights and privileges equal to, but never greater than, other employees in the workplace.

No one is any more important than anyone else in terms of intrinsic human worth. With this in mind, it is entirely possible that sometimes two or more sets of individual rights may need to be addressed and reconciled. Your organization is encouraged to approach such conflicting situations with sensitivity and respect for everyone concerned. Common sense, good judgment, and fair treatment can go a long way in such cases.

Loree Cook-Daniels of the Transgender Aging Network offers some additional ideas for consideration when developing transgender-inclusive policies for organizations.[5] Some of those ideas, as well as additional suggestions, are adapted and commented upon here:

Do your organization's programs, publications, and/or employee policies refer only to "sexual orientation," or do they also include "gender identity," "gender characteristics," and/or "gender expression"? If necessary, the organization can update by adding the appropriate phrase or phrases to the wording of its policies and literature. By mentioning only sexual orientation, organizations send an implied message to transpersons and their partners that they are welcome only if they are perceived as lesbian or gay. (As we have seen, most transpersons do not identify as gay or lesbian.) The organization thus infers that it is only concerned with sexual orientation issues and not with gender identity matters. It also subtly implies that the company does not take the concerns of transgender employees seriously.

Does your organization's employee policy specifically recognize that the needs and concerns of preoperative or nonoperative transsexuals will almost certainly differ from the needs of postoperative transsexuals? Does the company policy also acknowledge, affirm, and accommodate the unique needs and concerns of cross-dressers, bi-gendered persons, transgenderists, intersexuals, and other transpersons who may be transgender but not necessarily transsexual? The distinctive issues of transgender workers who are *not* transsexual are equally as important as those of transsexual and/or transitioning employees.

Does your organization offer adequate health care coverage for transsexual and/or transitioning employees? Many transgender workers have gender-specific health needs that necessitate certain types of coverage. Your organization should work to offer health insurance that will meet those needs and allow the transgender employee to function to the best of his or her ability.

How does your organization treat the spouses, partners, children, and families of transgender employees? Does the organization explicitly welcome them and make them comfortable? Does the company policy extend full domestic partner benefits to the spouses/partners of transgender workers? Many transpeople are partnered with someone who may not identify as lesbian, gay, bisexual, and transgender (LGBT). Those non-transgender partners may identify themselves as straight/heterosexual. Therefore, the organization should adopt a policy that articulates how the partners, spouses, children, and families of transpersons will be treated. Doing so will not only protect the loved ones of transgender employees but also help others in the company become more aware of the wide variety of relationships that may exist involving transpersons.

Does your organization have a specific written plan in place to deal appropriately with transition issues in the workplace? Are there specific guidelines for managers, HR, team members, and transitioning employees? Are transgender employees who transition on the job protected and assisted in that process? Does your organization have a list of reputable, informed, transgender-aware doctors, clinics, transgender consultants, and attorneys?

Are awareness training programs or other educational opportunities available to help all employees in your organization learn about transgender diversity issues? Is transgender-specific literature readily available for your organization's people to use as a resource in case questions should arise at work? Is a zero-tolerance approach to discrimination, bullying, and/or harassment of transpersons part of your organization's written employee policy?

Are your organization's leaders supportive of a transgender-inclusive policy? Do your leaders understand the significance of a transgender presence as part of an overall benefit for the organization? Do they affirm the need for transgender inclusion as part of a diverse workforce that will benefit the company?

Do the printed and/or online sales, marketing, and other materials that represent your organization include identifiably transgender persons? If not, why not? Is your business ashamed or afraid of including transpersons in such materials? Are transpeople expected to remain invisible in perpetuity? Is there some particularly valid reason why transgender people should be disqualified from appearing in your company's literature, Web site, marketing efforts, or other materials?

Fear of potentially making a few individuals a little uncomfortable is not a justifiable rationale for excluding transpersons from appropriate representation in your company's sales and marketing materials.

PRINCIPLES OF FAIRNESS

Eliminating discrimination in every American workplace is a worthy goal. Here are some basic principles of fairness for workplaces that can be directly applied to the concerns of transgender employees.

- Management should insist that workplace discrimination based on gender identity, characteristics, or expression must be eliminated. Such prohibitions should be clearly communicated in the organization's written company policy. All new hires should be informed and/or made aware of this policy before they begin employment with the organization.
- Employee records should always be updated to reflect personal changes on the date that a transgender employee begins a formal transition at work. Name badges, ID cards, HR records, etc., should be immediately updated to reflect the employee's new status.
- All employee groups deserve equal standing and treatment regardless of the gender identity or sexual orientation of their members.
- Pluralistic awareness training for all team members should specifically include and cover gender identity, gender characteristics, gender expression, workplace transitions, and other basic transgender-related issues. Annual reminders or review training about transgender topics are also recommended, since people can sometimes forget or become lax in their understanding of the organization's expectations in these areas.
- Spousal and family benefits for domestic partners of transgender employees should be made available on an equal basis and should be comparable to those offered to the spouses and families of heterosexual married employees.
- All negative stereotypes concerning gender identity, characteristics, and expression should be banned in organizational advertising, marketing, Web sites, and literature. Media advertising

should not discriminate on the basis of gender identity, characteristics, or expression.

- Organizations should not discriminate in the sale and purchase of
goods and services, and certainly not on the basis of gender identity, characteristics, or expression.

- Top management should make it clear that a transgender-
inclusive employee policy is to be fully supported throughout
the entire company. Such policies will not be effective over time
without the full, visible support of organizational leadership.
The encouragement, acceptance, and backing of management is
a critical aspect of any successful trans-inclusive workplace
initiative.

- Written, specifically worded organizational policies of inclusivity
concerning gender identity, characteristics, and expression should
be prominently posted, disseminated, and/or otherwise made
readily available throughout the organization. There is no excuse
for behaving in a discriminatory or disrespectful manner toward
others at work on the basis of gender-related attributes.

Additionally, business organizations (particularly Human Resources divisions) have a responsibility to offer diversified resources and
training, promote fair and equitable employee policies and guidelines,
and publicly recognize the professional competence and successes of
transgender workers.

To be most effective and beneficial, a transgender-based initiative
should be part of a larger and more strategically inclusive organizational plan that addresses appropriate workplace behaviors and
expectations throughout the company. Transgender individuals
deserve the same opportunities as anyone else to be employed and
make a living. In fact, organizations that hire transpersons often realize an added bonus in terms of creative thinking, innovation, and fresh
perspectives on important business topics. Increasingly, organizational decision-makers are discovering that "What is really important
is hiring somebody who doesn't think like you."[6] This implies a need
to recruit and hire people from different backgrounds who can add
unique or unusual life experiences, diverse knowledge, and different
viewpoints to the organizational mix. The goal is to bring different
kinds of people together and create a strong, creative, idea-rich workplace community—not a toxic, hostile battlefield. Judy Tso, a social
worker, speaker, consultant, and president of Boston-based Aha

Solutions Unlimited, says, "Other employees need to make it a welcoming environment, not just a begrudging tolerance."[7]

It helps if people can be invited to think in terms of "us" instead of "them." B. J. Gallagher, a Los Angeles diversity consultant and author, has issued an invitation to try a monthlong experiment in eliminating the word "they" from your organization's vocabulary. "Consider the possibility that there is only WE—there is no THEY … You'll see what this simple change in language does to how you and others think about solving problems, generating creative ideas, getting the work done."[8]

This chapter has touched on a few areas that deserve to be addressed by forward-thinking organizations seeking to take transgender inclusion issues seriously. Hopefully, these ideas will be catalysts that inspire and motivate your organization's leadership to take action on behalf of their transgender employees. The people of your organization—*all* of them—deserve no less.

CHAPTER 10

Insights for Coworkers of Transpersons

> *If you treat an individual as if he [sic] were what he ought to be and could be, he will become what he ought to be and could be.*
>
> —Johann Wolfgang Von Goethe

Interaction between people with differing worldviews and life experiences is an opportunity to learn something new. Unfortunately, sometimes it may also create workplace difficulties and/or misunderstandings.

It may be a test of professionalism or even of character for some individuals to deal with a coworker's transgender status. The experience may prove to be awkward and inconvenient for you, or it may become a source of growth and enlightenment. If you are like most people, however, it will probably fall somewhere in the middle—it might not be the easiest or simplest thing in the world, but it probably will not be the worst either. In any case, consider the potential business and performance advantages to be gained from having respectful interactions with a transgender coworker.

For workplace relationships to be effective, they require

1. a recognition and acceptance of behavioral differences among people.
2. clear, understandable verbal and nonverbal communication.
3. an ability to manage conflict.[1]

Learning to interact effectively and appropriately with a transgender coworker may necessitate paying attention to all three of these critical workplace relationship requirements.

A good place to start is by having a respectful dialogue, in good faith, with your transgender coworker. Let us be honest: marginalization and/or exclusion of gender-variant employees on the job are often rooted in the discomfort of others, and it usually centers around perceived sexual overtones. It has to do with innuendo and unspoken implications of perversity and depravity. Some people may choose to operate under the presumption that "As long as I don't have to know about it, whatever you do is fine with me." This approach may work to a degree when dealing with issues of sexual orientation, which can usually be hidden or at least downplayed on the job, but when it comes to gender expression in the workplace, it is almost impossible to hide the fact that someone looks, dresses, or behaves in a differently gendered manner. Therefore, people will know when a transgender person comes out at work—and if people are going to know, significant conversations between team members should take place to help eliminate confusion and deal with concerns.

By now most people have some idea of what the words "gay" and "lesbian" mean, and some people have an inkling about bisexuality, but there are still plenty of questions and misunderstandings that center around the terms "gender identity," "gender characteristics," and "gender expression." Meaningful, respectful conversations can help to address those questions, creating a foundation of knowledge and understanding that leads to acceptance. Most of us do not really care about a coworker's sexual orientation, and there is no valid reason why we should. It does not affect us one way or the other, and it is none of our business what someone else does in the privacy of his or her own bedroom anyway. (Do *you* share every detail of your sex life with your coworkers? It is not the kind of thing that is overly conducive to fostering productivity or professionalism in the workplace.) However, an innate transgender identity and correspondingly appropriate transgender expression are no reasons for silence. They are core human issues that do not deserve to be shamefully locked away at home and never discussed in the workplace.

A transgender identity is not about sexual behaviors or perversity: it is about being able to express who one truly is in a benign, healthy manner. If a person is transgender and makes the courageous decision to come out at work, it will be visible, if only by default. Because the individual's gender-variant status will be apparent on the job, the issue deserves to be discussed openly and respectfully so that dignity can be maintained, questions can be answered, concerns can be addressed, and fears can be dispelled.

Donna Rose, who successfully transitioned in her workplace, says that some confusion is a natural by-product of such an unusual circumstance and is probably to be expected in most organizations. Questions and puzzlement are perfectly understandable responses to the news of a coworker's pending change in gender status. "What could possibly make a person want to change their gender? To most people such a thought is unimaginable . . . unthinkable . . . unbearable. The fact that someone would even consider such seeming sacrilege often produces strong responses at a variety of levels. And this emotional disconnect often creates substantial communication barriers when trying to explain or understand."[2]

Because of these emotionally rooted communication barriers, extra effort should be made to create safe places and generate a variety of opportunities for open conversations and sharing between coworkers. Honest, candid dialogue between people can often be the beginning of progress and growth, since fears of "the other" are usually rooted in ignorance. When individuals can converse and get to know each other as real human beings, gender-based fear and bigotry can be set aside.

College professor Miqqui Alicia Gilbert, who occasionally cross-dresses openly in her classroom, has written about "the phenomenon of desensitization, wherein when people actually know a transgender [individual], the craziness of the idea quickly dissipates."[3] It is amazing how putting a human face on this issue, especially through the medium of personal, face-to-face conversation and interaction, can positively alter people's perceptions and alleviate fears.

Once connections between human beings are established, fear of the unknown can quickly subside. The transgender person will no longer be a mysterious or unknown (and therefore potentially dangerous) entity. As fear begins to dissipate and people realize that any major concerns they may have had were essentially groundless, the anxieties about interacting with a transgender coworker will lessen— and then everyone can get back to doing what they were hired to do in the first place: work together and get the job done.

WHAT COWORKERS SHOULD KNOW ABOUT THE TRANSGENDER COMING OUT PROCESS

Different Is Not Synonymous with Deviant.

Being transgender does not mean being mentally ill. However, being transgender sometimes can mean that a person may have gone through his or her entire life with no one knowing who he or she really is. Almost all transgender individuals who come out at work do so because they wish to stop hiding the truth. They want to be honest about who they are and be accepted. Such integrity and raw courage deserve to be appreciated and respected, not ridiculed or rejected.

Your transgender coworker is not trying to be frivolous or malicious. They are not trying to hurt anyone or purposely cause problems. They are not doing this on a capricious whim. They are not promoting some bizarre personal agenda, "recruiting," or trying to needlessly upset everyone in the organization. In fact, if they could simply express themselves in anonymity without calling attention, they would do so in a heartbeat. Unfortunately, that is usually not possible, since a public transition is far too visible. Therefore, do not patronize, ridicule, or ignore the transperson who comes out on the job, but treat them with dignity and professionalism just as you would any other coworker.

No one should be asking you to radically alter your life, discard your values or personal belief system, or change who you are. There is no law that says you have to agree with everything transgender people may say or do, and you do not have to become their best friend if you do not want to be. Just behave like a civilized human being, act with common sense and courtesy, and treat the transperson with respect. In short, be a nice person, a professional, and a responsible team member.

Here is something else you should know: You do not need to be afraid. Your transgender coworkers are not going to hurt or attack you. They are not going to attempt to prey on you sexually. Gender-variant people have not lost their senses: if anything, they have come to them and are simply making that known.

No form of transgender identity or expression is transmittable like a virus or other disease. In and of itself, transgender is harmless and always exists within a certain percentage of the population (2–3 percent, according to estimates by the National Transgender Advocacy Coalition,[4] although estimates by other groups have run from 1 percent to as high as 10 percent). These situations simply *are*, just like being short, tall, blond, brunette, right- or left-handed, brown- or blue-eyed.

DEALING APPROPRIATELY WITH THE SITUATION

Disparities in appearance and personal presentation can vary widely from person to person and even era to era. What is viewed as fashionable today will undoubtedly be perceived as quaint and out-dated tomorrow. Paisley shirts, polyester leisure suits, platform shoes, miniskirts, and ironed hair used to be in fashion, but now are considered to be anachronistic (and often hysterically amusing) relics of decades gone by.

Styles and presentations change. Nangeroni tells us, "Women wearing pants may not seem transgender today, but fifty years ago they were . . . [It's interesting to note that] crossdressing is enjoyed by both males and females, but appears more pronounced in males because of an imbalance in norms of attire and attitude (we see little transgression when a woman wears a suit)."[5] In other words, there is no reason to become upset over a coworker's external presentation as long as they meet reasonable standards for workplace behavior and professional appearance.

While there is little doubt that appearances do matter in business, they can also be deceiving—which is why it is often more helpful to focus on the person than on their appearance. Ask yourself this question: does someone else's physical presentation or clothing choice truly affect his or her ability to do his or her job, or am I unfairly forcing them to fit into my own limited paradigm of what is acceptable at work? We are all just human beings here, and we need to get past our preconceived biases about gender expression so we can start respecting each other as interesting, unique, intrinsically worthwhile people who happen to work for a living.

Admittedly, and especially at first, it may be something of a shock if someone with whom you work comes out as transgender. That is understandable. It may be even more of a surprise when you see them dress and/or present themselves publicly in their transgender persona for the first time. You may be horrified. You may laugh. You may stare in wonder (or in some cases, envy). You may gape in confusion and amazement at the unaccustomed sight. You may not know what to think, say, or do. We have all been taught and conditioned by society to think in certain ways about gender and gender presentation, so when confronted by an unfamiliar gender difference, it is not always easy for us to know how to respond appropriately. How do you process something like that? What should your feelings be? How are you supposed to react? Those are reasonable questions, and they deserve meaningful responses.

It is typical to be surprised or to have questions and concerns about such a situation, especially if it is new to you. But guess what? You will survive. Newness usually is not fatal, and the shock probably will not kill you. Lighten up, keep a reasonable perspective, and remember to be courteous and professional even if you do not understand much of what is going on. Your transgender coworkers may look different, but they are still human beings and they deserve to be treated with respect. Female-to-male transsexual Matt Kailey says, "I'm not a monkey in a cage. I do not exist for your amusement or your fascination. I am a person with a right to privacy and space."[6] Transgender workers are not there to put on a sideshow or to entertain you: they come to work to do their jobs.

You do not need to necessarily understand everything the transperson is doing. In fact, you probably will not understand much of it—and that is okay. You do not have to agree with all their decisions or behaviors, but you can still act responsibly and professionally toward your transgender coworker. Try to be polite and compassionate toward the transperson. They will need all the emotional support they can get, especially during the first few days or weeks of coming out on the job.

After some time goes by, the feelings of shock, confusion, or dismay will inevitably fade. They always do. The newness will wear off, and you will probably come to view your transgender coworker as a teammate, a fellow employee, perhaps your friend, and someone who incidentally happens to be transgender. Familiarity breeds complacency. In time, it will not be an issue any longer, and you probably will not even remember what all the fuss was about.

Dr. Renee Baker writes that in some organizations, "the system unfairly assumes that transgender people are cognitively dysfunctional until proven otherwise."[7] Keep in mind that despite the potential stresses of transitioning on the job, your transgender associate is there in the workplace because they have been hired to get the work done. The fact that they are involved in a gender change does not mean they have somehow lost the knowledge, skills, and abilities that enabled them to do their job previously, so their professional competence certainly should not become an issue now. The transgender employee is experiencing a gender transition, not a frontal lobotomy, and there is nothing wrong with their cognitive processes. Gender-variant people in all fields of employment have made successful workplace transitions. With your help and with the support of your organization, your transgender coworker can do the same.

Lauren works as an account executive for a national television network affiliate station. A few years ago, he became she, changed social genders, transitioned while on the job, and now lives and works full-time as a woman. However, the people skills and relational abilities that made him a valued salesperson were not lost or discarded in the transition to her. Lauren's coworkers and customers liked and appreciated him as a male before the transition. Fortunately, that has remained the case during and after her transition to female. Everyone continues to work successfully with her, and they have been able to discover that it is really the person inside that matters. Also, and just in case you are curious, no sales or customer accounts were lost due to the transition. If anything, business relationships between the television station and its advertising clients were strengthened because of the courage and personal integrity demonstrated by this transgender employee.

No matter what thoughts or questions may arise for coworkers upon discovering that a coworker is transgender, the transperson has almost certainly been dealing with gender-related issues for a long time before making the courageous choice to come out in the workplace. Coming out is not a decision that transgender individuals reach without a great deal of soul-searching. Most people have little idea of the sheer bravery it takes to openly reveal oneself as transgender in a work environment, for if they did they could only be awestruck by such courage. To come out in the workplace is to make an almost incomprehensibly powerful statement of trust and belief in one's inner strength and in the people of one's organization. It is a testament to the transcendent possibilities of the human spirit whenever anyone takes such a remarkable step. Hopefully, you will feel honored that your transgender coworker respects you enough to want to be honest with you. Consider their coming out in the workplace to be a sign of the esteem in which they hold you and your organization.

You may have known the transperson in his or her old gender role for some time. You may have viewed him or her as a "typical" male or female, at least before he or she was revealed as transgender. Perhaps you have known this person only as a woman, and now you are astounded to learn that she has a strong personality component that craves truth and honesty through a masculine form of gender expression. Or you may have worked daily with a man, perhaps even considered him a "regular guy" in every way, and now you learn that he has a deep-seated feminine persona that needs to be expressed openly at work. Why do these people suddenly seem so different?

They are not. They have not really changed at all, except on the outside. They have simply chosen to act responsibly, with courage and integrity, on what they already knew to be true about themselves but kept hidden until now. What makes the transperson seem different is our own set of filters, those personal assumptions that are culturally created and sustained. These filters may include unfounded fears, internalized transphobia, inaccurate social gender myths and expectations, misinformation, personal ambivalence, and misperceptions and/or ignorance about transgender issues. In short, *we* are the ones who make the transperson seem different.

Admittedly, that premise may be difficult for many of us to realize and perhaps even harder for us to accept. When we are confronted with something new and mysterious like transgender, the natural tendency is to point the finger of perceived blame at the transgender person instead of ourselves and our own firmly established cultural filters. (After all, how could we possibly be wrong about something so evident, so obvious, as someone's gender? Does not everyone know that there are only two genders and that everyone is supposed to line up with them according to their genitalia? And if someone does not fit into the gender box, they must be gay, right?) However, since we are the ones who make the transgender individual seem different, we can choose to shift our old, internalized paradigm of gender. We can help the transperson become more accepted and respected, first in our own minds and then in the minds of others within the organization.

You may want to try to understand it all. Forget it. You cannot. No one understands everything about transgender, not even your transgender coworker, and it does not really matter anyway. (It is a phenomenon, remember? That means there is no complete, definitive explanation. Much of it is still a mystery. You *cannot* understand it all.) Learn as much as you can, certainly, but do not expect to comprehend everything about transgender.

You may want to help the transgender employee get "fixed." You can—and definitely should—not. Gender-variant people do not need "fixing" or "repair." The fact that they are transgender does not mean there is something wrong with them. They are *different*, not diseased or broken. What they *do* need is acceptance, respect, and fairness from the people around them so they can get on with their lives and work. It is not your responsibility to mend, save, or set anyone straight, particularly in such a complex situation as this. You can help most by choosing to work together as colleagues, as members of the same team, and by discovering how to live and operate in respect and mutuality as effective, productive members of your organization.

Our actions always serve to influence the way we feel about something and the subsequent attitude we choose about it. Behaviors always preclude attitudes, and our actions can powerfully affect our feelings. If you are having trouble with your emotional response to a transgender coworker, perhaps you might want to try behaving in a more open and receptive manner toward that person. It is surprising how taking some simple but meaningful actions can help us shift our feelings about something or someone. We may not be able to change the other person or the situation/circumstances, but we always have the individual power to choose how *we* will respond—and that choice can sometimes make all the difference.

BECOMING AN ALLY

An ally may be defined as someone who joins together with another to encourage and support him or her in a common or shared purpose. A transgender ally is someone who is not necessarily transgender but who is willing to personally advocate for justice, equality, dignity, and legal protection for transpeople.

Often there is an event of some kind that motivates a person to become a transgender ally. It might involve witnessing the negative effects of oppression by seeing a transgender friend, teammate, colleague, acquaintance, or even a complete stranger being hurt by social injustice, unfair systemic organizational policies (or the lack thereof), or cruel acts by others. It might be the result of a personal decision to struggle against any form of bigotry and prejudice on general principles. Regardless of your motivation, become an ally for your transgender coworker. Provide encouragement, speak out when it is appropriate to do so, and affirm the transperson's right to be who they are without apology.

Another thing you can do to be an ally is to learn about the transgender community. Find out about the problems that transpeople face in our culture and discover the many contributions that transgender persons make to society. The more information you have, the more effective ally you can become. Try to understand as much as you can. Ask questions. Grow in your knowledge of transgender. Keep in mind that every employee is at work to do a job, and that a person's sexual orientation or gender identity has no bearing on his or her ability to do his or her work. Be aware that a transgender worker who comes out on the job is going through something that most people will never experience, and that experience will leave them much stronger than most. Think about your own blend of feminine and masculine characteristics as well as your various expressions of gender and recognize that, no matter how those attributes blend together, they provide you with certain opportunities and accountabilities in society. No person's blend is better than another's—they are just different and deserve to be respected. As we gain insight and learn to understand ourselves more fully through the process of self-examination and discovery, we also can learn to appreciate the worth and value of others. That awareness can strengthen and enrich our own lives immeasurably.

The key to relational progress is not necessarily found in always agreeing philosophically or ideologically with another person, but in choosing to value and respect the other person's intrinsic human merit. A transperson who exhibits the raw courage it takes to come out in the workplace is deserving of respect—and the opportunity to extend respect to another person is always within our power. It is a simple choice: all that is necessary is to extend the acceptance and human dignity that everyone needs and warrants from others.

Please do not waste your time and energy trying to turn the transperson into something or someone they are not and cannot honestly be. None of us are here to live up to someone else's expectations of how to live our lives, anyway. As Dana Rivers says, "Being transsexual is not a choice. You cannot will it into being nor can you erase it."[8] The same thing holds true for cross-dressers, intersex people, transgenderists, or other kinds of transpersons: these are not willful "lifestyle choices" or "preferences," and you cannot erase or eliminate a transgender identity at will. Perhaps those who insist that being transgender is a "lifestyle choice" might want to consider this question: "What is the attraction of a 'transgender lifestyle' that would lead someone to choose to be transgender?" Life is infinitely simpler if you operate the same way as most other people: just ask people who are left-handed.

Do the best thing for business and focus on developing an atmosphere of mutual respect on the job so that everyone on the team can work together cohesively. Why not create a work environment where everyone can perform to his or her highest potential in a supportive, encouraging, considerate, affirming, and trusting atmosphere that enhances everyone's ability to contribute? Surely we can all recognize the benefits of creating such a healthy and productive place in which to work.

Most people are friendly and well-mannered individuals who want to do what is right. Most are decent, caring, compassionate folks. Most do not want to discriminate against, judge, or isolate others. Hopefully, you are one of those nonjudgmental people. If so, consider becoming a supportive ally for your transgender associate.

CHAPTER 11

Tips for Transgender Workers

IF YOU ARE TRANSSEXUAL...[1]

Most persons who make the decision to fully transition in the workplace are transsexual. A transsexual employee has a unique set of circumstances with which to contend if he or she intends to come out publicly on the job. Personal fulfillment and the pursuit of happiness are obviously key considerations for a transitioning worker, but the primary reason for coming out is to be responsible and provide factual information about the situation to those who may be affected by the transition.

Transitioning on the job can be a tremendous opportunity for personal growth, not only for the transperson but for the entire organization. One of the challenges faced by many businesses is a comparative lack of experience and/or knowledge about transgender persons and their unique issues. One transitioning worker said, "The plant doctor and I are breaking new ground for my situation. I asked him if there were any [organizational] policies regarding transgender issues. He looked at me and said, 'You are the policy.' "[2]

This scenario is not necessarily unusual. Most organizations have not instituted a policy regarding transgender workers, and the transgender employee may therefore become a "test project" of sorts, if only by default. Gender-variant workers are encouraged to view this as an opportunity for everyone to learn. Their experience will almost surely help prepare the way for other transpersons who may follow.

There are many questions and areas of concern to be addressed if a transgender employee plans to transition on the job. One thing is for certain: you learn who your friends are. The Human Rights Campaign says, "The greater the [gender-based] nonconformity, the greater could be the need to negotiate with others (e.g., medical professionals, family, workplace management and co-workers) whose cooperation could influence the ease or difficulty of accomplishing your plans."[3] Transitioning workers will want to consider questions such as

- What is the extent and nature of the new transgender status you have in mind?
- Do you plan to change your body through surgery and/or the use of hormones?
- Will you transition fully and legally from one sex to another?
- How will you deal with potential harassment or other negative responses to your public transition?
- What about pronoun use?
- Restroom issues?
- The responsibilities of your job?

Transsexual persons who come out in a work environment have much to consider. Here are some issues that will need to be addressed in order to ensure a successful experience. Suggestions include

- Begin working with a qualified, fully licensed therapist before coming out on the job. Doing so will help you be more prepared psychologically and can provide additional credibility with your employer and coworkers. Working with a licensed therapist will demonstrate that this is an effort you are undertaking in conjunction with a recognized authority.
- Believe in yourself and in your ability to live your life on your own terms. Do not be obnoxious about it, but take pride and have confidence in your own self-worth as a transgender person. Remember the words of Eleanor Roosevelt, who said, "No one can make you feel inferior without your consent."
- Build a support system for yourself before you come out at work. It should include your therapist and/or doctor, an attorney, and as many caring friends and family members as possible. Going it alone can be a difficult proposition. You will probably want all the emotional help and encouragement you can get, especially in the beginning stages of the transition process.

- Begin hormone therapy and/or electrolysis, if those situations apply to you, before coming out. Doing so can help ease the stress of transitioning in a public setting such as the workplace. Such actions will provide additional proof to others that you are serious about this and want to look your best in your new gender role.

- Work on your appearance, practice your personal grooming, and acquire an appropriate professional wardrobe before you come out and/or begin your transition. It will be particularly important to make a good first impression in your new social gender role, so be sure to dress conservatively and professionally. Nancy Nangeroni offers this sound advice: "If you look dirty, smell bad, and sound unpleasant, people will turn away when they see you coming. But if you wear a smile, smell clean, and sound pleasant, you're much more likely to be welcomed. You don't have to be beautiful, but a little soap and water applied to your attitude can go a long ways. Take the time to make yourself presentable, and make the effort to be pleasant."[4]

- You owe it to management and yourself to establish a working relationship built on trust and honesty about your situation. If you plan to come out and/or transition on the job, talk with management first and tell them what you want to do. They deserve to know your plans and to have the opportunity to be supportive—and you deserve to receive their support. Honest, open dialogue will help you move toward your goal of coming out and/or transitioning successfully.

- Try to present the image of a competent, cooperative, congenial, and professional team player who is there to get your job done as efficiently as possible. Be careful not to come across as frivolous, a slacker, a clueless airhead, or a would-be sex object at work—you will only confuse people about your intentions, undermine your credibility as a person and an employee, and damage your hopes for a successful transition. Remember, you are there to work and help your organization succeed, not to turn the company on its ear and/or upset people unnecessarily. Keep in mind that, at least for most people, perception is reality, and how you are perceived by others will go a long way toward creating your new reality within the organization. Charlie Chaplin once entered a Charlie Chaplin look-alike contest: he came in third. It is up to you to create the perception that you are an asset to your company, not a freak or a clown.

- Learn about your organization's employee nondiscrimination policy (or lack thereof) before coming out, then carefully choose your actions based on that knowledge. If there is no specific written policy in place to protect gender-variant employees, have a conversation with your company's Human Resources department about creating and instituting such a policy before you come out to the rest of the organization. Then you can be officially protected and supported by the organization. (Besides, it is always a good idea to have the HR people on your side.)

- Honestly assess and unflinchingly evaluate your relationships with supervisors and teammates. Whom do you think might be supportive? Which people might be unreceptive or hostile toward your coming out at work? Be practical, rational, and even calculating about this. You may want to come out to certain individuals first in order to gain their support before coming out to the organization as a whole. It is important to have as many allies as possible in a situation such as this.

- Try to be as professional, calm, responsible, helpful, and non-problematic as possible. Your employer or supervisor is probably being confronted with a new and unfamiliar situation that deserves to be addressed, but the daily concerns and efforts of the organization will go on as usual. This is just one more piece of business for your management team, and that is how they will almost surely approach it. Do not be shrill, obnoxious, or a pain in the neck—you want to create friends and allies, not enemies, especially in the front office. After all, the squeakiest wheels do not always get greased: sometimes they get replaced.

- If you are planning to transition on the job, make the effort to legally change your name, driver's license, and social security card beforehand if at all possible. This will officially document your transition even further, providing a legally authorized and perceptual framework in case any questions of legitimacy should arise. (Remember: in the court of public opinion, perception is everything. You will want to demonstrate to others that you are serious about what you are doing.)

- Keep the names, addresses, and phone numbers of your physician, therapist, and attorney handy and available at all times. You never know when you might need them.

- Have discussions with management about your organization's restroom policy, since this issue will almost surely affect you. Talk about the situation with your supervisor and work out a plan beforehand so you will not be left high and dry (so to speak). When the restroom question comes up, and if it should become an area of contention, you and the management team will be prepared to respond based upon this strategy. It will be much more difficult for any detractors to effectively object to your approved use of the facilities if a specific restroom policy has been previously agreed upon with management.

- Keep a small notebook with you at all times. Immediately write down any negative workplace events that may occur relative to your transition. These entries should include any disparaging remarks someone may make about your coming out or transitioning, including the date and time, the speaker, any witnesses, and the circumstances. If an individual's speech/behaviors are rude or disrespectful toward you because of your gender status, note these incidents in your log. (Do not keep the information on your office computer. Type it up at home.) Having detailed records will be important if legal action should ever become necessary.

- Assure your employer that you have no wish to cause disruption in the workplace and you want business to continue as usual. Explain that you are there to work and get the job done, not to create problems and upset the team or the organization. With management's help and support, you should be able to move ahead successfully. Without the backing of management, however, you might want to begin preparing your résumé. A lack of support from management does not usually bode well for the long-term future of an openly transgender employee.

- Provide your employer, HR director, and supervisor with some quality literature and additional resources to help them more fully comprehend the scope of your situation. Also, make sure your employer/manager knows how to contact your therapist, physician, attorney, and/or next of kin if the need should arise.

- Request that your organization consider providing awareness training opportunities on transgender-related issues for everyone in the company. All employees can potentially benefit from such increased knowledge.

- Hope and plan for the best, but be mentally and emotionally prepared for the worst. Unfortunately, it is possible that you may lose your job if you disclose your transgender situation. It has happened to others. As stated previously, many states still have unjust laws that allow them to fire employees for being transgender (or even being perceived as such), so it would be wise to plan for that possibility. Update your résumé *before* you come out, set aside some money so you will not be destitute if you lose your job, do some quiet networking, and know who to contact if the worst should happen.

- Finally, *Illegitimi Non Carborundum*. According to *Safire's New Political Dictionary*, this is a pseudo-Latin phrase meaning "don't let the bastards grind you down." You have infinite worth and have no reason to be ashamed of who and what you are. Keep the faith and keep moving ahead. Thousands of others are transitioning successfully on the job, and you can do it, too.

There is much to consider if you are going to transition in the workplace, so a good deal of thought and careful planning is necessary. Please think this through, take care of yourself, act intelligently, behave with integrity and professionalism, and do what you know in your heart is right for you.

IF YOU ARE A CROSS-DRESSER . . .

Cross-dressers who come out in the workplace confront some of the same issues as transsexuals, yet they must also deal with unique and specific situations that apply directly to their distinctive status as cross-dressing transgender individuals. If you are someone who has made the decision to be open about cross-dressing at work, you may find that you encounter apprehension and/or misunderstanding from some quarters. Some people may question your motivations for coming out. There may be hostility or other opposition based on misinformation or misinterpretation of what you are doing and why. Some people may think you are trying to promote sexual perversity of some kind, so be ready to immediately dispel that notion with factual information and your own professional, reasonable behavior. You should be prepared to talk about your situation with others as the need arises, and it would be helpful if you were able to speak rationally about your transgender status and your valid reasons for cross-dressing on the job.

If your intent is to cross-dress full-time and permanently present yourself in a new gender role at work, then your primary name and accompanying personal pronouns should logically match that new full-time gender role. Doing so will make workplace interactions simpler for all concerned. In such a situation, many of the previously mentioned guidelines for transsexuals who transition on the job will probably apply. Communication, cooperation, and strategizing with management and HR will be essential in such instances.

If you do not plan to cross-dress full-time while at work but intend to do so only on occasion, be prepared for various types of reactions from others in your organization. There may be those who resist or object strenuously. Sometimes, these are individuals who are alarmed, angered, and/or terrified by the presence of a transperson: "Men in dresses! Women in suits, ties and wingtips! The world is surely coming to an end. Moral decay is all around us! It's a sign of the impending apocalypse!" This author's suggestion is to smile broadly, be friendly and rational, and try to have a nonconfrontational, behavior-based conversation with these folks. (Be warned: such efforts may prove to be somewhat less than fruitful, especially if the minds of detractors are already made up and are not willing to be influenced by the facts.) Let them know that you come in peace and reassure them that you are not out to destroy civilization as we know it. Do your best to focus on the personal integrity and honesty piece, which can open the door to a dialogue about ethics, morals, professionalism, best practices, and behaviors on the job as opposed to focusing on sensationalism or sex.

Some objectors may try a smoother, more legalistic type of approach by arguing that since you are not specifically transsexual and/or are not undergoing a medically supervised transition, you have no valid reason or legal right to cross-dress while on the job. They may insist that you dress or present yourself only in a manner consistent with your birth gender, especially if you do not plan to transition full-time as a member of the opposite sex. However, do not allow yourself to be distracted from the real issue that is at stake here. This is not about transitioning or sex changes, at least for those who are cross-dressers: it is about an individual's right to dress and express themselves in a way that allows them to feel psychologically comfortable when they are at work. (There is a little thing called the First Amendment to the Constitution that guarantees one's right to freedom of expression. This is an inalienable right which, in the view of many, includes freedom of gender expression. As long as you are not abusing it or trampling on the rights of others, you have a legitimate right to be your transgender self.)

You can always ask any detractors, "Why does this upset you so? Why does it cause you such anguish? I'm not asking you to do what I do, and I don't want anything from you other than the same respectful, professional treatment you would extend to anyone else in the workplace. Please explain to me why you feel as you do. Just who, exactly, am I hurting when I cross-dress, and in what specific ways are they hurt?" At this point, the burden of explanation and proof shifts to the other party. They will then be in the position of having to justify the rationale for their objections. After all, you are not asking *them* to cross-dress or to do what you do—you are only asking them to leave you alone, permit you to do your work without harassment, and allow you to express your internal gender identity in a harmless manner. Unless someone can produce solid, incontrovertible evidence— not just an opinion—to demonstrate that they are actually being harmed or damaged in some way by your cross-dressing, they have no reasonable grounds for protesting your transgender expression. Forcing another person to conform to a certain set of beliefs is not acceptable behavior in the workplace, especially if those beliefs are based on religion or if they interfere with anyone else's civil and/or human rights. Corporate policies are not supposed to be predicated upon religious beliefs or on an arbitrary emotional response to an individual's gender status.

In the end, this workplace diversity issue is not really about labels, social expectations, sex, or even gender. Instead, it is about two very specific concerns: getting the work done, and equality for everyone. Forward-thinking organizations will understand the powerful implications of these two key issues and will support freedom of gender expression on the job. It makes good business sense, and it is the fair and equitable thing to do for all employees.

CROSS-DRESSING MYTHS AND REALITIES

There are many misconceptions about cross-dressing and cross-dressers that remain pervasive throughout the culture. These mistaken beliefs continue to be obstacles to more widespread acceptance for transpersons in general, so it is important to dispel such inaccurate perceptions with the truth. To further our understanding of what cross-dressing entails, let us consider a few myths that have sprung up about cross-dressers, then respond to those myths with facts.

- Myth: The real reason people cross-dress is (fill in your own answer here).
  Reality: In *Trans Liberation: Beyond Pink or Blue*, Leslie Feinberg writes,

> Pink-blue dogma assumes that biology steers our social destiny. We have been taught that being born female or male will determine how we will dress and walk, whether we will prefer our hair shortly cropped or long and flowing, whether we will be emotionally nurturing or repressed. According to this way of thinking, masculine females are trying to look "like men," and feminine males are trying to act "like women." But those of us who transgress those gender assumptions also shatter their inflexibility.[5]

Feinberg implies that there are a myriad of reasons for the existence of cross-dressing as an element of human behavior. Behavioral psychologist Abraham Maslow's research indicated that although we have plenty of psychological theories about how people are motivated to do what they do, no one knows precisely what prompts any one individual to behave in a certain way. Everyone is different (which, as we have learned, is often a good and healthy thing), and everyone has his or her own reasons for his or her behavioral choices. For example, some people cross-dress because they are entertainers. Some cross-dressers may be demonstrating social or political rebellion against what they perceive as a repressive binary gender system. Some people cross-dress solely as a sexual fetish, while others cross-dress to be outrageous or humorous. Most cross-dressers, however, engage in the behavior as a means of accessing and expressing a highly significant aspect of their internal gender identity. Referring to male-to-female cross-dressers, Helen Boyd says,

> They don't all do it for a sexual turn-on, though some do. They don't all do it because they are unhappy being men [or women]. They don't all do it as a way to release stress. They certainly don't all do it to attract men, or to attract women. Most of them, however, will admit they do it for

pleasure of some kind. For some that pleasure is sexual, and for others it is a more tactile pleasure, a sensual appreciation of soft fabrics and fragrances. Others enjoy being able to express part of themselves they feel they can't otherwise express: to be able to cry easily, or giggle, or touch someone to whom they're talking. For every crossdresser there is a different reason to dress, and for each crossdresser there may be several reasons, but the only true thing I can say is that crossdressers dress for themselves and for the pleasure it brings them.[6]

The overwhelming majority of cross-dressers engage in the behavior for reasons of authentic, benign self-expression and personal fulfillment through the medium of gender expression.

- Myth: Only males engage in cross-dressing. Females do not need to do so.
  Reality: There are many females who cross-dress in masculine attire, though their actual numbers are difficult to ascertain. Since our culture adheres to a double standard for women with regard to clothing (i.e., it is easier for a woman to wear men's apparel in public than vice versa), the general public does not think much about female-to-male cross-dressers. However, and though the issue flies mostly below the cultural radar, it is believed that there are significant numbers of women who dress in men's clothing. They do so for the same reason some males wear the clothing of women: as a benign mechanism for gender expression. Just as some men have a need to express an innate femininity through the medium of cross-dressing, there are women who have a similar need to express a masculine gender identity through the wearing of men's attire. The internal motivations are similar. However, society tends to be a bit more forgiving when a woman wears clothing that is associated with men. This is because, despite the obvious inequity of the situation, masculinity is rigidly considered to be a more valuable status in this culture than femininity. Therefore, a woman who puts on men's apparel and/or seeks to pass as a man in public is, at least in a certain sense, attempting to elevate her social status. The wearing of certain clothing by a transgender individual usually has less to do with intentional power struggles or attempts to negotiate the social ladder than with an internalized need for

gender expression. In any case, the myth says that women do not cross-dress. The reality is that there are many women who do.

- Myth: People cross-dress to attract sexual partners.
Reality: Admittedly, males and females will sometimes use clothing to signal sexual availability. A person's chosen attire is usually an individualized reflection of attitude and personal style—and so it is with cross-dressers, both male-to-female and female-to-male. Sounds like a rather common human characteristic, doesn't it? Many people, possibly even you, wear certain clothing as an individual expression of their own personality or as a source of personal identification. (Just ask the jersey-wearing supporters of any major league sports team!) What we wear may indicate something about us or impart a personal message of some kind, but most of the time, it is not automatically a sexual come-on. Usually, our choice of clothing has more to do with how we feel about ourselves, what we are doing, or where we are going at any given time than it does about advertising that we are sexually available. And when we are at work, we have no business dressing for sex. We have a responsibility to dress in a professional manner that is appropriate for our work situation.

- Myth: Cross-dressers and/or other transpersons try to recruit or convert others.
Reality: This is one myth that richly deserves to be put to rest. Nobody can convert someone into "becoming" a cross-dresser— people either are or they aren't, and there is nothing anyone can do about that. Cross-dressers are not a religious or sexual cult, a social club, or a political party, and the transgender community does not need to solicit or "recruit" new members: they are being born and/or coming out on a daily basis anyway. Besides, there is no viable reason why anyone should want to attempt to conscript, recruit, or convert someone else to being transgender, nor is there a valid reason for previously non-transgender persons to choose to somehow "become" transgender (as if that were even possible, any more than it is possible for someone to choose to "become" left-handed or green-eyed or heterosexual). Who would intentionally decide to be a member of a socially disenfranchised minority group if they were not already identified with or predisposed toward such a status? Transgender persons have always comprised a certain percentage of the population. Mother Nature takes care of that on her own and needs no help from anyone.

Therefore, there is no reason or need for transgender persons to attempt to recruit, enroll, or convert others.

- Myth: People who cross-dress are gay.
  Reality: No, not usually, despite the shrill protestations and alarmist cries of those who continue to equate sex with gender. Research strongly indicates that most cross-dressers identify as heterosexual in terms of their orientation. The rate of gay-identified persons among the cross-dressing population appears to be about the same percentage as it is throughout the rest of society. Speaking of percentages, it has been estimated that anywhere from 1 to 10 percent of all males in this society are "closeted," or secret, cross-dressers, though there is currently no way of confirming the actual numbers with any real accuracy. Percentages of female-to-male cross-dressers among the wider population have not been estimated, probably due to a lack of research in this area. Besides, who cares whether someone else is gay, lesbian, bisexual, straight, or whatever? Why should it matter to anyone at all, unless they plan to pursue a sexual relationship with the person in question? We should all be at work to perform our jobs as well and productively as we can, not to speculate about or judge someone else's gender identity, sexual orientation, or personal relationship(s).

- Myth: Cross-dressers are only out to seduce others.
  Reality: The vast majority of transgender people are too busy trying to go to work, do their jobs, and build happy, productive, healthy lives for themselves and their families. They do not have the time, energy, or inclination to go around indiscriminately seducing other people. Frankly, most transpersons have more common sense than that, particularly when they are at work. "Transgender [workers] show up at the office every day to do their jobs, not to seek out sexual encounters."[7]

- Myth: Cross-dressing is a pathological, harmful compulsion.
  Reality: Sorry, but no. "Compulsion" is a clinical term that describes urges gone out of control and that cause harm to oneself and/or others. Common examples of destructive compulsions might include compulsive gambling, compulsive overeating, compulsive drinking or drug use, compulsive sex, or even compulsive cleaning. Clearly, gambling yourself or your family into financial ruin is not a healthy thing for anyone. Overeating is obviously detrimental to one's well-being. Excessive drinking and/or drug use are destructive behaviors. Sexual urges that are

uncontrolled can generate all sorts of devastating consequences, from emotional wounding to physical disease and possibly even death. By improperly applying the word "compulsion" to a trans-gender activity like cross-dressing, there is an inference that such behavior for males is somehow not quite as healthy and whole-some as, say, a genetic woman's innate desire to dress up and look her feminine best. We have been hearing for decades that women should enjoy all the opportunities in life that men have (and right-fully so). How about vice versa? Who or what could a personal desire on the part of a male for acquiring and expressing beauty possibly harm? Should not males have that same right to enjoy-ment, dressing up, and beautification if they desire it? What about female-to-male cross-dressers: should not they have the right to express an innate masculinity through dress and appearance if they desire it? And if they should not have that right, why not? Because some people may disagree or be uncomfortable with the idea? Because it is "different"? Cross-dressing is not a pathology or a damaging compulsion: it is an opportunity for gender expres-sion and personal fulfillment that hurts no one.

- Myth: All male-to-female cross-dressers are sissies and weaklings.
  Reality: It is suggested that you avoid risking a bloody nose by insisting on this one. Many male-to-female cross-dressers seem to end up in "macho" professions, motivated perhaps by emotional denial and/or overcompensation due to their internal need for transgender expression. Besides, it is not a weakness or a moral failing for a male to be feminine or to cultivate feminine qualities: it is merely human. As a general rule of thumb, one should probably be very careful about calling a cross-dresser a sissy—it could lead to some unexpected repercussions. The word "cross-dresser" describes an outward form of personal expres-sion. "Sissy," when used in the pejorative sense, is a belittling social term that implies an inferior or undesirable status.

- Myth: Cross-dressing is indicative of deeply rooted psychological problems.
  Reality: That is hardly the case for most people who cross-dress. Modern psychology accepts that cross-dressing is a benign expression of personality for a certain percentage of the popula-tion, and the behavior itself seems to be as immutable (and just as harmless) as left-handedness. Any psychological difficulties that cross-dressers may experience are usually due to the presence

of social stigma, prejudice, or bigotry, not to some type of mysterious "transgender mental disorder." Problematic cultural expectations with regard to gender identity and expression are not a credible basis upon which to assess or diagnose transgender as a mental disorder. According to the American Psychiatric Association, the singular behavior of cross-dressing is in no way indicative of a psychological disorder. Cross-dressing itself does not create psychological problems, but unwarranted social antipathy toward cross-dressers may.

- Myth: All cross-dressers desire to have their sex changed.
  Reality: A compelling need for surgically and/or hormonally assisted physical alignment with an internal psychological orientation/identity is legitimate for primary transsexuals, to be sure, but such desires are *not* typical for most cross-dressers. (As we have learned, a small percentage of transgender individuals feel so strongly about being a "woman trapped in a man's body" or "a man trapped in a woman's body" that sexual reassignment surgery is actively sought. These people are transsexuals. They comprise only a small minority within the much larger transgender population.) For the vast majority of cross-dressers, sex changes are simply not wanted nor are they ever pursued.

- Myth: Cross-dressing is against the law.
  Reality: With the possible exception of a few archaic and largely unenforceable "disguise" ordinances, people are generally free to wear whatever fashion and style of clothing they choose in public. (A few years ago, the city of St. Paul, Minnesota, did away with an outmoded law against cross-dressing in public. That law had been on the books for over one hundred years. It became evident to the city officials that such a statute was ridiculous, and when it was brought to their attention, they wisely chose to eliminate it.) People should not be compelled by civil authorities to restrict their apparel only to "gender-specific" attire. If such a concept were to be strictly enforced to its full extension, women would almost certainly be legally prohibited from wearing pants in public.

- Myth: Cross-dressing is "sinful" and a spiritual "abomination."
  Reality: No, not at all.[8] Theologians define "sin" as a rebellion of some sort against God or against scripturally based laws for human behavior as interpreted within a particular religious framework. Most reputable biblical scholars agree that certain biblical passages (particularly Deuteronomy 22:5, a verse often quoted out of its

appropriate historical and religious context for the purpose of oppressing transpersons[9]) are based on and/or pertain to the practice of pagan priests and priestesses exchanging clothing in their worship rituals. This scripture verse, a part of the Holiness Code, was directed toward the Hebrew people during the era of their exodus from Egypt and 40 years of wandering in the wilderness. Crossing or blurring the gender line was considered socially/religiously unacceptable and even culturally dangerous for the Hebrew people. In biblical times, the Deuteronomic prohibition against ritualistic cross-dressing enforced a strong sense of tribal unity through the mandating of specifically gendered appearance and behavior among the Israelites. This expectation about clothing-based gender expression was presumably structured and enforced to keep the Hebrews from engaging in the idolatrous worship behaviors that were commonly practiced by the surrounding indigenous peoples. The apparent fear was that any adoption of gender-variant ritualistic expression by the Israelites might lead to a breakdown and/or lack of distinction between the sexes, which was deemed to be the precursor to social chaos (and potential non-procreation), a state of affairs that could presumably weaken or destroy tribal cohesion and trigger the subsequent incurring of God's judgment upon the people of Israel. In any case, most modern biblical scholars recognize that the injunction of Deuteronomy 22:5 had nothing to do with any sort of innate psychological/emotional transgender identity or with legitimate forms of transgender expression as we know and understand them today. Rather, this particular scriptural sanction was a socioreligious form of codified dress/behavior control that was instilled to maintain tribal control and national identity. Such passages of scripture are not applicable or relevant to our modern culture or to an enlightened biblical hermeneutic (i.e., an interpretive lens or cognitive framework for understanding). In fact, the concept of an internal transgender identity was completely unknown in biblical times and is therefore never mentioned in scripture at all.[10] The legalistic, arbitrary religious argument equating cross-dressing with a spiritual "abomination" does not survive the scrutiny of modern theological understanding, a realistic biblical hermeneutic, and culturally accepted psychological insight. (Besides, use of the word "abomination" in the Old Testament merely implies an action or behavior that varied from the rigid socioreligious tribal/national norms of the time. It does not necessarily indicate a type of perversion, sin, or moral failing as we understand the word today.)

- Myth: All cross-dressers are sexually depraved.
  Reality: Flatly, no. This misunderstanding is, in large part, the unfortunate result of sensationalistic media-driven stereotypes and is not based on truth or on the actual life experiences of the vast majority of cross-dressers. For most people who cross-dress, the physical act of wearing specific clothing as a form of gender expression is a heartfelt, emotionally fulfilling expression of an inner awareness about their gender status. Spouses, children, family, friends, associates, and others need not feel threatened in the least. Most cross-dressers pose no danger to anyone; in fact, creating problems for themselves or their families is the last thing they want to do. Sexual perversion in its various forms, however, is another matter entirely: it sometimes involves activities that may potentially bring harm to people. In and of itself, cross-dressing is a form of behavior that harms no one and that can actually provide a healthy, emotionally beneficial outlet for specific, internal gender-based needs. Consequently, cross-dressing as a distinctive activity does not fit the definition of a sexual perversion and should not be considered as such.
- Myth: Cross-dressers go into restrooms to spy on others and get sexual kicks.
  Reality: Oh, come on! We all have the biological need to relieve our bodies, and when nature calls, we need to use the restroom. When cross-dressers enter the facility that is designated for their outwardly expressed gender role, they are logically and realistically using the restroom that presents the least risk to their personal well-being and that of others. Some males in this culture have a tendency to be transphobic and are potentially prone to violence toward other males who cross-dress, which makes restroom use a legitimate safety issue for the male-to-female cross-dresser. Think about it: if you were a cross-dresser (regardless of your sex and/or gender), would not it make sense to calmly and appropriately use the restroom that has been designated for the gender in which you are physically presenting at the time?
- Myth: Cross-dressing as a form of gender expression in the workplace is covered under state or federal laws and EEO "gender identity" language. Therefore, there is no need to include "gender identity, characteristics, and expression" in your own organization's employee policy.
  Reality: On a national basis, at least as of this writing, workplace discrimination based on gender expression is *not* fully addressed by legal

EEO language that includes gender identity. A handful of states have passed laws that protect the rights of transpersons, but there are no current federal protections. Transsexuals, cross-dressers, intersexuals, and other transpersons are different types of people with different types of gender-based needs. That is why every business should consider implementing organizational policies that include gender identity, gender characteristics, and gender expression.

While it is true that some cross-dressers dress primarily for sexual pleasure, such activities almost always take place in privacy (and are certainly not appropriate at work, which is hardly the place for overt sexual behavior). We should also note that sexual arousal associated with cross-dressing often tends to wane as the individual ages and the cross-dresser becomes more comfortable with accepting and expressing her or his transgender identity.

Many male-to-female cross-dressers feel there is something fascinating and compelling about seeing themselves in women's clothing, which is why a mirror is often said to be a cross-dresser's best friend. Emulating the beautiful women whom they appreciate makes these cross-dressers feel good about themselves. The same holds true, only in reverse, for many female-to-male cross-dressers who emulate masculine appearances. Some may perhaps find this behavior strange or unusual—and that is okay, since everyone is entitled to his or her own opinion and beliefs—but a critical, condemning attitude or response is hardly necessary.

IF YOU ARE INTERSEXUAL...

The distinctive issues and concerns of intersex persons have begun surfacing culturally only within the last few years. Until the 1990s, there were few, if any, social or political measures being actively pursued on behalf of intersex individuals.

A major concern for the intersex community involves the imposing of "reconstructive" surgery on babies born with "different" or statistically abnormal genitalia. Whether immediately in the delivery room or later on in the life of an intersex person, physicians often "enforce" gender through uninvited genital surgery, thus potentially inflicting both physical and psychological harm on their intersex patients.

Dr. Sharon E. Preves says, "Something that's important to keep in mind is that well over nine times out of ten, someone born with intersex anatomy is completely healthy physiologically."[11] Therefore, uninvited genital surgery is physically unnecessary in most intersex cases. The unsolicited imposition of such surgeries is a primary reason for the growth of a burgeoning intersex movement focusing on the premise that intersexuals have a right to be self-determining in every area that affects their lifelong physiological, mental, and occupational well-being. The goal of the movement is to destigmatize and demedicalize intersex persons, thereby empowering the intersex community and the individuals that comprise it.

Intersex people are beginning to come out of their closets, and many are purposely becoming more visible throughout society. Some are openly revealing themselves as intersex in their workplaces. Accordingly, business organizations have a responsibility to institute appropriate policies, methods, and procedures for dealing with these employees in a respectful manner.

Some people may become anxious, concerned, irritable, and/or even hostile when they cannot immediately discern someone's gender. Because intersex persons can sometimes be androgynous and/or ambiguous in their gender presentation, their gender-neutral appearance may occasionally spark non-positive and/or less-than-respectful reactions on the part of others. However, a person's physical appearance is certainly no reason to be rude or discriminatory toward him or her, regardless of his or her gender status. Once again, the issue is workplace behaviors, not beliefs or values.

INTERSEX MYTHS AND REALITIES

Since we have already done so for cross-dressing individuals, let us list a few myths about intersex and then respond to them with realities.

- Myth: Intersex is extremely rare.
  Reality: Apparently, it is not as rare as many people think. According to Dr. Alice D. Dreger, research indicates that 1 in every 2,000 persons appears to be intersexual to some degree, and that figure may end up proving to be even higher than originally thought.[12]
- Myth: Only "true hermaphrodites" are really intersexual.
  Reality: Technically, no. The term "intersex" is used to refer to anybody who was born with anatomy other than what the cultural Powers That Be define as "standard male" or "standard female."

That can cover a lot of territory. Also, the term "hermaphrodite" is considered disparaging by most intersexuals.

- Myth: If you are transsexual, then you are also intersexual.
  Reality: This myth arises from a faulty cultural assumption which insists that gender identity must always find its basis in anatomy. As we have learned, the seat of gender identity is located in the brain, not in the genitalia or chromosomes. Transsexuals are rarely people who are born intersexual. Far more often, transsexuals are born with "standard" male or female anatomy. By a common definition of transsexuality, transsexuals were assigned a gender at birth that does not work for them. Later in life, they desire to change their anatomy to be more congruent with the gender that they internally know and understand to be valid for them. Based on this understanding, not all transsexuals are intersexual and not all intersexuals are transsexual.

- Myth: You cannot raise an intersex child as a boy or girl without surgery.
  Reality: Says who? Is there some rule that says we have to show people the genitals of a child whenever they ask about the child's gender? Note that "male" and "female" are terms that refer to one's biological/physical/chromosomal status, while "girl," "boy," "woman," and "man" are culturally created terms that have specific meanings and are framed within our social construct of gender. This means that "boy" and "man" do not necessarily have to align with "biological male" as a personal designation or description, nor do "girl" and "woman" always have to mean "biologically female." Based on this understanding, it is entirely possible to be a male woman or a female man or a gender-neutral individual. It is unusual and perhaps somewhat confusing at times, but it is true—and it is all part of the mystery of transgender.

- Myth: Surgery creates normal-looking genitals.
  Reality: No. Intersex genitals are not diseased, only different. Besides, what is "normal-looking"? Who gets to decide what is normal and what is not? The delivery room physicians? (Who anointed them as the sole arbiters of cultural normality?) As noted elsewhere in these pages, "normal" is only a statistical average, not a value judgment. Beauty is in the eye of the beholder—and so is "normal," at least when it comes to aesthetics and genitalia.

- Myth: Once surgery is completed, intersex concerns will be over.
  Reality: Dreger says,

When is it ever going to be ok to risk a baby's future sexual function, fertility, and even life, just because her genitals force you to realize gender and sex aren't simply dichotomies? Who are you to decide she wouldn't be happy with the genitals she was born with? If it is true that intersex cosmetic surgeries are getting better (and we lack the data to know), then why not let the intersexed person himself decide when, in his own opinion, the likely benefits to him of the surgery outweigh the burdens and risks to him of that surgery? Keep in mind, too, that surgeries designed to "correct" intersexed genitals will always, by definition, carry with them the message that intersex is shameful and bad.[13]

Viewed from this perspective, the common medical practice of genital surgery at birth for intersex persons is not necessarily a good thing. Perhaps such surgeries should be delayed until the individuals in question are old enough to make a qualified, informed determination about genital surgery for themselves.

• Myth: "Corrective" cosmetic surgeries make parents forget their kid was born "different" and undo all their confusion, shame, guilt, and fear.
Reality: Not a chance. All this does is convince parents that their child is some sort of freak with a horrible condition that needs to be "normalized." Genital surgery that is unnecessary can be damaging to the child, potentially causing physical, psychological, sexual, and/or emotional difficulties throughout adolescence and into adulthood.

The sex and gender issues of intersex persons can be intricate and multifaceted. In the workplace, discrimination toward intersexuals may occur due to an androgynous physical appearance or presentation, or perhaps because of some confusion about the "legitimate" sex category of the person in question. Once again we see the potentially negative ramifications that can accompany a fear of the unknown when it comes to gender variance. The existence of that fear and accompanying negativity is why business organizations must find ways to become more informed and educated about transgender issues.

CHAPTER 12

What to Do about, with, and for Transgender Customers

> *Our chief characteristic [at IDEO] has been that we constantly reconfigure what we do in order to catch the wave of what is new in industry.*
>
> —David Kelley, IDEO

You may be wondering why this book includes a chapter on transgender customers, especially since we have been focusing so much on the issues of transgender workers. That is a fair question, and here is the answer, in several parts:

- Unless companies are willing to continuously reassess and update what they do and how they do it, they will miss the wave of new ideas in their industries and be left behind. Just because something has always been done a certain way does not mean that it is a smart business practice to continue operating in that same manner indefinitely, especially if better alternatives are available. Transgender in the workplace is a new idea for the corporate world, but it is a significant issue that is growing in its impact on workplace cultures. Acceptance for transgender individuals in business will eventually become the norm around the world.

- Most organizations will come in contact with transgender customers at some point and in some way (if it has not happened already). As the transgender phenomenon becomes more visible within the larger society, clients who are openly transgender will

increasingly be purchasing goods and services from all kinds of
businesses. The everyday presence of transgender persons is
becoming a fact of business life and will eventually be at least a
somewhat routine occurrence. Therefore, it is in an organization's best interests to welcome the paying transgender customer
(along with their money—which, as authorities have determined,
is definitely just as green and spends just as well as anyone else's).
Bottom lines and corporate bank accounts know no gender.

- In a few states and in a growing number of municipalities, it is
  now illegal to discriminate against transgender persons in a place
  of business. Since your organization probably does not want to
  be the defendant in a potential discrimination lawsuit or receive
  the negative publicity that such an event might foster, it might
  be a prudent move to inform your people that transpersons are
  to be welcomed and treated with respect like every other customer. This can present an excellent opportunity for employees
  to brush up on their customer relations skills in general. It can
  also create an opening for your people to talk about those particular skills in a new, helpful, leading-edge business context, and the
  result may well be that all of your organization's customers will be
  treated more courteously and fairly.

- There are businesses that have told potential transgender customers, "We're sorry, but we can't (or won't) serve you. We can't
  afford to risk offending our real customers." *Real* customers?
  Does that mean transgender customers are somehow artificial,
  or that their dollars are less valuable than those of other people?
  Turning away a customer who has the money and is sincerely
  interested in spending it on your product or service is usually
  not a sound business idea. Purposely rejecting and/or offending
  an openly transgender customer is not conducive to long-term
  business growth, either. The unwanted transperson will probably
  never darken your door again, will almost surely tell others
  (perhaps even the media) about your discrimination, and can
  potentially cause you to lose future sales. All of this can be easily
  avoided by simply treating paying transgender customers as you
  would like to be treated. Besides, one day in the foreseeable future
  it will become illegal for any business in the United States to
  discriminate against transgender persons. After all, business is
  business and money is money, no matter what the person's sex

or gender. Your accountant, banker, and stockholders certainly are not going to ask or care about the gender of the people who brought revenue into your organization!

- Cindy Laughlin, Human Resources Senior Manager at electronics mega-retailer Best Buy, has said, "Profit means tapping into multicultural markets, and mirroring a multicultural base ... you sell to all people. If you don't understand those people, including the purchase motivators and needs of GLBT buyers, then you lose their significant spending power."[1] The GLBT population of the United States is estimated to have over $600 billion in purchasing power.[2] Gender-variant persons are a growing segment of that minority population. As transgender customers become more of a visible entity and a legitimate economic factor in the marketplace, learning about their purchase motivators and buying needs will become increasingly important if your organization seeks access to their "significant spending power." Personalization is an excellent way to create lasting customers, but you cannot effectively personalize your marketing approach unless you learn about your customers and their specific needs.

Additionally, business organizations can improve customer service by encouraging team members to take the following ideas under consideration as they interact with transgender clients:

- Matt Kailey says, "True respect for a trans person is either correct gender acknowledgment or none at all ... Employees of every company [should] be trained in these types of issues so as not to offend paying customers of their products and services."[3] Once again we see the significant value of improving an organization's customer relations skills by educating employees about transgender issues.
- "A true trans-friendly business should have a unisex restroom in addition to the traditional men's and women's rooms meant for those stuffy people who define themselves by their genitalia."[4] Note the importance of helping everyone, regardless of gender identity, feel comfortable and welcomed in your organization's cultural environment. It does not take much to make a difference: just a little thought and planning should do the trick. The rewards in terms of customer approval and satisfaction (as well as repeat business) will be worth the effort.

MARKETING TO A TRANSGENDER CLIENTELE

Today's successful businesses understand the importance of con-
tinually expanding their organization's customer base as well as retaining existing customers on a lasting basis. Marketing surveys
consistently indicate that it is much more difficult and expensive to
initially gain a customer than it is to keep a customer once they are
already in the fold. Logic says that if your organization already has
transgender customers (and many businesses do, whether they are
aware of it or not), then your company should do its best to recognize,
welcome, and retain them, for that will prove to be the most profitable
and cost-effective practice over time.

From a marketing perspective, organizations that welcome transgender clients can gain a unique business advantage by

- Accepting the reality that, as society becomes increasingly
  enlightened, transpeople are becoming more visible throughout
  the business world. Therefore, eventual encounters with paying
  transgender customers are almost a foregone conclusion. Since
  this is becoming the case, organizations may as well be prepared
  to view this circumstance as a new and exciting opportunity to
  expand the scope of their business sales efforts.

- Actively seeking out and specifically marketing to transgender customers as a legitimate and even desirable target group. Try not to
  focus so much on "customer service" or even "customer satisfaction." Instead, choose to emphasize the cultivation of ardent *customer loyalty* with transgender clients. (The Ken Blanchard/
  Sheldon Bowles concept of creating "raving fans" for your business
  might well apply here.) Discerning organizations can make significant inroads into the transgender market demographic by getting
  there first and demonstrating the company's continuing interest in
  meeting their needs. Being first means that a company can begin
  developing a strong brand loyalty among transgender customers
  that will extend far into the future. What price might your business
  put on that kind of long-term customer loyalty for its product or
  service?

- Creating and maintaining a trans-friendly environment for everyone involved with your organization, including transgender
  customers. Marketing professionals are aware that a successful
  sales campaign works primarily because of the nurturing of

lasting relationships with customers. Developing and maintaining relationships and connections with all kinds of people should be the goal for businesses that want to grow and thrive.

- Identifying and cultivating new customers, including transpersons. The transgender community is a relatively untapped market group that is ripe and even hungry for engagement with forward-thinking business organizations. Such efforts will almost certainly be welcomed by transpersons and will generate positive responses from the gender-variant community. Getting in on the ground floor with this target group will surely work to an organization's long-term advantage in terms of profitability, brand identification, and lasting customer loyalty.

- Working even harder to retain existing customers who may be transgender. Think about how your organization might nurture and expand those current relationships. Demonstrating an honest, ardent appreciation for existing customers is always a prudent business move. It usually leads to more sales and increased revenue as the relationship with those customers continues to deepen and improve.

Businesses specializing in selling personal items like wigs, cosmetics, jewelry, breast prostheses, and larger shoe/clothing sizes will probably be used to dealing with transgender customers. Those businesses should logically view the transgender community as a clear and intentional part of their overall marketing strategy.

Julie Forster says that an "incentive for companies ... is adding marketing muscle. The buying power of the gay and lesbian market [as well as the bisexual and transgender market] is pegged at $690 billion for 2007, according to a report by market research firm Packaged Facts in collaboration with Witeck-Combs Communication."[6] Any organization that overlooks and/or rejects the significant purchasing power of a legitimate percentage of the buying population does so at its own peril.

The challenge for today's organizations is to create a business culture that welcomes everyone and provides a positive purchasing experience. However, many companies are unaware of the existence of a growing transgender community, nor have they ever given a moment's thought to actively pursuing a transgender customer base. Perhaps the time has come for your organization to consider the financial feasibility of such an initiative. If and when you do, you might want to reflect on the words of "poet Audre Lorde, who wrote that, instead of viewing our human differences as 'insurmountable barriers,' we should develop the tools necessary to use them as 'a springboard for creative change.' "[7] Transgender customers may be "different" in some respects, but they are not all *that* different. They may be unique people, but they are still human beings with the same kinds of basic human needs that everyone has, and they purchase goods and services like everyone else.

The first ones into new territory invariably gain the right to plant their stake in the ground and create their own rules. What about your organization: are you willing to successfully seize the future and plant a new stake of your own by welcoming gender-variant customers? Millions of potential transgender clients, along with their families, friends, and allies, are waiting to see how you will respond to this new business opportunity.

CHAPTER 13

What *You* Can Do

The challenge lies in creating a workplace in which people can be the best they can be.

—Frederick W. Smith, *The Book of Leadership Wisdom*

By now you have hopefully acquired a more in-depth understanding of why transgender is increasingly relevant in terms of its impact on today's business community. The times are indeed changing, and organizations that want to succeed will change with them. It is not enough to sit back passively with this knowledge and allow the negativity that has historically been directed toward transgender individuals to continue unabated. The time for specific, meaningful action is here.

To quote Peter Singer, the transgender-in-the-workplace "movement demands an expansion of our moral horizons and an extension or reinterpretation of the basic moral principle of equality. [When that movement toward equality occurs,] practices that were previously regarded as natural and inevitable come to be seen as the result of an unjustifiable prejudice."[1] This leading-edge workplace dynamic is beginning to shift the public perception of transgender workers in a new and positive direction. As a result, the transgender phenomenon is becoming increasingly accepted into the fabric of mainstream society.

In addition to its other business implications, the moral issue of transgender civil and human rights deserves to be taken seriously in our workplaces and not be looked upon only as a "minority flavor-of-the-month" topic. Giving lip service to business fads will not end discrimination against transgender workers. It will take strategic leadership, decisive action, and wholehearted, long-term commitment on the part of many—beginning with ownership and top management—to achieve that worthy goal.

Transgender workers are not asking for the moon. Genuine equality, a level playing field, common courtesy, professionalism, and human decency are all that is necessary. However, transpersons who work for a living must do more than just come with cap in hand, bowing and scraping and begging humbly for their rights. History repeatedly demonstrates that human rights are attained through insistent, insightful action, not by pleading or some vague hope that they will be handed out. In the words of Frederick Douglass, "Power concedes nothing without demand. It never has and never will."

Transgender workers cannot afford to simply pass the time waiting for fate to deliver their rights, nor can they count on the kindness of others to deliver those rights to them. Instead, transpersons must strategize, organize, mobilize, and work untiringly to obtain and sustain those rights for themselves. The world is not going to automatically cede human rights to someone just because he or she may desire or deserve them.

Transgender voices must become an integral part of the conversation within the larger society, including the workplace, for until trans voices are heard and taken seriously, they can never truly be perceived as equal. But while attempting to encourage, legislate, and/or otherwise promote broader cultural acceptance of transgender appearance and behaviors, transpersons must also do their part to help the world understand and recognize that they are valuable, contributing members of society who happen to be gender-variant. Such efforts will help transgender individuals set a positive tone for success, thereby further legitimizing the movement toward wider public recognition of transpeople as human beings and workers who deserve protection and full equality under the law.

According to the American Civil Liberties Union, "The ways in which the freedoms of . . . transgendered [sic] people are limited is rooted in . . . stereotypical and tightly bound notions of gender (including gender roles, attributes assigned to either gender, and the expression of gender identity)."[2] Culturally based limitations on human freedom and potential are valid reasons for business organizations to establish specific antidiscrimination policies that protect transgender employees and other organizational stakeholders as well as transgender customers. Hopefully, your company will choose to be an inclusive working community that celebrates the inherent worth and the remarkable gifts of every person, regardless of gender identity.

The right to live means little if it does not include the right to make a living. Every person deserves to perform his or her work in an environment that rejects intolerance, unfounded bigotry, and oppression leveled at the "have-nots" by the "haves." The effort toward transgender equality at work is not about securing "special" or undeserved treatment for anyone, nor is it about furthering some sort of destructive and/or perverse sociopolitical agenda to weaken or undermine the culture. This movement is about protecting a group of people who have historically been disenfranchised by unjust social expectations and arbitrary gender rules. It is about making it possible for each person, no matter what his or her gender identity, to have a legitimate opportunity for happiness and fulfillment in life. It is about valuing and appreciating our common humanity so we can all operate successfully in workplaces that are as free from prejudice and injustice as we can make them. Professional job performance and results must be the criteria by which people are evaluated in the workplace. Those should always be the standards for everyone, transgender or not, who works for a living.

If you are a transgender worker, look deep within yourself and find your self-confidence and courage so you can move ahead in whatever ways you believe are best for you and your organization. Those remarkable human qualities are already there inside you, waiting to be fulfilled. Tap into them. Apply them wisely and courageously.

Hopefully, you will work hard to make increasingly valuable contributions to your company. The best way to achieve acceptance and respect while becoming an appreciated member of your organization is to produce solid, measurable results. (It is amazing how receptive and affirming people, especially those in management, can become toward transpersons when the transgender individual is visibly contributing to the organization's success.) It is much more difficult for businesses to demote or terminate people who are making a strong, positive difference through their work. If you feel that perhaps you have not been doing all you can or that you have not been giving your best effort while on the job, you have an ethical responsibility to your employer and yourself to find ways to make more significant contributions. Conscientious, hardworking transpersons are doing that every day in organizations throughout society. "[The] future is already evolving in many places. [You are urged to] look with new lenses at . . . your own organization and discover ways you can contribute to a positive future."[3]

STRUGGLING FOR THE BIRTHRIGHT

> *It had long since come to my attention that people of accomplishment rarely sat back and let things happen to them. They went out and happened to things.*
>
> —Elinor Smith

W. E. B. Du Bois once said, "We claim for ourselves every single right that belongs to a freeborn American, political, civil, and social; and until we get these rights we will never cease to protest and assail the ears of America! The battle we wage is not for ourselves alone but for all true Americans. It is a fight for ideals."[4]

The struggle for those noble, transcendent, life-affirming ideals is as relevant for transgender persons in the workplace today as it was for the African American community that Du Bois was addressing back in 1906. Following his example, we must not "cease to protest and assail the ears of America" until transgender citizens have achieved full equality in every part of society, including the workplace.

Today, some of the same tired, discriminatory charges that have historically been directed against women, African Americans, and gays/lesbians in society and in our workplaces are being directed toward transgender persons. It is encouraging to know that, just as with the invalid arguments against racial and sexual equality of the past, baseless attacks on transgender equality are also beginning to crumble under the weight of their own inauthenticity.

Transgender workers are increasingly refusing to stand idly by and allow themselves to be ignored or denied any longer. The growing visibility of transpeople throughout society, coupled with the fledgling transgender-in-the-workplace movement for justice and equality, will doubtless bring about some negative, highly emotional responses to transgender inclusivity. The journey toward transgender egalitarianism will almost certainly take the form of an ongoing struggle. But struggling against injustice by actively demanding equality and fair treatment for everyone is a just and worthy cause, and for this good reason transgender people will ultimately win the acceptance and respect they seek. Transpeople will win not because they are better or smarter than others, but because they deserve the same human and civil rights as everyone else—and holding fast to that ideal is what will make the difference.

SPECIFIC ACTIONS YOU CAN TAKE

You may be asking yourself, "How can *I* make a difference? I'm only one person." First, be aware that here is a remarkable power in small, personal actions that are performed in a just cause. Whenever someone takes action for something that is good and right, the impact of that action is multiplied and enhanced by the force of the moral authority that defines and sustains the action. When many people perform individual acts in a just cause, the result is often a combination of effort that generates significant power. Such power can change hearts, minds, lives, and societies. Here are a few things that one person, perhaps *you*, can do to make a substantive impact on behalf of transgender workers.

- Speak out. Speak truth to power if necessary. Speak boldly: you have that right because you are speaking in the name of justice. Refuse to be silenced. Speak the truth as you know and understand and have lived it, and never stop speaking it. Speak logically, rationally, and courageously. If transpeople and their allies remain silent, then only the voices of their opponents and detractors will be heard in the public discourse. Do your best to be calm, reasonable, factual, and sensible. (Hysteria, anger, and shrillness are unattractive qualities, and they rarely achieve any desired results.) All you have to do is share your personal experiences and feelings, which are completely valid and which no one can legitimately dispute. You may choose to write letters to your CEO, supervisor, or others in influential positions, including your elected officials and the media. They need to hear from you as well. (E-mails can communicate, too, but substantive, short, direct, and well-crafted letters wield a good deal of influence and can be highly effective.) Let people know where you stand and why you believe transgender issues are significant for society and for your organization. Make your point and then stop. Be honest and lucid, not judgmental, irrational, or extremist in your comments. Focus on the benefits to society and/or your company, not on negativity, attacks, or a personal agenda. Then you can take pride in knowing that you are lifting your voice and doing something for good. It does not matter whether you are transgender or not—right is right and fair is fair. Justice and equality are for everyone, not only the traditionally gendered.

- You do not need to be ashamed or afraid of benign human difference. The world is filled with all kinds of people, and transfolk are people, too. There is no legitimate reason why anyone should be embarrassed to be transgender, and there is no justifiable reason why others should be afraid of transpersons. Fear of the unknown is almost always a major ingredient in conflict situations, so make the decision to move beyond your fear and start living your life as a worthwhile, happy, whole, and contributing person.

- Stand up for yourself. It is great to be unashamed, unafraid, and committed to being transgender or an ally, but it is equally important to make the issue become real by making yourself visible and known to others whenever possible. How will public awareness of transgender be increased without people standing up and being counted as proud transpersons and allies who refuse to be diminished or silenced by the power brokers and gatekeepers of the status quo?

- If you are a transgender worker, come out to others as often (but always as safely and strategically) as you can. A dynamic human power is manifested whenever a transperson comes out to someone else. Such an act of honesty, authenticity, and integrity can make a significant difference, not only for your life but also in the lives of others. Acts of courage generate character, and the moral impact of character combined with appropriate action can change the world (witness Mahatma Gandhi, Martin Luther King, Jr., Lech Walesa, Nelson Mandela, etc.). As you become more visible, you become more acceptable. As you become more acceptable, you become more respected. Most people genuinely appreciate honesty and integrity. They know it when they see and experience it in others. Coming out with dignity and self-confidence is a powerful way to make a difference.

- Focus on things that matter in your workplace. The worst thing for any organization is a falsely perceived sense of unity, especially when that false unity is actually shallow and therefore ineffective. In such cases, there is no genuine unity because the organization's culture/community is grounded not in shared values and concerns about the welfare of its people but in an absence of firm ethics, standards and principles, and a spiritual core. Pursuing common cause at work is a worthy goal, but it can only happen if that common cause is shared by the entire organization and springs from a genuine desire to operate within an ethical framework of equality and mutual respect.

- Support people and organizations that are working to obtain human rights and equality for everyone. You can give money, time, and energy to social, political, religious, or professional groups that share your values and purpose. Become part of and contribute to something larger than yourself. You will feel good about that involvement, for you will be making a positive difference in the world alongside others who are also passionate about your cause.

- It is okay to be who you are. People respect and can even come to admire those who live with authenticity and without phoniness, whether they agree with them or not. You are a unique and valuable person with much to offer the world. Take quiet pride in that knowledge—let it motivate you to act in honorable, ethical ways that will truly make a difference for others and yourself. If enough people choose to act for justice and equality with strong moral conviction, then creating a profound, lasting impact on society will be a foregone and inevitable conclusion.

Here are a few suggestions about how anyone can be more open and understanding of gender-variant persons in a workplace environment. Some helpful actions might include

- Speaking the word "transgender" with respect.
- Not using the suffix "ed" at the end of "transgender."
- Ensuring that single stall and/or unisex restroom facilities are available in your workplace.
- Respecting everyone's personal identity along with his or her rights to self-identification and self-labeling.
- Consciously choosing not to make assumptions about someone's gender identity or sexual orientation.
- Not assuming that every transperson is completely knowledgeable or even wants to talk about transgender issues in depth. Allow them to make such decisions for themselves.
- Not assuming that a transperson can speak only about transgender topics or issues. In fact, do not assume that transgender is or is not an issue for someone else at all. It certainly does not have to be a major workplace concern or a problem unless people choose to make it so.

- On organizational forms where gender is requested, draw in a new box labeled "transgender" or "other." Also, ask for a person's gender, not their sex, on company forms. It is time for businesses to start formally recognizing that sex and gender are not the same thing. Companies need to start using personnel forms that offer more gender-inclusive options.

- Make sure that accurate information and resources on transgender topics are readily available for everyone in your organization. Your Human Resources office or a transgender diversity consultant can be helpful in this regard.

- Do not patronize or tokenize persons who happen to be transgender. They are human beings who have human worth, brains, skills, and abilities, so treat them with respect.

- Encourage your organization to include identifiably transgender persons in its marketing/advertising initiatives.

- Try an experiment: spend a day or week purposely avoiding the use of gender-specific pronouns when referring to someone important in your life. (You will probably discover that it is more difficult than you might think.) See what insights you can glean from this experience, then try to apply those insights in every area of your life.

- Learn about your local laws regarding

  ◦ hate crimes
  ◦ name changes
  ◦ changing gender
  ◦ changing sex
  ◦ discrimination against transpersons in the areas of employment, housing, medical care, public facilities, etc.

BECOMING AN AGENT OF POSITIVE WORKPLACE CHANGE

The Rev. Dr. Martin Luther King, Jr., once said, "Injustice anywhere is a threat to justice everywhere." The existence of injustice and unwarranted negativity directed toward transgender people in the workplace is why business organizations need to address that situation for the benefit of all.

Those who are transgender have a distinct responsibility and must be expected to do their part as well. Matt Kailey tells us, "If we don't speak up, if we don't make ourselves visible and let our voices be heard, if we don't come out and let people know who we are, our lives, and our destinies, will continue to be decided for us. We will continue to be discriminated against, receive substandard medical care, lose our jobs and our housing and even our lives."[5] Transgender persons must be honest, courageous, open, verbal, and visible so that all may benefit and learn from their contributions to the world.

Challenging and changing society for the better is a worthy task and a magnificent opportunity. Speaking out and taking action on behalf of transgender persons will increase awareness and improve the situation, but remaining silent and apathetic will do neither.

> *Nightfall does not come at once, and neither does oppression. In both instances, there is a twilight when everything remains seemingly unchanged. And it is in such twilight that we all must be most aware of change in the air—however slight—lest we become unwitting victims of the darkness.*
>
> —Supreme Court Justice William O. Douglas

Admittedly, change is almost never simple or easy for us, either as individuals or as members of an organization. We fear change because we do not know what the outcome will be. We tend to prefer the illusion of stability, for it helps us feel more emotionally comfortable and secure. We are only human, after all, and change always requires giving up something old in order to acquire something new. Change can feel like a death to us: the death of the familiar. But the reality of life is that we cannot become who we want to be by remaining who we are. Life is not meant to be about seeking a perceived sense of safety and security at all costs, but about meeting and overcoming challenges in order to achieve freedom and growth. The true richness and satisfaction of human existence comes from meeting life's tests and surmounting them through individual and/or combined efforts in a worthy cause.

There may be resistance from powerful, fiercely traditionalist "gender enforcers"—but out of that intense struggle for human equality and justice, we will surely see the true greatness of people emerge. In the words of Peter Koestenbaum, "We all have the capacity to be great. Greatness comes with recognizing that your potential is limited only by how you choose, how you use your freedom, how resolute you are, how persistent you are—in short, by your attitude. And we are all free to choose our attitude."[6]

Transgender in the workplace is not a far off, unattainable vision: it is a relevant call to action for today's business leaders who operate boldly and decisively in the here and now. The ways in which you and your organization respond to that call will say a great deal about the business leadership and future success of your company.

In the context of the transgender-in-the-workplace movement, extraordinary new opportunities for successful growth and learning and business achievement are beginning to arise. Each day more people and organizations choose to join in this movement toward a new and brighter future. When they do, they discover that such golden opportunities can help create successful, inclusive workplace cultures that are somehow far greater than the sum of their visible parts. With this noble goal in mind, you and your organization are encouraged to flatly refuse to be anything other than great and remarkable.

LIVING AND WORKING WITH HOPE AND COURAGE

Whether you are transgender or not, you are encouraged to always respect, appreciate, and honor yourself, for as Margaret Wheatley has so profoundly reminded us, when we do so we also offer everyone else their humanity.[7] What greater gift can anyone possibly offer to another?

In the end, we must believe and act in the belief that "truth, acceptance and equality will always find a way to prevail."[8] If you believe in that premise, join transpersons, family members, friends, colleagues, allies, and all people who care about fairness, justice, and equality on a remarkable journey toward creating positive change for transgender individuals in the workplace. When people come together and pool their talents, they are capable of creating genius, power, and unstoppable transformation. Alone, we are limited—but when people unite around a shared idea that is rooted in a just cause, they can accomplish anything. As Lisa M. Hartley says, "We must never give up. We must educate, educate, educate. We must advocate, advocate, advocate. Persistence is the only way to move the cultural paradigm."[9]

Whether you are transgender or not, straight, gay, lesbian, bisexual, or other, come out to the leading edge of social and organizational change where good and extraordinary things are happening within the realm of human understanding and mutual cooperation. Come out to the front of the curve and move away from the pedestrian centers of limited and outmoded Industrial Era thinking. Come out to a place where diverse people are valued for their uniqueness, not viewed as worthless entities, faceless numbers, or part of a giant inhuman machine. Come out and join in the noble pursuit of workplace justice and equality for all people. Come out joyfully into the Age of Values: a sparkling new era for organizations, an amazing moment in history when people are becoming liberated to fully live into their human potential. Come out to the frontier of the human experience, far ahead of the pack and the mundane, to a place where the view of the future is spectacular and the transformative possibilities are so limitless and brilliant that they glitter and sparkle in the light. Choose to be remarkable, and never settle for anything less.

Here at this book's end, it seems appropriate to quote Mara Keisling, executive director of the Washington, D.C.-based National Center for Transgender Equality (NCTE). Keisling is a tireless worker for transgender rights and a champion for the entire trans community. She observes, "We sometimes like to say that transgender people are just ordinary people. I think that misses the point. Unlike most people, we have had to evaluate who we are and who we need to be. We have faced our fears and risked just about everything. By coming out as transgender, we have engaged in a humbling act of courage that would frighten almost anyone. Transgender people are not simply ordinary; we are extraordinary."[10]

No matter what your gender status, try to celebrate each day by living as the whole person that you are capable of being. Choosing to respect and fully include transgender persons as equals can be a meaningful way to begin your—and your organization's—journey of transformative difference.

Cherish and support the people in your life.
Value those around you and invite them in, whether or not you understand them or agree with them.
You will be serving not only your particular [organization] but a higher ideal marked by openness, kindness, and justice.
And that action will prevail over any words that attempt to divide and diminish us.

—Ann Marie DeGroot

APPENDIX 1

Answers to the "So, Whaddya Know?" Quiz

True or False

1. True. As of this writing, there is no definitive explanation for transgender's existence, though evidence increasingly indicates that there may be a biological cause.

2. False. In fact, most persons who identify as transgender do not desire or seek sex/genital reassignment surgery.

3. False. Many organizations with openly transgender workers discover that they are among their best employees.

4. False. Most transgender persons identify as heterosexual.

5. True. Transgender is not a sickness: it is an internal identity and a state of being. No cure is necessary.

6. False. As of this writing, there are no federal statutes that protect the rights of transgender citizens.

7. True. Due to misunderstanding and social stigma connected with the transgender phenomenon, most transpersons keep their gender-variant identity hidden.

8. True. Transgender employees who are permitted to be themselves openly on the job are often among the most creative and hardworking in an organization.

9. False. Transitioning from one gender to another is a complex, usually well-monitored, and very serious initiative that is pursued as a way to more effectively align the transperson's external presentation and appearance with his or her internal identity. It is

not an act of sexual immorality. It is, if anything, an ethical, intelligent choice that allows the transgender individual to become more fully self-actualized.

10. True. Transgender people have always been part of the human family, and always will be.

Multiple Choice

1. a—no; b—yes; c—no; d—yes; e—potentially; f—yes; g—yes, but with an asterisk, since many transpersons reject the term; h—yes, but with an asterisk, since many intersex persons reject the term

2. a—no; b—yes; c—no; d—perhaps, but "b" is a better answer; e—no

3. a—no; b—no; c—no; d—no; e—yes

4. a—no; b—no; c—yes; d—no; e—no

5. a—partially correct; b—partially correct; c—partially correct; d—yes; e—no

APPENDIX 2

Recommended Reading

This is only a brief list of suggested readings on the extremely complex subject of transgender. The list is not intended to be comprehensive, but the books mentioned here can serve as helpful, informative resources.

- Allen, J. J. *The Man in the Red Velvet Dress*. New York: Carol Publishing Group, 1996.
- Bornstein, Kate. *Gender Outlaw: On Men, Women, and the Rest of Us*. New York: Routledge Press, 1996.
- Bornstein, Kate. *My Gender Workbook: How to Become a Real Man, a Real Woman, the Real You, or Something Else Entirely*. New York: Routledge Press, 1997.
- Boyd, Helen. *My Husband Betty: Love, Sex, and Life with a Cross-dresser*. New York: Thunder's Mouth Press, 2003.
- Boyd, Helen. *She's Not the Man I Married: My Life with a Transgender Husband*. Emeryville, CA: Seal Press, 2007.
- Boylan, Jennifer Finney. *She's Not There: A Life in Two Genders*. New York: Broadway Books, 2002.
- Brown, Mildred L., and Chloe Ann Rounsley. *True Selves: Understanding Transsexualism—For Families, Friends, Co-workers, and Helping Professionals*. San Francisco, CA: Jossey-Bass, Inc., 1996.
- Bullough, Vern, and Bonnie Bullough. *Cross Dressing, Sex, and Gender*. Philadelphia, PA: University of Pennsylvania Press, 1993.

- Cole, Dana. *The Employer's Guide to Gender Transition*. Wayland, MA: International Foundation for Gender Identification, 1992.
- Currah, Paisley, Richard M. Juang, and Shannon Price Minter, eds. *Transgender Rights*. Minneapolis, MN: University of Minnesota Press, 2006.
- Denny, Dallas. *Identity Management in Transsexualism*. King of Prussia, PA: Creative Design Services, 1994.
- Devor, Holly. *FTM: Female to Male Transsexuals in Society*. Bloomington, IN: University Press, 1997.
- Dreger, Alice Domurat, ed. *Intersex in the Age of Ethics (Ethics in Clinical Medicine Studies)*. Hagerstown, MD: University Publishing Group, 1999.
- Ettner, Randi. *Confessions of a Gender Defender: A Psychologist's Reflections on Life among the Transgendered*. Evanston, IL: Chicago Spectrum, 1996.
- Fausto-Sterling, Anne. *Myths of Gender: Biological Theories about Women and Men*. New York: Basic Books, 1992.
- Feinberg, Leslie. *Stone Butch Blues*. Ithaca, NY: Firebrand Books, 1993.
- Feinberg, Leslie. *Trans Liberation: Beyond Pink or Blue*. Boston, MA: Beacon Press, 1998.
- Feinberg, Leslie. *Transgender Warriors: Making History from Joan of Arc to RuPaul*. Boston, MA: Beacon Press, 1996.
- Garber, Marjorie. *Vested Interests: Cross-Dressing and Cultural Anxiety*. New York: Routledge Press, 1997.
- Gershick, Lori B. *Transgender Voices: Beyond Women and Men*. Lebanon, N.H.: University Press of New England, 2008.
- Heath, Rachel Ann. *The Praeger Handbook of Transsexuality: Changing Gender to Match Mindset*. Westport, CT: Praeger Publishers, 2006.
- Kirk, Sheila, and Martine Rothblatt. *Medical, Legal & Workplace Issues for the Transsexual*. Blawnox, PA: Together Lifeworks, 1995.
- MacKenzie, Gordene Olga. *Transgender Nation*. Bowling Green, OH: Bowling Green State University Press, 1994.
- Meyerowitz, Joanne. *How Sex Changed: A History of Transsexuality in the United States*. Cambridge, MA: Harvard University Press, 2002.

- Namaste, Viviane K. *Invisible Lives: The Erasure of Transsexual and Transgendered People*. Chicago, IL: University of Chicago Press, 2000.
- Rubin, Henry. *Self-Made Men: Identity and Embodiment among Transsexual Men*. Nashville, TN: Vanderbilt University Press, 2003.
- Rudd, Peggy J. *Crossdressing with Dignity: The Case for Transcending Gender Lines*. Katy, TX: PM Publishers, 1990.
- Rudd, Peggy J. *My Husband Wears My Clothes*. Katy, TX: PM Publishers, 1990.
- Walworth, Janis. *Transsexual Workers: An Employer's Guide*. Los Angeles, CA: Center for Gender Sanity, 1998.
- Weiss, Jillian Todd. *Transgender Workplace Diversity: Policy Tools, Training Issues and Communication Strategies for HR and Legal Professionals* (Charleston, SC: BookSurge Publishing, 2007).

APPENDIX 3

Suggested Web sites

This is a (very) brief list of potentially helpful Web sites that deal with transgender subjects. There are many other sites online that may be useful as well, but these should certainly be able to get you started. A search engine such as Google or Yahoo! can be an excellent place to begin your journey of discovery. Try typing in "transgender resources" and see what comes up.

- Vanessa Sheridan—http://www.vanessasheridan.com
- International Foundation for Gender Education—http://www.ifge.org
- Intersex Society of North America—http://www.isna.org
- National Center for Transgender Equality (NCTE)—http://www.nctequality.org
- Transgender at Work—http://www.tgender.net/taw
- Center for Gender Sanity—http://www.gendersanity.com/index.shtml
- Transworkplace (Transgender Workplace Diversity Network)—http://www.transworkplace.ning.com
- FTMInternational (FTMI)—http://www.ftmi.org
- Human Rights Campaign Foundation: Workplace Issues—http://www.hrc.org/worknet
- Gender Education and Advocacy (GEA)—http://www.gender.org
- Transgender Employment Links—http://www.gendersanity.com/resources.shtml

- Bodies Like Ours—http://www.bodieslikeours.org/forums
- OutFront Minnesota, Fairness in the Workplace: Transgender Minnesotans—http://www.outfront.org/library/issues/trans-workplace
- Gender Public Advocacy Coalition (GenderPAC)—http://www.gpac.org
- Transgender Law and Policy Institute—http://www.transgenderlaw.org
- Our Transgender Children, sponsored by the Transgender Network of Parents, Families and Friends of Lesbians and Gays (PFLAG)—http://community.pflag.org/Page.aspx?pid=380

APPENDIX 4

XYZ Company: Guiding Principles, Procedures, and Best Practices for Transsexual Employee Transitions in the Workplace

Contents

- General Information
  - An Organizational Guide to Transsexual Employee Transitions
  - XYZ Company's Approach to Issues of Transsexuality and Workplace Transitions
  - Helpful Sources of Information
  - Transgender-Related Terms and Definitions
  - Transsexualism and Transitions: An Overview
  - Transsexual Transitions: Frequently Asked Questions

- Information for Transitioning Employees
  - A Checklist for Transsexual Employees Who Desire to Transition on the Job
  - For the Transitioning Employee: Questions and Answers

- Information for Coworkers of Transitioning Employees
  - For Coworkers: Questions and Answers

- Information for Managers
  - For Managers: Information about Transsexual Employees and Workplace Transitions

AN ORGANIZATIONAL GUIDE TO TRANSSEXUAL EMPLOYEE TRANSITIONS

In today's modern culture, with its astonishing advances in medical knowledge and technology, thousands of members of society have changed their physical sex. More are in the process of doing so. Until relatively recently, such persons were advised to quit their jobs, find other employment elsewhere, and start over as members of the opposite sex.

Increasingly, however, transsexual employees are choosing to visibly remain on the job while they transition from male to female or from female to male. Transgender is an area of emerging concern and interest to employers, and growing numbers of employers are supportive of the unique workplace situation that confronts transgender workers. These organizational leaders wisely recognize the intrinsic value of a diverse and pluralistic workforce that values the skills, talents, and contributions of every employee, regardless of gender identity or sexual orientation.

According to the Human Rights Campaign, an organization that carefully tracks workplace diversity issues, over 175 *Fortune* 500 companies have adopted employee policies that protect individual rights to gender identity and/or gender expression. This is no trendy, flavor-of-the-month business topic: transgender is the last great human rights issue to be addressed in the workplace.

WHY A GUIDE LIKE THIS?

XYZ Company is fully committed to protecting the worth and dignity of every employee, stakeholder, and customer. For this reason, we have established a nondiscrimination policy that includes gender identity and gender expression. Taking such a step is an indicator of this organization's leadership in our industry and within the local and national community. It is good for business and it is the right thing to do.

Developing and implementing workplace strategies that prohibit discrimination against transgender employees is a significant component of our overall diversity initiative. Taking this action will enhance our company's reputation while increasing job satisfaction, improving teamwork, and boosting employee morale.

When a gender identity Equal Employment Opportunity (EEO)/ nondiscrimination policy like ours is established, specific guiding principles and procedures for successfully implementing that policy also become necessary in order to avoid potential confusion or misunderstanding within the organization.

Since transsexuality and gender transitions are often new and/or mysterious issues for many in our society, and since workplace transitions by transsexual employees directly influence our organization, there is an understandable need to articulate XYZ Company's guidelines and expectations regarding these situations. We must be clear about how our company will deal with transgender issues as they affect the workplace environment.

That is why this document exists: to help our people become more aware of XYZ Company's organizational guiding principles and procedures for dealing with transsexual transitions on the job. The goal of this Guide is to present answers to questions, provide a variety of resources, and offer helpful information for managers, coworkers, and transitioning employees to make workplace transitions as smooth and productive as possible.

WHAT WE WANT TO ACHIEVE

We want to help everyone at XYZ Company—including executives, middle management, frontline employees, sales and marketing teams, as well as transsexual/transitioning employees—move forward in a healthy, respectful, nonjudgmental, and productive manner that will enhance our overall organizational culture and improve our business. Our company takes these issues seriously, and we fully expect each employee to do the same.

If you take nothing else away from this Guide, we hope you will remember this: in business or in life, it is always a wise policy to treat people—even those whom you may not understand or with whom you may not agree—the way you would want to be treated. The Golden Rule still works.

We will continuously strive to make XYZ Company an even better place to work. This Guide is a part of that ongoing effort toward improvement. If you have questions or concerns about the content and/ or interpretation of the information contained in the Guide, please check with XYZ Company's Human Resources department.

XYZ COMPANY'S APPROACH
TO ISSUES OF TRANSSEXUALITY
AND WORKPLACE TRANSITIONS

You should be aware that XYZ Company's EEO policy prohibits discrimination based upon gender identity or expression. Please note that harassment of an employee based on gender identity or expression is also prohibited by company policy.

Workplace policies are not intended to alter people's personal beliefs or infringe on their thoughts, but exist solely to prevent inappropriate and/or nonproductive workplace behavior. XYZ Company's antidiscrimination policies are designed to guard the human rights, dignity, and privacy of transgender employees along with those of every other employee, transgender or not. This means it is unacceptable to fire, refuse to hire, evict, deny service to, or in other ways discriminate against a person because he or she is or may be perceived as being transgender.

Ensuring Fairness

Why is it important to have and enforce such a policy in the workplace? In a nutshell, it is because the only issue that should really matter is whether a person can do the job or not. Their biological sex should not matter. Their sexual orientation should not matter. Their race, religion, or age should not matter. Their gender identity should not be a factor, nor should their form of gender expression. What is important is doing the work and conducting our business in a professional manner that always strives for excellence.

XYZ Company's EEO policy exists to guarantee fairness and equality for every employee throughout our entire organization. Fairness for one category of employee further establishes and reinforces an organizational culture of fairness for every other category of employee. Everyone wins and our organization is elevated when all of our people are treated justly, respectfully, and equitably.

How This Guide Can Help

Based on these important principles, we believe it is vital to have a specific set of guidelines and procedures available to help managers, gender transitioning employees, and other employees better understand their rights and responsibilities on the job. Since transsexual transition is admittedly a little known and often misunderstood phenomenon in our society, having this information readily available will create a useful resource and smooth the way for everyone who is directly or indirectly involved with a XYZ Company employee's gender transition at work.

It is understandable that most people will have no experience in dealing with a transsexual person's transition. Some people may even be fearful of transgender persons, usually because they do not know much about them. We often have a tendency to fear what we do not understand, but the antidote for such fears is knowledge and awareness. Once people become personally familiar with a situation, fear tends to dissipate quickly because they discover that there was really nothing to fear in the first place. We do not have to be afraid of benign human difference—in fact, we should welcome it as an opportunity to learn more about the amazing and inherent possibilities that exist within humankind.

As we have said, most individuals will have little or no frame of reference to help them deal with a unique circumstance like a transsexual transition. That is to be expected. Because this is so, a basic understanding of what is involved can be very useful. This Guide was created to help provide such an understanding.

Transgender issues can be extremely complex. There are unique and distinctive elements of human behavior, psychological and emotional factors, physical/biological/genetic/hormonal issues, and other multifaceted elements that may come together to create a gender-variant identity within an individual. To help provide a knowledge framework for this remarkable complexity, this Guide will offer some basic information about transsexuality and transitioning.

HELPFUL SOURCES OF INFORMATION

You will probably have some questions. That is a natural and expected response to a unique situation like transsexual transitioning on the job. In order to help you, we want to provide as many useful and practical sources of information as possible.

There are several existing resources for any XYZ Company employee who wants to learn more in general about transsexual transitions on the job:

- Within XYZ Company itself, general information resources and support are available through the company's Employee Assistance Program at 1-800-xxx-xxxx.
- Other helpful information about transgender in the workplace is also available online at http://www.vanessasheridan.com and at http://www.hrc.org.
- Concerns related to benefits, medical questions, insurance, or other relevant workplace issues should be directed to the company's Human Resources department.

If you are an employee who is considering, planning to, or already involved in the process of a gender transition at work, you should

- Contact your manager or Human Resources Generalist immediately to begin discussions of your personal situation, your concerns, and what is needed to help with workplace issues. It is safe (and responsible) for you to do this, and you will not be punished or retaliated against in any way.
- For general questions or concerns, you should research the programs, phone numbers, and/or Web sites listed above.
- For questions about medical benefits to which you may be entitled, contact your health benefits provider. If you do not know that contact number, check with the Human Resources department.

TRANSGENDER-RELATED TERMS
AND DEFINITIONS[1]

Cross-dresser: An individual who presents or dresses in the clothing that is characteristic of the opposite sex. This is usually done as a means of personal gender expression and is not necessarily an indication of transsexual desire. In fact, most cross-dressers are not interested in changing their sex or transitioning and do not consider themselves to be transsexual. Also, most cross-dressers appear to be heterosexual in terms of their orientation.

Gender: A way of perceiving appearance, dress, and behavior as either masculine or feminine. The term is often used inaccurately as a synonym for sex. We tend to associate gender—e.g., masculine and feminine meanings—with features that may include

- physical sex or genitals;
- other physical characteristics (for instance, height, weight, and body hair);
- sexual orientation (gay men are often considered more feminine than their heterosexual counterparts, and lesbian women more masculine);
- behavior or dress (a man who cries may be considered unmanly by some, or a woman who wears short hair and a suit coat may be considered unfeminine).

Gender Expression: Manifesting a feeling of being masculine or feminine through clothing, behavior, or grooming. This can include dress, posture, hair style, jewelry, vocal inflection, and so on.

Gender Identity: An inner sense of being either male or female. Though they may occasionally intersect or overlap, gender identity is *not* the same thing as sexual orientation. It is important to keep these distinctions clear.

Gender Stereotypes: Social expectations and/or mental templates for how each sex should look, act, or dress.

Gender Stereotyping: Enforcing conformity to certain expectations of how an individual should look, act, or dress.

Intersexuality: A biological condition that occurs when a person's sexual or reproductive organs (or secondary sexual characteristics) do not necessarily match his or her chromosomal makeup or external appearance.

Sex: An individual's legal assignment at birth as either male or female. Also, biological sex, as evidenced by chromosomes, body type, genitalia, and other physical characteristics.

Sexual Orientation: The direction of one's sexual interest toward members of the same, opposite, or both sexes. In short, sexual orientation is about whom one is attracted to. (And yes, we know you should never use a preposition to end a sentence with.) Sexual orientation and gender identity are *not* the same.

Transgender: An umbrella term for people whose gender identity, characteristics, or expression does not necessarily conform to that associated with their sex. It includes transsexuals, who transition from male to female or female to male, as well as intersexuals and people who dress in another gender's clothing, i.e., cross-dressers, and others who find themselves in different places along the gender spectrum.

Transsexual: A person who identifies with the roles, expectations, and expressions more commonly associated with a sex that differs from the one he or she was assigned at birth. A transsexual often seeks to change his or her physical characteristics and manner of gender expression for greater happiness, personal fulfillment, and to satisfy the social requirements for membership in another gender (i.e., transition). This may or may not include hormone therapy and eventual sex reassignment surgery. Upon transitioning, transsexuals may refer to themselves as male-to-female (MtoF) or female-to-male (FtoM) as a way of acknowledging that their change in appearance is designed to match their internal gender identity. *A transsexual status has no direct or predictable connection to their sexual orientation.*

Transition:

- In medical terms, transition involves the various steps that a transsexual person takes to express and live into their internal gender identity more fully. Most transsexual people are involved with a program of medical care and supervision in their transition. This process usually consists of diagnostic assessments, psychotherapy, the "real life test," hormonal therapy, and surgical therapy. Some transsexual people may undergo some type of surgery as part of their transition but, for any number of reasons, only a small percentage of transsexuals actually go through genital reconstructive surgery. Some transsexual persons do not access any medical care and simply transition through the way they express their gender and present themselves to the world.

• In business terms, transition in the workplace involves a series of strategic steps that are designed to help the transsexual worker move smoothly into their new gender while remaining on the job. Therefore, the transition process also affects and involves the transsexual worker's organization, from management through coworkers. For these reasons, it is important to have specific policies, guidelines, and procedures in place to make a workplace transition as easy and non-interruptive as possible for all concerned.

TRANSSEXUALISM AND TRANSITIONS:
AN OVERVIEW

The information in this section is in no way intended to be a complete or comprehensive examination of transsexualism or of the transition process. However, you should be able to gain at least a basic understanding of some of the elements that are involved in such complex human situations.

WHAT IS A TRANSSEXUAL?

Transsexuals are people who identify with the roles, expectations, and expressions more commonly associated with a sex different than the one he or she was assigned at birth.

The term *transsexual* is used to describe an apparently biologically normal individual who has an overwhelming desire to be identified and/or live their life as a member of the opposite sex. Increasingly, such individuals seek chemical (hormone) therapy and sexual reassignment surgery to conform their body to that of the opposite biological sex.

A dictionary definition of *transsexual* is "a person who has a psychological urge to belong to the opposite sex and to live as a member of the opposite sex and who may be motivated by the urge to acquire the necessary physical appearance (as by surgery or hormone use) or to adopt the social role typical of the opposite sex."[2]

CAUSES OF TRANSSEXUALISM

As you read this, many people are devoting their lives to exploring the potential causes of transsexualism. To date, however, there are no specific, indisputable, and/or scientifically proven genetic or organic explanations for the existence of transsexualism.

From a current research perspective, the presence of transsexualism or a transsexual orientation in an individual appears to be strongly associated with the neurodevelopment of the brain, more specifically the hypothalamus area.

Without going into extensive medical detail, it is now generally accepted by most reputable professionals in the field that transsexualism stems from a physiological cause and is in no way a mental illness, perversion, moral failing, or "lifestyle choice." The consensus of opinion is that a person's gender identity is determined before birth, *en utero*, and is immutable thereafter. Transsexuals simply desire to align their physical bodies with their internal gender identity in order to achieve greater happiness and personal fulfillment.

DEALING WITH BEING A TRANSSEXUAL

Transsexuals may deal with their personal situations in different ways. As we will discover, some of those ways appear to be more helpful than others.

- For example, at some point in their lives, most transsexuals go through a form of denial and try to convince themselves that they are not transsexual, or that they will "grow out of it," or that they should "ignore it and it will go away." However, denial does not usually work for long. Unfortunately, there is considerable evidence to indicate that transsexuals who fail to escape this stage frequently commit suicide. Some figures suggest that as many as 30 percent of transsexuals are not diagnosed and treated soon enough to prevent them from taking their own lives. Obviously, repression/denial is not the way to go. (We at XYZ Company certainly do not want our transsexual team members committing suicide, inflicting bodily harm on themselves, or taking other destructive actions that can potentially be avoided.)

- Another way of dealing with transsexualism is to simply take no action and to consciously choose to live with the pain and discomfort of an inappropriate body and gender role. Since a core need is not being met, this path is nearly always found to be unsatisfactory for the true transsexual.

- For transsexuals, the most pressing need usually requires altering their gender role and living in accordance with their internally recognized gender identity. For a male-to-female transsexual, this means living completely as a woman. For a female-to-male transsexual, it obviously means living completely as a man. This approach is taken as a step in a journey that may eventually lead to hormonal therapy and/or surgical gender reassignment.

- Transsexual persons may benefit from a comprehensive, medically supervised strategy that includes, among other things, a program of hormones and corrective surgery to achieve a more congruent realignment of the physical body with the internal gender identity. These efforts are usually accompanied by well-integrated psychological help designed to support the individual and assist in his or her adaptation to the appropriate social role.

WHAT IS INVOLVED IN TRANSITIONING?

Transsexual persons who seek sexual reassignment are usually placed into a medical/psychological program that is conducted under the auspices of the World Professional Association for Transgender Health Standards of Care (SOC).

The SOC are intended to provide flexible directions for the humane and positive treatment of transsexual individuals. The general goal is to provide lasting personal comfort with the gendered self in order to maximize overall psychological well-being and self-fulfillment. The SOC comprise a comprehensive and medically centered approach to matters of transsexuality and/or eventual sex reassignment, including all aspects of treatment directed toward such reassignment.

For most transsexuals, a full transition will probably take several years and many thousands of dollars. Such a transition may involve extensive medical costs, counseling and/or psychotherapy, a variety of surgical procedures, the "real life test" (wherein a person undergoing a gender change is required to live in the desired gender role for one to two years before being recognized as ready to undergo sexual reassignment surgery), and other medically supervised procedures/requirements.

A supervised medical program for transsexual persons will usually involve a combination of any or all of the following:

A. Diagnostic assessment
B. Psychotherapy
C. Real life experience
D. Hormonal therapy
E. Surgical therapy

Generally speaking, persons who enter transition will begin with a diagnostic assessment, followed by extensive sessions of psychotherapy. Many questions are addressed in the therapeutic setting, and these questions are designed to gather critical information such as the person's true motivation for pursuing transition. (The goal of such questions is to differentiate between persons who are indeed transsexual and those who demonstrate other types of gender-based disorders.) The individual is diagnosed in accordance with the DSM-IV, and further treatment plans are based upon this initial diagnosis.

If the therapist or endocrinologist agrees to prescribe them, the transsexual may begin taking appropriate doses of hormones to help move the transition process along. Female-to-male transsexuals may also begin electrolysis to remove unwanted facial or body hair.

The next step is usually a period of one to two years that involve cross-living while continuing with hormone therapy. The transsexual actually lives 24 hours a day in the gender of choice, which is why this period is called the "real life test." During this time, the individual must demonstrate stability and prove functional ability, become self-supporting, and be socially active.

At the end of the designated cross-living period, some initial surgeries can be the next step in the transition process. However, any such surgeries must be approved by the appropriate medical authorities. For example, an orchidectomy (i.e., removing the sex glands of a male) may be performed for male-to-female transsexuals. Implants or breast augmentation and other optional nongenital surgical sex reassignment procedures may be performed at this time as well.

For female-to-male transsexuals, mastectomy (i.e., removing the breasts) and hysterectomy (i.e., removing the uterus) surgeries usually occur after one year of cross-living. Most female-to-male transsexuals consult a plastic surgeon for the mastectomy and a gynecologist for the hysterectomy.

Some female-to-male transsexuals will desire the creation of a penis. This operation is called phalloplasty (i.e., implanting the male sex organ). Some female-to-males who have been on androgen for a while tend to get so much clitoral enlargement that they may choose not to have that phalloplasty at all.

At this point, a final psychological evaluation takes place before the complete sexual reassignment surgery will be decided. Two written evaluations are required by at least two clinical behavioral scientists, one of which must be a doctoral level clinical behavioral scientist and one of whom has known the patient in a professional relationship for at least six months, before approval is given for surgery.

Finally, the sexual reassignment surgery takes place.

After completion of the surgery, postoperative or follow-up care for a period of at least three months is required. However, six months are generally recommended. This is a period of recovery which is considered necessary for immediate psychological and social readjustment.

As we can readily see, transsexual transitions are not something to be entered into or taken lightly. There is much to consider, and there are many obstacles to be overcome before a transsexual can be fully transitioned. The scope, complexity, and intensity of this remarkable human experience are deserving of respect. Transsexual persons who undergo such rigorous undertakings should be supported, and XYZ Company has committed to doing exactly that for its transsexual employees who choose to transition.

TRANSSEXUAL TRANSITIONS: FREQUENTLY ASKED QUESTIONS

1. **What language is in XYZ Company's official EEO policy that protects transgender employees?** [Hopefully, the answer to this question will be "Gender identity, characteristics, or expression."] These factors do not affect the company's decisions about any aspect of a person's employment or decisions about applicants for employment. A supportive workplace transsexual transition policy goes beyond adding the words "gender identity, characteristics, or expression" to our EEO policy. In addition, it is also necessary to address issues like communication to management and coworkers, updating of employee records to reflect the new name and gender, organizational dress codes, and even use of the restroom. It is the responsibility of managers to ensure a work environment free from all forms of discrimination and harassment.

2. **What laws are in place to protect transgender workers?** No current federal laws exist to directly protect transgender employees. "However, courts have increasingly recognized that workplace discrimination based on the failure to conform to sex stereotypes (that is, discrimination against a woman who is considered too masculine or a man who is considered too feminine) is prohibited by Title VII, the federal workplace sex discrimination law."[3]

   - [Check your state laws to see if there are statutes pertaining to this issue.]
   - Approximately a dozen states have now passed antidiscrimination laws to protect transgender persons in the area of employment. This is obviously a growing societal and business trend that bodes well for the future of all transgender workers.

3. **If a transsexual employee comes to HR and/or management and discloses a need to transition to the opposite gender, how will it be handled?** The situation should always be addressed with great care and with respect to the employee, with education and HR support to the personnel in the area, and with the objective of enabling a smooth and dignified transition.

   - The company will be supportive of the employee and of the employee's desire for transition. Working together, management and HR will learn about and review the issues. They will then determine how best to proceed. Within Human Resources, the staff member's HR generalist and their Employee Relations manager would provide

206

Appendix 4

assistance in working with the employee and his or her department/team/work group.

- A plan will be created for an announcement as well as an initial date for beginning the employee's transition on the job. The announcement of the employee's transition should be made in person by management to the employee's work group. It will be made clear at that time that the transsexual employee has the full support of management, and that XYZ Company's policy is to treat the transitioning employee just like anybody else—with all the respect and dignity befitting any XYZ Company worker.

- On the designated day of transition, the transitioning employee reports to work in the new gender role. A new badge (with new photo and new name, if necessary) is issued on the first day. Also, all personnel records pertaining to the transitioning employee are updated as necessary (e.g., name changes and sex or gender designations).

- The transitioning employee should use the restroom appropriate to his or her new gender. However, the employee may be restricted by HR and instructed to use certain designated restrooms during the transition period that historically has lasted from one to three months. Since there may potentially be concerns from other employees about restroom use, discussions and dialogue on this delicate issue should be held prior to the transsexual employee's designated date of transition. Management's expectations regarding restroom use should be made very clear to everyone concerned so there will be no confusion about the issue.

4. **Does XYZ Company's EEO policy extend to other gender-variant employees, such as feminine men, masculine women, or cross-dressers?** Yes. This is specifically covered by the company policy's "gender expression" language. Issues relative to other and/or non-transsexual persons who may still be gender variant may be addressed in a separate "Guide to (Non-Transsexual) Transgender Issues in the Workplace."

5. **What about changes in dress, accessories, cosmetics, hairstyle, or other personal appearance concerns?** Organizations have the right to regulate employee appearance and behavior in the workplace for reasonable business purposes. XYZ Company already has a dress code policy in place, and regardless of gender status, every employee's individual appearance remains subject to that policy. Transsexual employees are expected to dress consistently so as to be congruent with their gender identity and are required to comply with the same standards of dress, clothing, and general appearance that apply to all other employees in the workplace and/or in

similar work situations. Regardless of gender identity, every XYZ Company employee is expected to dress and present themselves in a competent, professional manner at all times while on the job or when representing XYZ Company in public.

6. **How will the restroom issue be handled during a transsexual employee's transition?** This can be the most sensitive and potentially volatile issue to be addressed, but it can almost always be handled successfully if everyone will approach this topic in a calm, sensible, and professional manner.

- An excellent and eminently practical rule of thumb is that a person should use the restroom appropriate for the gender in which he or she is presenting at that time.
- While a transitioning employee certainly has a right to restroom access, so do their coworkers. Concerns of safety, respect, personal dignity, and individual needs for everyone must be considered. Therefore, it is incumbent upon the transitioning employee, his or her manager, and the HR generalist to strategically develop a workable system for restroom use that will meet the transsexual employee's personal needs while simultaneously respecting the needs and concerns of others.
- The agreed-upon restroom system should *not* be revealed to coworkers until the day of the transitioning employee's disclosure. At that time, the restroom guidelines should be explained only by the manager—*not* by the transitioning employee. This way everyone will know that the restroom issue has already been considered by management and that management is genuinely concerned about the rights of all employees. Explaining the restroom strategy in this way will also subtly and strategically underscore management's firm support of the transitioning employee.
- Questions and/or concerns from coworkers may arise with regard to the restroom issue. The manager should explain, as comprehensively as possible, why this particular restroom strategy has been chosen. People should be permitted to raise questions and share their concerns as long as they are voiced respectfully, but management must make it very clear that the company's decisions about the restroom system are to be honored by everyone. It should be emphasized, too, that this is not about willfully imposing a negative situation on anyone; instead, it is an honest effort to deal successfully with a delicate (but certainly not insurmountable) issue and to treat all employees, transgender and non-transgender alike, with dignity and respect.

A CHECKLIST FOR TRANSSEXUAL EMPLOYEES WHO DESIRE TO TRANSITION ON THE JOB

As is almost always the case with any new and/or complex workplace issue, clarity of communication will be essential. You—the transsexual employee—must do your best to communicate clearly with your manager, your HR generalist, and any other key associates as you prepare to transition. Without continuous and clear communication your transition experience can quickly become a nightmare for both you and the company. No one wants that to happen, so be sure to talk frequently with the appropriate people as you begin this part of your journey.

After you have worked strategically with management and HR to prepare for your transition on the job, and once the announcement about your transition has been publicly announced, you will probably have many opportunities to dialogue with your coworkers and other team members. Keep in mind that although you may have been dealing with your transsexual issue for many years, all of this will be new to them. Patience and a sense of humor are qualities that will serve you well during this initial period.

After some time has passed (probably a few weeks at most), the early curiosity factor will have worn off and most people will simply accept you as the person you present yourself to be. If you have prepared yourself and planned appropriately for success, you should have a fulfilling and rewarding experience as you transition to your new gender role.

PREPARATION IN ADVANCE

1. Contact the lesbian/gay employee resource group at XYZ Company. Hopefully, this group will be receptive to and supportive of your situation. Also, the group may have someone who can advise you, and may know people in HR or other parts of the company who can also support you in your transition.

2. Talk to your HR generalist and share your intent to transition. HR is an important resource and should be an ally for your transition.

3. Talk to your manager and share your intent to transition. This conversation should take place in a face-to-face, one-on-one meeting where you can be honest, candid, and forthright about your situation. If you are uncomfortable or fearful of your manager's potential reaction, you may find it helpful to include one or two allies from HR or your employee resource group in the

meeting. Note: this step is critical and should never be skipped under any circumstances. You must not surprise your manager by transitioning without an advance agreement. That would be ill-advised and would almost guarantee failure, so make sure to bring your manager into the loop as early as possible. He or she will need to be part of the planning process. Frankly, you will need your manager as an ally if you want to have a successful transition on the job.

4. Your manager will probably want to share your situation with a small portion of your management chain. This is to be expected and should be welcomed by you. It is an opportunity for you to learn more about who is on your side and who will be supportive of you during your transition.

5. Your management team and others involved in the planning should become familiar with educational resources, including XYZ Company's EEO policy and this Guide on the subject. You should ask if you can help them in any way.

6. Strategically plan for your transition:

   - Involve a local transgender expert (your therapist, for example, or an expert transgender consultant).
   - If necessary, involve other appropriate individuals. Examples of persons who may need to be involved are the Employee Assistance Program, Security, and the HR department.
   - Whatever you do, make sure you have some kind of support group available. This may potentially include friends, family, and medical/psychological professionals. You will want to be supported emotionally and psychologically as you enter this new phase of your personal journey.
   - Establish a reasonable time line for your transition, including the date for an announcement to your work group.
   - Plan solutions to the usual issues that accompany such events (e.g., restroom, new name, other personal records, and e-mail accounts).
   - Involve all the behind-the-scenes people in the planning process to ensure they are in agreement with the plan and that there are no surprises.

THE DAY OF THE ANNOUNCEMENT

1. Hold a department meeting, or include your transition news in an already-scheduled face-to-face meeting. It is permissible to

teleconference with any nonlocal people. Everyone with whom you interact often at work should be there if at all possible. *Do not do this by e-mail!* It is acceptable to have a written paper letter to be distributed in conjunction with the face-to-face meeting.

2. The manager of your work group (the department head, for example)—*not you*—should make the announcement about your transition. It is important, significant, and symbolic for the highest level manager in the group to demonstrate and model the company's support. The manager should

   • Make it clear that the person transitioning is a valuable employee of the organization and has management's full support in making this transition.

   • Briefly explain XYZ Company's EEO policy, company expectations, and recommendations.

   • Emphasize that on a designated upcoming date, the employee will be recognized by the company as a woman (or man, depending on the circumstances) and should be called by the new name and new pronouns only.

     ◦ A note on pronouns: if someone is unsure or uncertain about which pronouns to use when referring to a transsexual/transitioning individual, it is appropriate for them to respectfully ask the transsexual person's name as well as which pronouns he or she prefers. Generally speaking, it is considered insensitive and/or rude to refer to someone by incorrect pronouns once you have established which set of pronouns he or she prefers. (Calling a woman "he" or "him" is discourteous if you have established that the person is indeed presenting as a woman. By the same token, referring to a man as "she" or "her" is equally ill-mannered. Respect for others should always be the primary focus in any conversation.)

   • Answer people's questions honestly and candidly, and emphasize that this is "no big deal." The work of the organization will continue as before, and getting the job done should be everyone's primary focus.

AFTER THE TRANSITION ANNOUNCEMENT

1. Suggest some general education on the subject for the other employees. Informational transgender workshops, seminars, and other training opportunities should be discussed and considered. You (the transitioning employee) should choose whether to

be present at these educational/training events, depending on your comfort level. If you agree, coworkers may be invited to ask questions and/or engage in dialogue with you about your workplace transition.

2. Make arrangements with the Payroll Department and with your bank to ensure that payroll checks in your new name can be deposited in your existing account. This may potentially be as simple as adding a new signature to the bank card.

TRANSITION DAY

On the day of your transition, your manager should take the following steps, just as he or she would probably do for any new or transferred employee:

1. Issue a new company identification badge with the new name and photo as necessary.
2. Arrange for a new name tag on your door/desk/cubicle.
3. Update any organizational charts, mailing lists, and other references to the old name.
4. Issue paperwork for the HR employee database, to be effective on the day of transition, to change the following:

   - New name.
   - Change the gender marker ("M" or "F").
   - Computer and account IDs may need to be changed if the old ID is inappropriate.
   - Update the e-mail address if it contains the old name.

5. Address restroom use and communicate the decision, as planned earlier. The suggested recommendation (unless prohibited by local law) is to use the restroom corresponding to the gender being presented (e.g., use the women's restroom starting the first day of presenting as a woman; do *not* go back and forth between the men's room and the women's room). If someone objects, which may potentially happen, they should be heard respectfully and then informed that this valued employee has the same rights to the restroom as all other employees.
6. If any restrictions have been placed on restroom usage, a date should be planned to revisit those restrictions. Two months after the transition is usually about right for this meeting.

7. The first few hours on the first day of transition will probably involve many new introductions. It is especially helpful if any informal social groups are inclusive, especially those relevant to the new gender. If at all possible, the manager should plan to spend time with you on the first day to make introductions, support you, ensure respectful and inclusive treatment, and see that work returns to normal as quickly as possible.

8. You will be talked about and probably stared at by some people, especially during the first few hours and days. Expect it, and do not let it throw you. It is natural for people to want to be curious about something that is so new and different.

   • Keep in mind, though, that you are not a monkey in a zoo and you are not there to entertain the troops. You deserve to be treated respectfully, even if some people are inquisitive.

   • Much of the attitude of others will be determined by your own responses and actions during this time; if you behave in a dignified manner and act as though you deserve respect, you will almost certainly receive it.

   • The novelty will wear off soon enough and things will return to normal, which means getting on with the actual business of doing business. Over time, as people get to know you and become used to seeing you in your new gender role, you will become old news.

FOR THE TRANSITIONING EMPLOYEE: QUESTIONS AND ANSWERS

1. Is there medical coverage available for the special needs of a transsexual/transitioning employee? Transsexual employees should contact their health benefits provider. If they do not know that contact number, check with the HR department.

2. Are hormones and/or doctor visits for lab work in support of hormones for transsexual/transitioning employees covered under XYZ Company's medical coverage? What about concerns such as mental health coverage for Gender Identity Disorder diagnosis, drugs, and electrolysis? Again, transsexual/transitioning employees should contact their health benefits provider or the HR department for information about these issues.

3. How will my time away from work for medical procedures associated with my gender transition be handled? XYZ Company's standard leave and paid time off policies will apply. For more information, call the HR department.

4. Can I work in another position or location at XYZ Company while I undergo my gender transition? An important part of your transition at work involves sharing your personal situation with your manager and HR generalist. Working with you, they will explore opportunities and alternatives to accommodate your needs as the organization's business realities dictate. They will explain their decision and, if they are unable to accommodate your request to work in another position or location, will do their best to support you in other ways. You have specific needs, to be sure, and those needs deserve to be respected and carefully considered. However, as a XYZ Company employee you must also realize that sometimes business realities may not permit every request to be granted.

5. How do I go about introducing changes in my dress, accessories, hairstyle, or other personal appearance elements? It is your responsibility to decide when the visible transition will begin and how you will choose to share it with others. However, keep in mind that no matter what, as an employee you are still subject to and must comply with XYZ Company's dress code policy.

FOR COWORKERS: QUESTIONS AND ANSWERS

As the coworker of a transitioning employee at XYZ Company, you have a unique opportunity to do several important things:

- You can learn about a growing social phenomenon called transgender. It is always healthy to increase one's general knowledge base, perhaps especially in areas of human difference. Doing so will make you a better and more informed employee of this organization, and probably a better citizen as well.

- You can be kind to and supportive of your transitioning coworker. Imagine how you might feel if you were in their position: you would probably be nervous, perhaps more than a little scared about the reactions of others, and concerned about your future with the organization. You can reach out, be respectful, and be a friend. By supporting your transsexual coworker, you will help improve morale, strengthen teamwork in your department, and be part of creating a more diversified (and, therefore, a better) organizational culture at XYZ Company. Offering dignity to others is a mark of maturity and professionalism.

- You can help solidify and reinforce XYZ Company's commitment to diversity in our organization. Remember, everyone comes to work to help the organization be successful; this is just one more way to achieve that goal. By recognizing the significance of accepting and respecting your transitioning coworker, you will further validate our company's diversity leadership within our industry.

LEARNING AND GROWING

When the announcement of your transsexual coworker's transition is made publicly, you may be taken by surprise. However, rest assured that work will continue as always and that the sky is not falling. It is really not that big a deal, and you will soon become accustomed to seeing your transsexual coworker in his or her new gender role.

If you are like most people, you know little about transsexuals or transitioning in the workplace. You may have never (knowingly) met a transgender person before and may not understand the importance of the need to transition. You may have misconceptions or be misinformed about a transition or about XYZ Company's company policy.

This can potentially lead to inappropriate behavior, such as use of improper names and pronouns, fear of the unknown, or possibly even harassment or discrimination in some form.

This Guide offers some initial information to help demystify the transition experience, and there are plenty of other resources available to inform you as well. Do not allow fear or ignorance to keep you from respecting and supporting your transitioning coworker.

RESTROOM ISSUES

Keep in mind that transgender workers need and deserve the same access to restrooms as other workers. (Transsexuals have bodily needs just like you do, and their dignity should be respected just as you would want your own to be.) The management/HR team and your transsexual coworker have already discussed the restroom issue and have developed a workable strategy to help minimize any discomfort for everyone concerned. If you have questions, be sure to check with your manager.

ASKING QUESTIONS AND HAVING CONVERSATIONS

If you are not sure about what to say or do around your transitioning coworker, there is nothing wrong with asking respectfully. This is a delicate and "different" situation, it is true, but it is still within the realm of human experience. Transsexuals are still human beings with feelings and emotions, and your transitioning coworker will probably appreciate the opportunity to dialogue personally with you about this new situation.

It is natural to be curious about something new, but allow your transsexual coworker to retain his or her dignity. Remember, they are on the job site to work, not to provide amusement or entertainment for you or anyone else.

At XYZ Company, we are all in this together. It is in everyone's best interests to focus on teamwork and collaboration instead of centering attention on issues that can divide us or be nonproductive. Talk to your transitioning coworker and discuss how you can move forward together to get the work done in an effective, professional manner.

Obtaining Further Information

If you have questions or concerns, or if you would like more information about transsexualism or transitions in the workplace, be sure to check with your manager or your HR generalist. Also, you may contact the company's Employee Assistance Program.

FOR MANAGERS: INFORMATION ABOUT TRANSSEXUAL EMPLOYEES AND WORKPLACE TRANSITIONS

As a manager at XYZ Company, your support will be critical to an employee who informs you that he or she wishes to transition on the job, or is already in the process of transitioning. Your attitudes and actions will almost certainly influence and impact the outcome of that employee's transition at work. (Also, you will be modeling appropriate behaviors for the other employees, so it is vital that you act with professionalism and respect in this matter.)

If you are not familiar with transsexuality or with the issues related to transition—and chances are you will not be—be polite, respectful, curious, supportive, compassionate, and permit the transsexual employee to help educate you. In-depth conversations are certainly in order. In addition, refer to the other resources listed in this Guide. Information and education will be the keys to a successful experience for everyone involved with the transition.

A gender change is unlike most other personal issues in that the person undergoing the change must eventually "come out" to almost everyone who is directly involved in his or her life, including his or her employer. It is almost impossible and unrealistic to continue hiding the physical changes that accompany a major life event such as a gender change. At some point, the transitioning individual is going to have to go public about his or her decision to transition. That is where you come in.

A transsexual person who is undergoing a medically supervised transition to the opposite sex is required to live full-time in his or her new gender role for at least a year before irreversible surgery takes place. Given this requirement, XYZ Company must necessarily become involved in the employee's transition. You, as a manager, have a responsibility to be supportive. Also, you must be prepared to take an active role as may be necessary in the transition process for an employee who works under your direction.

QUESTIONS AND ANSWERS

1. I have no experience in the area of transgender, transsexualism, or transition. Whom should I contact about these issues?
Contact the HR department and request assistance. You can also

find helpful information at http://www.vanessasheridan.com or http://www.hrc.org.

2. **What should an employee going through transition expect from XYZ Company (and, therefore, from me as a manager)?** Since XYZ Company prohibits discrimination based upon gender identity or expression as outlined in the company's EEO policy, the organization's role is to be supportive, provide information and resources, and assist the employee in making a successful transition to his or her desired gender role. Your role is to follow company policies, guidelines, and procedures, and to be supportive and helpful for your employee before, during, and after his or her transition process.

3. **If an employee comes to me and tells me that he or she wants to transition, what should my response be?**

   - First, assure the employee that his or her information and your conversation will be held in the strictest confidence. Be kind and supportive. Let the employee know that you want to discuss how XYZ Company can assist and support him or her during his or her transition.

   - Next, ask the employee for his or her thoughts and ideas on what he or she would like to see happen and what you can do to help.

   - Ask the employee if he or she plans to change his or her name. If the answer is yes, ask what name and pronouns the employee will want to use. The new name and pronoun change at work should begin on a designated date (which, at this point, has yet to be determined) to coincide with the public announcement of the employee's transition.

   - The employee will almost certainly be nervous and/or concerned about the impact the transition will have on him or her at work. Reassure the employee that he or she is covered by existing XYZ Company organizational policies such as confidentiality, EEO, and harassment.

   - Offer to help the employee contact his or her HR generalist and the Employee Assistance Program.

   - Finally, conclude the conversation by once again assuring the employee that you and XYZ Company will be supportive during his or her transition. Remind him or her of the resources that are available, including the lesbian/gay employee resource group. Ask him or her to inform you of anything else you can do to be of assistance, and make sure he or she understands that you are there to be supportive and helpful.

4. **If a transsexual employee notifies me that he or she is being harassed, what should I do?** Help the employee contact the

HR department. XYZ Company's company policy prohibits harassment of any employee based on gender identity or expression.

5. **What if I have other questions or specific concerns about the employee's transition?** The Employee Assistance Program and/or the Human Resources department should be able to answer most of your questions and address your concerns. However, if you need additional help or advice, a knowledgeable transgender expert/consultant from the outside may be the answer.

APPENDIX 5

International Bill of Gender Rights

(As adopted June 17, 1995 in Houston, Texas, U.S.A.)

The International Bill of Gender Rights (IBGR) strives to express human and civil rights from a gender perspective. However, the ten rights enunciated below are not to be viewed as special rights applicable to a particular interest group. Nor are these rights limited in application to persons for whom gender identity and gender role issues are of paramount concern. All ten sections of the IBGR are universal rights which can be claimed and exercised by every human being.

The International Bill of Gender Rights (IBGR) was first drafted in committee and adopted by the International Conference on Transgender Law and Employment Policy at that organization's second annual meeting, held in Houston, Texas, August 26–29, 1993.

The IBGR has been reviewed and amended in committee and adopted with revisions at subsequent annual meetings of ICTLEP in 1994 and 1995.

The IBGR is a theoretical construction which has no force of law absent its adoption by legislative bodies and recognition of its principles by courts of law, administrative agencies and international bodies such as the United Nations.

However, individuals are free to adopt the truths and principles expressed in the IBGR, and to lead their lives accordingly. In this fashion, the truths expressed in the IBGR will liberate and empower humankind in ways and to an extent beyond the reach of legislators, judges, officials and diplomats.

When the truths expressed in the IBGR are embraced and given expression by humankind, the acts of legislatures and pronouncements of courts and other governing structures will necessarily follow. Thus, the paths of free expression trodden by millions of human beings, all seeking to define themselves and give meaning to their lives, will ultimately determine the course of governing bodies.

The IBGR is a transformative and revolutionary document but it is grounded in the bedrock of individual liberty and free expression. As our lives unfold these kernels of truth are here for all who would claim and exercise them.

This document, though copyrighted, may be reproduced by any means and freely distributed by anyone supporting the principles and statements contained in the International Bill of Gender Rights.

THE RIGHT TO DEFINE GENDER IDENTITY

All human beings carry within themselves an ever-unfolding idea of who they are and what they are capable of achieving. The individual's sense of self is not determined by chromosomal sex, genitalia, assigned birth sex, or initial gender role. Thus, the individual's identity and capabilities cannot be circumscribed by what society deems to be masculine or feminine behavior. It is fundamental that individuals have the right to define, and to redefine as their lives unfold, their own gender identities, without regard to chromosomal sex, genitalia, assigned birth sex, or initial gender role.

Therefore, all human beings have the right to define their own gender identity regardless of chromosomal sex, genitalia, assigned birth sex, or initial gender role; and further, no individual shall be denied Human or Civil Rights by virtue of a self-defined gender identity which is not in accord with chromosomal sex, genitalia, assigned birth sex, or initial gender role.

THE RIGHT TO FREE EXPRESSION OF GENDER IDENTITY

Given the right to define one's own gender identity, all human beings have the corresponding right to free expression of their self-defined gender identity.

Therefore, all human beings have the right to free expression of their self-defined gender identity; and further, no individual shall be denied Human or Civil Rights by virtue of the expression of a self-defined gender identity.

THE RIGHT TO SECURE AND RETAIN EMPLOYMENT AND TO RECEIVE JUST COMPENSATION

Given the economic structure of modern society, all human beings have a right to train for and to pursue an occupation or profession as a means of providing shelter, sustenance, and the necessities and bounty of life, for themselves and for those dependent upon them, to secure and retain employment, and to receive just compensation for their labor regardless of gender identity, chromosomal sex, genitalia, assigned birth sex, or initial gender role.

Therefore, individuals shall not be denied the right to train for and to pursue an occupation or profession, nor be denied the right to secure and retain employment, nor be denied just compensation for their labor, by virtue of their chromosomal sex, genitalia, assigned birth sex, or initial gender role, or on the basis of a self-defined gender identity or the expression thereof.

THE RIGHT OF ACCESS TO GENDERED SPACE AND PARTICIPATION IN GENDERED ACTIVITY

Given the right to define one's own gender identity and the corresponding right to free expression of a self-defined gender identity, no individual should be denied access to a space or denied participation in an activity by virtue of a self-defined gender identity which is not in accord with chromosomal sex, genitalia, assigned birth sex, or initial gender role.

Therefore, no individual shall be denied access to a space or denied participation in an activity by virtue of a self-defined gender identity which is not in accord with chromosomal sex, genitalia, assigned birth sex, or initial gender role.

THE RIGHT TO CONTROL AND CHANGE ONE'S OWN BODY

All human beings have the right to control their bodies, which includes the right to change their bodies cosmetically, chemically, or surgically, so as to express a self-defined gender identity.

Therefore, individuals shall not be denied the right to change their bodies as a means of expressing a self-defined gender identity; and further, individuals shall not be denied Human or Civil Rights on the basis that they have changed their bodies cosmetically, chemically, or surgically, or desire to do so as a means of expressing a self-defined gender identity.

THE RIGHT TO COMPETENT MEDICAL AND PROFESSIONAL CARE

Given the individual's right to define one's own gender identity, and the right to change one's own body as a means of expressing a self-defined gender identity, no individual should be denied access to competent medical or other professional care on the basis of the individual's chromosomal sex, genitalia, assigned birth sex, or initial gender role.

Therefore, individuals shall not be denied the right to competent medical or other professional care when changing their bodies cosmetically, chemically, or surgically, on the basis of chromosomal sex, genitalia, assigned birth sex, or initial gender role.

THE RIGHT TO FREEDOM FROM PSYCHIATRIC DIAGNOSIS OR TREATMENT

Given the right to define one's own gender identity, individuals should not be subject to psychiatric diagnosis or treatment solely on the basis of their gender identity or role.

Therefore, individuals shall not be subject to psychiatric diagnosis or treatment as mentally disordered or diseased solely on the basis of a self-defined gender identity or the expression thereof.

THE RIGHT TO SEXUAL EXPRESSION

Given the right to a self-defined gender identity, every consenting adult has a corresponding right to free sexual expression.

Therefore, no individual's Human or Civil Rights shall be denied on the basis of sexual orientation; and further, no individual shall be denied Human or Civil Rights for expression of a self-defined gender identity through sexual acts between consenting adults.

THE RIGHT TO FORM COMMITTED, LOVING RELATIONSHIPS AND ENTER INTO MARITAL CONTRACTS

Given that all human beings have the right to free expression of self-defined gender identities, and the right to sexual expression as a form of gender expression, all human beings have a corresponding right to form committed, loving relationships with one another, and to enter into marital contracts, regardless of their own or their partner's chromosomal sex, genitalia, assigned birth sex, or initial gender role.

Therefore, individuals shall not be denied the right to form committed, loving relationships with one another or to enter into marital contracts by virtue of their own or their partner's chromosomal sex, genitalia, assigned birth sex, or initial gender role, or on the basis of their expression of a self-defined gender identity.

THE RIGHT TO CONCEIVE, BEAR, OR ADOPT CHILDREN; THE RIGHT TO NURTURE AND HAVE CUSTODY OF CHILDREN AND TO EXERCISE PARENTAL CAPACITY

Given the right to form a committed, loving relationship with another, and to enter into marital contracts, together with the right to express a self-defined gender identity and the right to sexual expression, individuals have a corresponding right to conceive and bear children, to adopt children, to nurture children, to have custody of children, and to exercise parental capacity with respect to children, natural or adopted, without regard to chromosomal sex, genitalia, assigned birth sex, or initial gender role, or by virtue of a self-defined gender identity or the expression thereof.

Therefore, individuals shall not be denied the right to conceive, bear, or adopt children, nor to nurture and have custody of children, nor to exercise parental capacity with respect to children, natural or adopted, on the basis of their own, their partner's, or their children's chromosomal sex, genitalia, assigned birth sex, initial gender role, or by virtue of a self-defined gender identity or the expression thereof.

APPENDIX 6

Alcatel-Lucent Technologies Equal Opportunity Policy Statement

The following policy statement from Alcatel-Lucent Technologies' (then Lucent Technologies) top management is offered as a model: a potential guide and/or template for organizations that may wish to create their own antidiscrimination policy with regard to gender-variant workers. To the best of our knowledge, in 1997 Alcatel-Lucent Technologies was the first major U.S. company to include specific language in its employee policy to protect the rights of transgender employees.

Lucent's policy contains language that is designed to prohibit discrimination on the basis of gender identity, characteristics, or expression. The policy's wording protects transsexuals ("gender identity"), intersex persons ("gender characteristics"), and cross-dressers ("gender expression"). In addition, the policy's language goes beyond these three narrow categories to include people whose gender presentation is nontraditional, including masculine women and feminine men.

Diversity and the equal opportunity it affords is strategically important to [Alcatel-]Lucent. It makes [Alcatel-]Lucent more competitive in the marketplace. It has been [Alcatel-]Lucent's long-standing tradition, as well as our corporate policy, to treat each individual with dignity and respect. This is both a question of equity and of market success. To guarantee this, we will effectively utilize all of our human resource talent and continue to pursue this effort.

[Alcatel-]Lucent's policy is to:

- *Comply with both the letter and the spirit of all applicable laws and regulations governing employment;*

- *Provide equal opportunity to all employees and to all applicants for employment;*
- *Take appropriate affirmative action to make equal opportunity a reality;*
- *Prohibit discrimination or harassment because of race, color, creed, religion, national origin, citizenship, sex, marital status, age, physical or mental disability, one's status as a special disabled veteran, veteran of the Vietnam era, or other covered veterans, or because of a person's sexual orientation, gender identity, characteristics or expression, in any employment decision or in the administration of any personnel policy;*
- *Make reasonable accommodations to the physical and/or mental limitations of qualified employees or applicants with disabilities;*
- *Ensure that maximum opportunity is afforded to all minority and women-owned businesses to participate as suppliers, contractors, and subcontractors of goods and services to [Alcatel-]Lucent Technologies; and comply with regulatory agency requirements and with federal, state, and local procurement regulations and programs;*
- *Advise employees of their rights to refer violations of this policy to their supervision, or to the appropriate [Alcatel-]Lucent Technologies organization charged with the administration of the Equal Opportunity/ Affirmative Action policy, without intimidation or retaliation of any form for exercising such rights.*

I want to reaffirm [Alcatel-]Lucent's commitment of providing equal opportunity to all employees and applicants for employment in accordance with all applicable laws, directives, and regulations of federal, state, and local governing bodies and agencies thereof.

I expect all managers throughout [Alcatel-]Lucent Technologies to comply fully with all aspects of this policy, and to conduct themselves in accordance with the principles of equal opportunity.

Demonstrated commitment to equal opportunity is an investment in our people and our future growth. Consequently, a company that attracts, selects, develops, and retains the best will remain the industry leader. [Alcatel-]Lucent's ongoing efforts in this direction will provide us with a critical competitive advantage in the marketplace.[1]

Courtesy of Alcatel-Lucent.

APPENDIX 7
IBM Corporation Equal Opportunity Policy

Equal opportunity
October 20, 2005

Business activities such as hiring, training, compensation, promotions, transfers, terminations and IBM-sponsored social and recreational activities are conducted without discrimination based on race, color, genetics, religion, gender, gender identity or expression, sexual orientation, national origin, disability, age or status as a special disabled veteran or other veteran covered by the Vietnam Era Veterans Readjustment Act of 1974, as amended.

These business activities and the design and administration of IBM benefit plans comply with all applicable federal, state and local laws, including those dealing with equal opportunity. IBM also makes accommodation for religious observances, which IBM determines reasonable.

In respecting and valuing the diversity among our employees and all those with whom we do business, managers are expected to ensure that there is a work environment free of all forms of discrimination and harassment.

To provide equal opportunity and affirmative action for applicants and employees, IBM carries out programs on behalf of women, minorities, people with disabilities, special disabled veterans and other veterans covered by the Vietnam Era Veterans Readjustment Act of 1974, as amended. This includes outreach as well as human resource programs that ensure equity in compensation and opportunity for growth and development.

Effective management of our workforce diversity policy is an important strategic objective. Every IBM manager is expected to abide by this policy and uphold the company's commitment to workforce diversity.

APPENDIX 8

The Equality Principles

(As Amended by the Equality Project (501c3) Executive Board, copyright 2001.)

The Equality Principles were originally developed in 1995 by the Equality Project[1] with the support of a variety of individuals and organizations.

1. *The company will prohibit discrimination based on sexual orientation and gender expression or gender identity as part of its written employment policy statement.*

2. *The company will disseminate its written employment policy statement company-wide.*

3. *The company will not tolerate discrimination on the basis of any employee's actual or perceived health condition, status or disability.*

4. *The company will offer equal health insurance and other benefits to employees to cover their domestic partners regardless of the employee's marital status, sexual orientation, gender expression or gender identity.*

5. *The company will include discussions of sexual orientation, gender expression and gender identity as part of its official employee diversity and sensitivity training communications.*

6. *The company will give employee groups equal standing, regardless of sexual orientation, gender identity or gender expression.*

7. *The company advertising policy will avoid the use of negative stereotypes based on sexual orientation, gender identity or gender expression.*

8. *The company will not discriminate in its advertising, marketing or promoting events on the basis of sexual orientation, gender expression or gender identity.*

9. *The company will not discriminate in the sale of its goods or services based on sexual orientation, gender expression or gender identity.*

10. *The company will not bar charitable contributions to groups and organizations on the basis of sexual orientation, gender expression or gender identity.*[1]

Courtesy of Equality Project for Equality Principles, www.equalityproject.org.

Notes

INTRODUCTION

1. Heath, Rachel Ann, *The Praeger Handbook of Transsexuality: Changing Gender to Match Mindset* (Westport, CT: Praeger Publishers, 2006), 2.
2. Ibid., xii.
3. Carlson Marketing, *Employees as Assets: The New Innovation Paradigm* (Minneapolis: Carlson Marketing, 2006), 2.
4. Lacey Leigh, "Conquering Outreach," from *TG Life*, www.tglife.com.
5. From an e-newsletter by the NCTE. Their Web site is www.ncte quality.org.
6. For this book's purposes, "coming out" means to openly reveal oneself as transgender. It is important to make an intentional differentiation between coming out as transgender as opposed to coming out as gay, lesbian, or bisexual. While there can be some similarities between the two experiences, we are really talking about two divergent forms of behavior with their own distinct dynamics and nuances. A transgender person's coming out is about disclosing one's gender status and/or identity, while coming out as a lesbian, bisexual, or gay person has to do with divulging one's sexual orientation. The former is about who one *is*, while the latter is about who one is attracted to. Some coming out issues can overlap and be relatively comparable for these groups, but other, more specific concerns are extremely different—and those human differences should be acknowledged and respected. Neither type of coming out is necessarily better or worse than the other, only different.

CHAPTER 1: WHAT IS TRANSGENDER?

1. Emi Koyama, for the Survivor Project, *Guide to Intersex and Trans Terminologies*, www.survivorproject.org/basic.html.

2. For more information about the growing global transgender community, see the Web site of the International Foundation for Gender Education (or IFGE) at http://www.ifge.org.

3. Christine Burns, "Why 'Phrasebook Diversity' Is Not Enough," http://www.pfc.org.uk/files/Why_Phrasebook_Diversity_is_Not_Enough.pdf.

4. Heath, *Praeger Handbook of Transsexuality*, 41.

5. Helen Boyd, *My Husband Betty: Love, Sex, and Life with a Crossdresser* (New York: Thunder's Mouth Press, 2003), 12.

6. Donna Rose, *Wrapped in Blue: A Journey of Discovery* (Round Rock, TX: Living Legacy Press, 2003), 21.

7. Helen Boyd, *She's Not the Man I Married: My Life with a Transgender Husband* (Emeryville, CA: Seal Press, 2007), 136.

8. David Steinberg, *Gender and Genteelness: The Southern Comfort Transgender Conference*, http://www.spectator.net/1160/pages/1160_steinberg.html.

9. Matt Kailey, *Tranifesto: Selected Columns and Other Ramblings from a Transgendered Mind* (Philadelphia: Xlibris Corporation, 2002), 71.

10. Dallas Denny, *Transgender Tapestry* 102 (Summer 2003): 27.

11. Miqqui Alicia Gilbert, "Bigenderism," *Transgender Tapestry* 102 (Summer 2003): 16.

12. Daniel Sorid, "Transsexuals New Focus of Companies' Legal Protection," http://www.gpac.org/pressroom/clippings/2003-forbes.html.

13. In *The Praeger Handbook of Transsexuality*, Rachel Ann Heath states that "many people of transsexual background are sensitive to the labels used to describe them. In particular, they detest being called 'transgendered,' [*sic*] a term that includes part-time crossdressers and drag performers with whom those of transsexual background do not identify. I apologize in advance if my choice of terminology causes offense." Like Heath, this author does not wish to offend anyone, especially transsexual persons, by including them in the large gender-variant family, that is transgender.

14. Adapted from Boyd, *My Husband Betty*, 127.

15. Most writers apply the term "sexual reassignment surgery" or "genital reconstruction surgery" when referring to what is commonly known as a "sex-change operation." However, increasing numbers of transgender advocates are referring to this as "gender affirmation surgery." Using this term indicates that the surgery is affirming the transperson's brain sex from birth by surgically altering the genitals.

16. Heath, *Praeger Handbook of Transsexuality*, 155.

17. Kailey, *Tranifesto*, 18.

18. Amy Bloom, *Normal: Transsexual CEOs, Crossdressing Cops, and Hermaphrodites with Attitude* (New York: Random House, 2002), 134.

19. ICTLEP, the International Conference on Transgender Law and Employment Policy, *Discrimination Against Transgendered People in America*, http://www.ibiblio.org/gaylaw/issue5/frye1.html.

20. Jennifer Warner, "Tomboys May Be Born, Not Made: Testosterone Levels During Pregnancy Linked to Behavior," *Child Development* (November–December 2000).

21. Gilbert, "Bigenderism," 16–17.

22. Bloom, *Normal*, 36.

23. Ellen Sherman, "The Real Truth about Crossdressing," *Selfhelp Magazine*, http://www.selfhelpmagazine.com/article/node/1218.

24. www.shpm.com/articles/sex/xdress.html.

25. American Psychiatric Association, *Diagnostic and Statistical Manual of Mental Disorders, Fourth Edition (DSM-IV)*. This is the primary resource on mental health disorders for the psychiatric community.

26. John Townsend, "Breaking New Ground in Intersex Research: An Interview with Sharon E. Preves," *Lavender Magazine* 12, no. 288 (June 9–22, 2006): 83.

27. Ibid.

28. Judy Osborne, "Transgender Diversity," *Transcending Genders: A Monthly Look into Transgender Lives for Mental Health Therapists*, www .soulforce.org/transgender/issue_7.pdf.

29. Boyd, *She's Not the Man I Married*, 133.

30. Osborne, "Transgender Diversity."

31. GLAAD, "Issues Facing the Transgender and Intersex Communities," http://www.glaad.org/publications/resource_doc_detail.php?id =3120.

32. American Medical Student Association, "Transgender Health Initiative Learning Seminar," http://www.amsa.org/advocacy/lgbtpm/ transterms.cfm#3 (accessed April 6, 2009).

CHAPTER 2: WHO ARE TRANSGENDER PEOPLE?

1. Virginia Ramey Mollenkott's *Omnigender: A Trans-Religious Approach* (Cleveland: The Pilgrim Press, 2001) examines the issues inherent in our society's rigidly bipolar concept of gender identity from a theological perspective.

2. Miqqui A. Gilbert, "A Sometime Woman: The Limits of Social Construction," http://www.pfc.org.uk/node/178.

3. Nancy Nangeroni, for the International Foundation for Gender Education, *Transgenderism: Transgressing Gender Norms*, http://www.gendertalk .com/tgism/tgism.shtml.

4. LEAGUE@NCR, "GLBT Issues in the Workplace: Coming Out as Transgender," http://www.league-ncr.com/data/Training%20-%20GLBT %20Issues%20in%20the%20workplace/wbt-tr1.htm.

5. Sabrina Marcus Taraboletti, *Written Statement of Sabrina Marcus Taraboletti to the Subcommittee on Health, Employment, Labor, and Pensions,*

Committee on Education and Labor, United States House of Representatives (Washington, D.C.: United States House of Representatives, 2008), 3.

6. Ibid.

7. Katrina C. Rose, "A No-Nonsense Transsexual Lawyer's Take on the T-Word," http://web.archive.org/web/20010417001214/http://content .gay.com/channels/home/trans_stories/rose_katrina.html. Courtesy of Katrina C. Rose, attorney and transgender legal historian.

8. Ibid.

9. Stephanie Armour, "Transgender Employees See Changes in Colleagues, Too," *USA Today*, http://www.usatoday.com/money/jobcenter/workplace/2005-06-09-transgender-usat_x.htm.

10. *Holt v. Northwest Pennsylvania Training Pshp. Consortium*, 694 A.2d 1134 (Pa. Commw. Ct. 1997).

11. *Oiler v. Winn-Dixie La., Inc.*, 89 Fair Empl. Prac. Cas. (BNA) 1832 (E.D. La. 2002).

12. Dana Rivers, "An American Woman," http://danarivers.net/mystory.html (accessed June 11, 2007).

13. Veronica Vera, *Miss Vera's Crossdress for Success* (New York: Random House, 2002), 161.

14. Found online at www.trans-yorks.org.uk/features/feature07.htm.

15. Found online at http://www.amazon.com/gp/richpub/syltguides/fullview/223qtzj3dsfqx.

16. Ibid.

17. Ibid.

18. Mike Reynolds, *The New Girl* (Baltimore: PublishAmerica, 2003), 185.

19. Ibid., 185–86.

20. Bloom, *Normal*, 19.

21. Nancy Nangeroni, *Advocating for Gender Identity*, http://www .gendertalk.com/articles/oped/advocating/shtml.

22. LEAGUE@NCR, "GLBT Issues in the Workplace."

23. Ibid.

24. Monica F. Helms, "And That's the Way It Is," *Transgender Tapestry* 103 (Fall 2003): 12.

25. Transgender at Work, *Workplace Guidelines for Transgendered Employees: Guidelines for Bigendered People Crossdressing Part-time*, http://www.tgender.net/taw/tggl/bg.html.

CHAPTER 3: WHY TRANSGENDER INCLUSION MATTERS TO YOUR BUSINESS (EVEN IF YOU DIDN'T KNOW IT)

1. As quoted by Robert W. Bly, *Become a Recognized Authority in Your Field in 60 Days or Less!* (New York: Alpha, 2002), 85.

2. Abraham H. Maslow, from the foreword by Warren Bennis, *Maslow on Management* (New York: John Wiley & Sons, Inc., 1998), xv.

3. Found online at http://www.charthouse.com/content.aspx?nodeid =1074.

4. Peter Drucker, as quoted in "The Guru's Guru," *Business 2.0* (October 2001): 72.

5. Jeff Immelt, as quoted by Geoffrey Colvin, "What Makes GE Great?" *Fortune*, found online at http://money.cnn.com/2006/02/21/magazines/ fortune/mostadmired_fortune_ge/index.htm?cnn=yes.

6. Carlson Marketing, *Employees as Assets*.

7. Analytic Technologies, "Gender Diversity in the Workplace," http:// www.analytictech.com/mb021/gender.htm.

8. Foothill-De Anza Community College District, "Diversity in the Workplace," http://hr.fhda.edu/diversity/.

9. Terrance Griep, "Reading, Writing, and Respecting," *Lavender Magazine* no. 310 (August 17–30, 2007): 50.

10. *The American Heritage Dictionary of the English Language*, 4th ed. (New York: Houghton Mifflin, 2006), http://dictionary.reference.com/ browse/pluralism.

11. American Society of Mechanical Engineers Professional Practice Curriculum, "What Is Workplace Diversity?" http://www.professionalpractice .asme.org/communications/diversity/index.htm.

12. Ibid.

13. Maslow, *Maslow on Management*, xvi.

14. Transgender at Work, http://www.tgender.net/taw/about.html.

15. Armour, "Transgender Employees See Changes in Colleagues, Too."

16. Ibid.

17. Jillian Weiss, *Adoption of Transgender HR Policies in US Employers*, http://phobos.ramapo.edu/~jweiss/metrics.htm.

18. Gilbert, "Bigenderism," 17.

19. Terry Howard, *Diversity: The Business Case for Sexual Orientation: It's about Presence, Policy, and Productivity*, http://www.tialumni.org/2002/08ed1/ diversity.htm (accessed August 28, 2007).

20. Weiss, *Adoption of Transgender HR Policies in US Employers*.

21. Julie Forster, "Getting Gay Workers," *St. Paul Pioneer Press* (September 22, 2007): 1C.

22. Ibid., 4C.

23. Ibid.

24. Kathryn Tyler, "The Boss Makes the Weather," *HR Magazine* 49, no. 5 (May 2004): 93.

25. "Work Safety a Growing Concern," *CNN Money*, http://money .cnn.com/2004/04/29/news/economy/job_satisfaction_survey/index.htm ?cnn=yes (accessed April 29, 2004).

26. Howard, *Diversity*.

27. Emily Jones, quoted in "Ernst & Young Becomes First Big 4 Professional Services Firm to Ban Gender Identity-Based Discrimination," *Living OUT* (Minneapolis) 1, no. 26 (June 1, 2005): 11.

28. Weiss, *Adoption of Transgender HR Policies in US Employers.*

29. Nevena Kraguljevic, "Welcoming the Transgender Workforce," *GayWired.com*, http://www.gaybusinessworld.com/page.cfm?ID=385&storyset =yes&typeofsite=storydetail.

30. Harvey Robbins and Michael Finley, *The New Why Teams Don't Work* (San Francisco, CA: Berrett-Koehler Publishers, Inc., 2000), 87.

31. Http://sites.target.com/site/en/company/page.jsp?contentId =WCMP04-034164.

32. Allan Gilmour, "Talking Shop with Allan Gilmour," *Equality*, Human Rights Campaign (Winter 2003): 23.

33. Margaret J. Covert, "Gender Expression Protections Added to Workplace Policies at Connecticut Company," http://www.northstarasset .com/mediacontent/NS4Q06.html.

34. Ibid.

35. John Weiser and Simon Zadek, *Conversations with Disbelievers: Persuading Companies to Address Social Challenges* (New York: The Ford Foundation, 2000), 4.

36. "More Than Just Commerce," http://www.morethanjustcommerce .org/resources/diversity.html.

CHAPTER 4: THE GREAT RESTROOM DEBATE

1. Joanne Herman, "Transgender? You're Fired!" From a commentary in *The Advocate*, http://www.advocate.com/exclusive_detail_ektid34806.asp (accessed July 28, 2006).

2. Kailey, *Tranifesto*, 109–10.

3. David Crary, "Transgender Activists Making Gains," *Minneapolis Star Tribune* (Minneapolis, January 7, 2003): E4.

4. American Civil Liberties Union, found online at www.aclu.org/news/ NewsPrint.cfm?ID=7332&c=105.

5. Dan Woog, "Transsexual Transition: Manage a Gender Change at Work," http://diversity.monster.ca/10457_en-CA_p1.asp.

6. Lisa M. Hartley, "Culturally Induced Stress: It Only Hurts Because You Are Different," in *Transgendering Faith: Identity, Sexuality and Spirituality*, ed. Leanne McCall Tigert and Maren C. Tirabassi (Cleveland: The Pilgrim Press, 2004), 13.

7. Transgender at Work, "Restroom Access Issues," http://www.tgender .net/taw/restroom.html.

8. Ibid.

9. "Transgender at Work," http://www.tgender.net/taw/restroom.html.

10. OutFront Minnesota, "The Goins vs. West Group Case: Workplace Implications," http://www.outfront.org/library/wgcase.html (accessed May 2, 2006).

11. Justin Tanis, National Center for Transgender Equality, "Make a Restroom More Accessible for Trans People (52 Things)," from an e-mail sent on June 19, 2006.

CHAPTER 6: COMING OUT AS TRANSGENDER AT WORK

1. National Lesbian & Gay Journalists Association, "A Newsroom for Everyone: NLGJA's Campaign to Protect Gender Identity and Expression," http://www.nlgja.org/workplace/newsroom_campaign.htm.

2. Susan Bryant, "Coming Out at Work," http://diversity.monster.ca/375_en-CA_p1.asp.

3. Margaret J. Wheatley, *Turning to One Another: Simple Conversations to Restore Hope to the Future* (San Francisco: Berrett-Koehler Publishers, Inc., 2002), 140.

4. Matt Krumrie, "Coming Out at Work," *Minneapolis Star Tribune* (Minneapolis, February 12, 2006): W-1.

5. Forster, "Getting Gay Workers," 4C.

6. Fergus M. Bordewich, *Bound for Canaan: The Epic Story of the Underground Railroad, America's First Civil Rights Movement* (New York: Amistad, 2006), 117.

7. Ruthann Rudel, "On Visibility," in *Out in the Workplace: The Pleasures and Perils of Coming Out on the Job*, ed. Richard A. Rasi and Lourdes Rodríguez-Nogués (Los Angeles: Alyson Publications, 1995), 52.

8. Ibid.

9. Lourdes Rodríguez-Nogués, "I Shall Not Be Silent," in *Out in the Workplace: The Pleasures and Perils of Coming Out on the Job*, ed. Richard A. Rasi and Lourdes Rodríguez-Nogués (Los Angeles: Alyson Publications, 1995), 14–15.

10. Associated Press, "Boston Writer Comes Out of Closet," http://espn.go.com/moresports/news/2003/0930/1627588.html. Also see Ed Gray, "Out and Proud," *Boston Herald* (Boston, September 30, 2003): 88.

11. Paraphrased and adapted from Rodríguez-Nogués, "I Shall Not Be Silent," 13–14.

12. Kipp Cheng, "Workplace Lessons from Transgender People," *DiversityInc*, October 2002.

13. From a presentation by Dr. Richard Rasi, "Gay, Lesbian, Bisexual, Transgender Issues in the Workplace," New England Human Resources Association, Cambridge, Massachusetts, on September 22, 2000, www.rasiassociates.com/elements/nehra.htm (accessed November 16, 2007).

14. Planned Parenthood of Tompkins County, "What's Up with That? Talking about Transgender," *Transgender Tapestry* 101 (Waltham, MA: IFGE, Spring 2003): 34.

15. For names and statistical information about transgender people who have been the murder victims of domestic or international hate crimes since 1970, see www.rememberingourdead.org.

16. OutFront Minnesota, "Fairness in the Workplace: Transgender Minnesotans," http://www.outfront.org/library/issues/transworkplace.

17. B. M. Goldman, S. S. Masterson, E. A. Locke, M. Groth, and D. G. Jensen, "Goal Directedness and Personal Identity as Correlates of Life Outcomes," *Psychological Reports* 91 (2002): 153–66.

18. Dan Woog, "What to Do When Your Boss Is a Homophobe," http://diversity.monster.co.uk/364_en_p1.asp.

CHAPTER 7: TOOLS FOR ORGANIZATIONAL LEADERS

1. Tim McGuire, "More Than Work: Create Code That Can't Be Broken," *Minneapolis Star Tribune* (Minneapolis, November 8, 2003): B7.

2. William Isaacs, *Dialogue and the Art of Thinking Together* (New York: Currency, 1999), 3.

3. Liz Winfeld, "Business Case: Sexual Orientation in the Workplace," from DiversityCentral.com, http://www.diversitycentral.com/business/business_case_diversity.html.

4. Gary Hart, "Obama Offers Presidential Leadership among the Ruins," *Alternet*, February 4, 2008.

5. Selisse Berry, quoted by Kipp Cheng, "Creating 'Safe Spaces' for GLBT Employees in the Workplace," *Diversity Inc.*, http://www.diversityinc.com/public/5266.cfm (accessed July 14, 2003).

6. Human Rights Campaign, "Transgender 101: An Introduction to Issues Surrounding Gender Identity and Expression," http://www.wsd1.org/grantpark/clubs/gsa/resources/Transgender%20101.pdf.

7. Http://www.nlgja.org/gender/gender.html (accessed December 4, 2006).

8. Ibid., 189–90.

9. Jonathan Capehart, "Transsexuals Come Out as a Workplace Issue," National Transgender Advocacy Coalition, October 2000.

10. Cheng, "Workplace Lessons from Transgender People."

11. Ibid.

12. Grietje Wijbenga, "The Truth at Work," in *Out in the Workplace: The Pleasures and Perils of Coming Out on the Job*, ed. Richard A. Rasi and Lourdes Rodríguez-Nogués (Los Angeles: Alyson Publications, 1995), 145.

13. Polly Labarre, "Do You Have the Will to Lead?" *Fast Company*, December 19, 2007, http://www.fastcompany.com/magazine/32/koestenbaum.html?page=0%2c3.

14. Ibid.

15. "How Microsoft Changed Its Mind," *BusinessWeek Online*, http://www.businessweek.com/technology/content/may2005/tc20050512_7358_PG4_tc024.htm.

16. For an insightful perspective on how to avoid potential clothing/dress code problems in the workplace, see Kate Lorenz, *What Not to Wear to Work: 15 Things*, http://msn.careerbuilder.com/custom/msn/careeradvice/viewarticle.aspx?articleid=711&SiteId=cbmsnhp4711&sc_extcmp=JS_711_home1&GT1=7864.

17. Linda Ellinor and Glenna Gerard, *Dialogue: Rediscover the Transforming Power of Conversation* (New York: John Wiley and Sons, 1998), 175.

18. NSW Health, "Transgender People—Managing Workplace Issues," http://www.health.nsw.gov.au/policies/pd/2005/pdf/pd2005_165.pdf.

19. Ibid.

20. Human Rights Campaign, "Transgenderism and Transition in the Workplace," http://www.ren.org/hrcworkers.html.

21. Wijbenga, "The Truth at Work."

22. Jim Kouzes and Barry Posner, "Learning Is the Master Skill," http://thinksmart.typepad.com/good_morning_thinkers/2004/01/learning_is_the.html.

23. For an excellent overview of transgender-related workplace policy suggestions in the area of organization leadership, the Human Rights Campaign Web site (www.hrc.org) is recommended.

24. Ibid.

25. Timothy White, *The Nearest Faraway Place* (New York: Henry Holt and Co., 1995).

26. Cam Lindquist, "Thank You for Your Lack of Support," *GayWired*, www.gaywired.com.

CHAPTER 8: HELP FOR HUMAN RESOURCES PROFESSIONALS

1. From a presentation by Rasi, "Gay, Lesbian, Bisexual, Transgender Issues in the Workplace."

2. Rosalind Bentley, "Transgenderism: A Workplace Issue for Employers," *Minneapolis Star Tribune*, May 11, 1998, http://www.debradavis.org/gecpage/startrib2.html.

3. Jillian Todd Weiss, "The Cutting Edge of Employment Diversity: Transgender Human Resources Policies in U.S. Employers," http://phobos.ramapo.edu/~jweiss/disssumm.htm.

4. Freely adapted from *Conflict: Getting to Win/Win*, a pamphlet by Shelly Melroe of Balanced Excellence, LLC. Their Web site's URL is www.balancedexcellence.com.

5. Paraphrased from Transgender at Work, "Policy FAQ for Employers of Transgender Workers," http://www.tgender.net/taw/policyfaq.html #Time%20off%20for%20Medical%20Treatment.

6. Heath, *Praeger Handbook of Transsexuality*, 141.

CHAPTER 9: PRACTICAL IDEAS FOR ORGANIZATIONS

1. Jeff Wuorio, "What Makes a Good Boss?" http://www.hrpao.org/HRPA/HRResourceCentre/KnowledgeCentre/newscluster2/What+Makes+a+Good+Boss.htm.

2. Jim Jenkins, "One True Voice," in *Out in the Workplace: The Pleasures and Perils of Coming Out on the Job*, ed. Richard A. Rasi and Lourdes Rodríguez-Nogués (Los Angeles: Alyson Publications, 1995), 84.

3. Http://www.att.com/gen/press-room?pid=4800&cdvn=news &newsarticleid=23565.

4. Loosely paraphrased/adapted from the Wheaton College, IL, student handbook and from Bianca Cody Murphy, "Once Is Not Enough," in *Out in the Workplace: The Pleasures and Perils of Coming Out on the Job*, ed. Richard A. Rasi and Lourdes Rodríguez-Nogués (Los Angeles: Alyson Publications, 1995), 42–43.

5. Loree Cook-Daniels, Transgender Aging Network, "Is Your 'T' Written in Disappearing Ink? A Checklist for Transgender Inclusion," *Transgender Tapestry* 101 (Waltham, MA: IFGE, Spring 2003): 41–44.

6. Rosanna Fiske, diversity committee chair for the Public Relations Society of America and a principle at Miami's Rise Strategies, as quoted by Tim Bentley, "The Search for True Diversity," *Worthwhile* 1, no. 2 (March 2005).

7. Judy Tso, as quoted by Bentley, "The Search for True Diversity."

8. B.J. Gallagher, as quoted by Bentley, "The Search for True Diversity."

CHAPTER 10: INSIGHTS FOR COWORKERS OF TRANSPERSONS

1. Tyler, "The Boss Makes the Weather," 94.

2. Rose, *Wrapped in Blue*, 11.

3. Gilbert, "Bigenderism," 17.

4. Woog, "Transsexual Transition."

5. Nancy Nangeroni, "Transgressing Gender Norms," *Transgender Tapestry* 102 (Waltham, MA: IFGE, Summer 2003): 23.

6. Kailey, *Tranifesto*, 58.

7. Renee Baker, "Transgender Pilot Regains Her Wings," *Dallas Edge*, June 20, 2008, http://www.edgedallas.com/index.php?ch=news&sc=local &sc2=features&sc3=&id=76237.

8. Rivers, "An American Woman."

CHAPTER 11: TIPS FOR TRANSGENDER WORKERS

1. Note: this chapter is in no way intended to be a comprehensive exploration of the complex topics of transsexualism, cross-dressing, and/or intersex. The book's scope does not permit an in-depth discussion of such multifaceted subjects. Instead, this chapter is intended solely to provide some suggestions, ideas, concepts, strategies, and tools for dealing with workplace situations if you happen to be a transgender worker. There are other books that address these individual transgender manifestations in greater detail if that is your interest. Please see the recommended reading list for suggestions.

2. Http://www.debradavis.org/gecpage/genederempl.html.

3. Human Rights Campaign, "Transgenderism and Transition in the Workplace," http://www.ren.org/hrcworkers.html.

4. Nancy Nangeroni, "Building Bridges," *GenderTalk*, http://www .gendertalk.com/articles/stories/bridges.shtml.

5. Leslie Feinberg, *Trans Liberation: Beyond Pink or Blue* (Boston: Beacon Press, 1998), 9.

6. Boyd, *My Husband Betty*, 29.

7. OutFront Minnesota, "Fairness in the Workplace: Transgender Minnesotans," http://www.outfront.org/library/issues/transworkplace.

8. I am the author of *Crossing Over: Liberating the Transgendered Christian* (Cleveland: Pilgrim Press, 2001) and *Transgender Journeys*, cowritten with Virginia Ramey Mollenkott (Cleveland: Pilgrim Press, 2003). These books explore the spiritual connotations of various aspects of transgender from a Christian perspective, providing a solid hermeneutical basis for a nonjudgmental view of the phenomenon. If you have questions or concerns about the spiritual validity of transgender, particularly from a Christian standpoint, you may want to explore these books as a way of gaining insight into the question.

9. For a unique visual representation of this scripture verse, see http:// www.thebricktestament.com/the_law/transvestism/dt22_05a.html.

10. It is critically important to understand that putting bible verses into their proper context for appropriate interpretation is necessary for any valid understanding of scripture. Even then, scriptural interpretations may vary widely, depending upon the worldview and background of the interpreter. Do not always believe the person who insists, "The bible says what it means

and means what it says." That is too simplistic. Things are a bit more—actually a great deal more—complex than that!

11. Townsend, "Breaking New Ground in Intersex Research," 83.

12. Alice Dreger, "Top Ten Myths about Intersex," *ISNA News*, February 2001, 3, http://www.isna.org/files/hwa/feb2001.pdf.

13. Ibid.

CHAPTER 12: WHAT TO DO ABOUT, WITH, AND FOR TRANSGENDER CUSTOMERS

1. Gwendoly Freed, "Gays and Lesbians Report Friendlier Workplaces," *Minneapolis Star Tribune* (Minneapolis, October 2, 2003): D4.

2. Lisa Leff, "More Companies Boost Gay Pride," *St. Paul Pioneer Press* (St. Paul, June 25, 2005): C1.

3. Kailey, *Tranifesto*, 38.

4. Ibid.

5. See Ken Blanchard and Sheldon Bowles, *Raving Fans: A Revolutionary Approach to Customer Service* (New York: William Morrow, 1993).

6. Forster, "Getting Gay Workers," 4C.

7. Paula Martinac, "Teaching the Value of Difference," *PlanetOut*, April 15, 2003, http://www.gay.com/news/roundups/package.do?sernum=517&-page=1.

CHAPTER 13: WHAT *YOU* CAN DO

1. Peter Singer, *All Animals Are Equal*, http://www.fortunecity.com/emachines/e11/86/singer.html.

2. American Civil Liberties Union, "The Work of the ACLU: Linking Gender Identity and Gay Rights," December 31, 2000, http://www.aclu.org/lgbt/transgender/12022res20001231.html.

3. http://cogpsy.skku.ac.kr/cwb-bin/crazywwwboard.exe?mode=read&num=2141&page=78&db=article.

4. W. E. B. Du Bois, from a speech given at the 1906 Niagara Movement's conference held in Harper's Ferry, Virginia.

5. Kailey, *Tranifesto*, 83.

6. Koestenbaum, "Do You Have the Will to Lead?" 222.

7. Wheatley, *Turning to One Another*, 140.

8. Lindquist, "Thank You for Your Lack of Support."

9. Hartley, "Culturally Induced Stress," 12.

10. Human Rights Campaign, "Introduction to Issues Surrounding Gender Identity and Expression," http://www.hrc.org/issues/1435.htm.

APPENDIX 4

1. Partially adapted from *Workplace Fairness*, Gender Public Advocacy Coalition, p. 2; located online at http://www.gpac.org/workplace/WorkplaceFairness.pdf and at http://www.gpac.org/gpac/glossary.html.

2. *Merriam-Webster's Medical Dictionary* (Merriam-Webster, Inc., 2002).

3. Lambda Legal, *Transgender People in the Workplace*, located online at http://www.lambdalegal.org/our-work/publications/facts-backgrounds/page.jsp?itemID=31986950.

APPENDIX 8: THE EQUALITY PRINCIPLES

1. The Equality Project (501c3) is a consumer, employee, and investor advocacy coalition working to support and monitor workplace awareness and adoption of the progressive policies expressed in the Equality Principles as endorsed by leading LGBT organizations.

Index

About the Author

VANESSA SHERIDAN has been researching, writing, and speaking about transgender issues on a national basis since 1991. As a corporate consultant, speaker/presenter, and transgender awareness trainer, she works with client organizations to provide practical information and helpful resources on transgender in the workplace. Sheridan is the author of *Crossing Over: Liberating the Transgendered Christian* and coauthor of *Transgender Journeys*.